Praise for *Accountable Leaders*

"*Accountable Leaders* outlines a compelling vision of leadership. Through our work at Mighty Networks, I know that when you create community and connection, it will fuel people to come together to do the extraordinary. Vince Molinaro shows exactly how you can build a vibrant community of leaders in your own company to tackle challenges, drive change, and create incredible results."

Gina Bianchini, Founder & CEO, Mighty Networks

"Vince has created a simple, profound, and practical masterpiece to guide the mobilization of leadership accountability. The examples and tools he shares are clear, user-friendly, and resonate well regardless of industry you work in or size of your organization. He continues to demystify what it takes to develop great leaders."

Giulia Cirillo, Senior Vice President and Chief Human Resources Officer
Human Resources, PSP Investments

"Building on Vince's prior work, *Accountable Leaders* is a roadmap for leveraging talent and culture to drive transformational change. The performance driven organization achieves results through individuals and teams that are empowered and highly committed to the success of each other and the enterprise. As I reflect on what it means to me to be an accountable leader, I am excited to put these lessons into practice and share them with my team."

Kurt Ekert, President and CEO of CWT

"As the future of work continues to evolve at breakneck speed having a group of moti-vated and aligned leaders is critical to attaining real competitive advantage. In his latest book, Vince Molinaro gives the leaders concrete strategies, whether they are the CEO or just starting their leadership journey, to step up, and be more accountable."

Brad Furtney, President, Fieldpoint Service Applications Inc.

"Dr. Molinaro has once again written a great book needed in today's organizations. It was with great promise that I read this book after implementing key concepts from *The Leadership Contract* and seeing the game-changing impacts it had. And this book does not disappoint—filled with great stories, insights, and practical strategies, *Accountable Leaders* provides the roadmap to help all your leaders truly step up and drive the success of your company."

Olga Giovanniello, Executive Vice President, People and Culture,
Sienna Senior Living

The book, *The Leadership Contract* contributed to strengthening our leadership and elevate our whole organization toward excellence. Now in *Accountable Leaders*, Vince Molinaro has written a grounded, practical, and easy-to-read book with new insights every company can implement to deal with today's uncertain and unstable markets."

Matthias Goebel, General Manager Region Europa South,
Bosch Rexroth

"Vince Molinaro's latest work gets at the heart of the leadership challenges companies face today. More than ever, we need leaders who can step up to drive real innovation and change. *Accountable Leaders* provides practical insights and proven strategies that any company can implement to drive stronger leadership accountability at every level. If you need your leaders to be more effective and accountable, this book is your guide. A masterful work and a must read!"

Josh Linkner, New York Times Bestselling Author, 5-Time Tech Entrepreneur, and
World-Renowned Innovation Expert

"*Accountable Leaders* presents a vision of leadership where leaders need to step up to drive the success of their organizations, create inspiring and inclusive cultures and drive fundamental change at a personal, team, and organizational level. Our world needs great leaders today more than ever, and Vince Molinaro's book provides a roadmap for a compelling future."

Laura A. Liswood, Secretary General, Council of Women World Leaders and author
of The Loudest Duck, Moving Beyond Diversity.

"This book unapologetically calls all leaders and organizations to step up and hold accountability front and center. Making a compelling case through insightful examples, Dr. Molinaro paints a startling and accurate picture of the price we pay for lack of accountability. He then offers hope and direction by providing a clear way forward. Read this book and be inspired to be an accountable leader for yourself, for your team, and for your organization!"

Tricia Naddaff, President/Owner, MRG

"In his new book, Dr. Vince Molinaro, dives deeply into what he believes is at the core of a leadership dilemma facing organizations—the lack of accountability—of leaders failing to step up and own their results, their people, and societal impact. The book is, however, full of hope and optimism, with a rigorous and systematic roadmap to instill and sustain leadership accountability throughout an organization. An essential read for any leader."

Andrew Pateman, Vice-President, People, Culture and Performance Canadian Blood
Services

"*Accountable Leaders* addresses one of the most important qualities that every organization, leader, and employee must take seriously in order to have a successful culture and business. Through compelling stories, first-hand experiences, and thoughtful strategies, Vince makes a direct link between accountability and higher performance. Ignore this book at your own peril."

Dan Schawbel, author of Back to Human, Promote Yourself & Me 2.0

"Wow! At last a leadership book cast in reality! The notion of accountability leadership sums it all. One who wants to lead any organisation must understand the meaning of leadership accountability and its outward focus...its accountability to others, to the organisation, to society, and more. This book is a must read!"

Sylvain Toutant, Board Director, Strategic Advisor and Speaker

"In *Accountable Leaders*, Dr. Vince Molinaro clearly shows how organizations can scale accountable leadership at every level. This book will be the go-to manual for any CEO, head of human resources or board looking to establish a strong leadership culture and drive successful transformation."

Dr. Ricardo Viana Vargas, Executive Director,
Brightline Project Management Institute

ACCOUNTABLE LEADERS

INSPIRE A CULTURE WHERE EVERYONE
STEPS UP, TAKES OWNERSHIP, AND
DELIVERS RESULTS

DR. VINCE MOLINARO

WILEY

Published by John Wiley & Sons, Inc., Hoboken, New Jersey.

Published simultaneously in Canada.

For general information on our other products and services or for technical support, please contact our Customer Care Department within the United States at (800) 762–2974, outside the United States at (317) 572–3993 or fax (317) 572–4002.

Wiley publishes in a variety of print and electronic formats and by print-on-demand. Some material included with standard print versions of this book may not be included in e-books or in print-on-demand. If this book refers to media such as a CD or DVD that is not included in the version you purchased, you may download this material at http://booksupport.wiley.com. For more information about Wiley products, visit www.wiley.com.

Library of Congress Cataloging-in-Publication Data:
Names: Molinaro, Vince, author.
Title: Accountable leaders : inspire a culture where everyone steps up,
    takes ownership, and drives extraordinary results / Vince Molinaro.
Description: Hoboken, New Jersey : Wiley, [2020] | Includes index.
Identifiers: LCCN 2019053448 (print) | LCCN 2019053449 (ebook) | ISBN
    9781119550112 (hardback) | ISBN 9781119550136 (adobe pdf) | ISBN
    9781119550150 (epub)
Subjects: LCSH: Leadership. | Responsibility. | Teams in the workplace.
Classification: LCC HD57.7 .M6347 2020 (print) | LCC HD57.7 (ebook) | DDC
    658.4/092—dc23
LC record available at https://lccn.loc.gov/2019053448
LC ebook record available at https://lccn.loc.gov/2019053449

Cover image: © Thomas Vogel/Getty Images
Cover design: Kevin Youngsaye
Figure design: Kevin Youngsaye

Printed in the United States of America

10 9 8 7 6 5 4 3 2 1

To Liz, for your friendship and unending support.

To Mateo, Tomas, and Alessia, for your daily inspiration.

To Mom and Dad, for your tremendous encouragement.

I am grateful to have you all in my life.

CONTENTS

INTRODUCTION

Why do so many of us have such negative experiences with leadership? Why do our organizations have so many mediocre leaders? Why do so many of us work on terrible teams? Why do we spend our careers in organizations with uninspiring and even dreadful cultures? More importantly, why do we put up with all of this?

You deserve better. We all deserve better. However, changing things means that you will need to be a better and more accountable leader. We will all need to be better and more accountable leaders. Why? Just look at the daily headlines or the newsfeeds on your smartphone. What do you see? Far too many stories of prominent leaders embroiled in scandal, corruption, sexual harassment, demonstrating unacceptable and even unethical behavior. Whether they are corporate CEOs, politicians, or other prominent figures, there are many disgraceful examples of leadership. These stories happen so often that we don't even notice anymore. We have become conditioned to accept this as the norm. Well, it's not—and we need to hold all leaders to a higher standard of behavior. You need to hold yourself to a higher standard of behavior.

Our experience with teams isn't much better. Research shows that only three in 10 employees believe that their co-workers are committed to doing quality work.[1] Most employees do the bare minimum to get by. We need to improve the quality and accountability of teams.

While business leaders talk about the importance of corporate culture, the sad reality is that very few of them have created compelling ones. Research estimates that only 15 percent of companies have the culture they need to succeed.[2] If an organization can't build an inspiring culture, it will not be able to attract and retain the best talent in their industry or drive sustained business results.

We must do better, and this book will show you how.

Twenty-Five Countries and 80 Cities—the Story Is the Same

I spend a lot of time talking to people about leadership. I've traveled to 25 countries and about 80 cities in the last few years. In that time, I conducted hundreds of presentations, speeches, and media interviews. I've met with senior executives, boards, leaders at all levels, and employees. During my travels, I have also had the incredible experience of touching down in a city or country that was in the middle of a significant leadership story.

For example, on one business trip, I landed in São Paulo on a sunny Sunday morning. Little did I know that on that day, an estimated five million Brazilians would take to the streets to protest their corrupt political and corporate leaders. On another business trip, I arrived in the United Kingdom a few weeks after the initial Brexit vote. People were still bewildered by what had happened and were concerned about their future. I traveled to Madrid when the country was dealing with a crisis in government. Spaniards were at their wits' end with the lack of leadership shown by their politicians. I traveled to many cities in the United States during the 2016 presidential election. Many Americans kept asking, "How did we get here?" After the election, many I spoke to asked, "Now what are we going to do?" As worried as people were, I'm sure no one could have predicted the kind of leadership style that President Trump would unleash on the world. Since he's been in office, everyone has had a front-row seat to see how he leads every day. A day doesn't pass when someone asks me to comment on U.S. President Donald Trump's leadership—everyone is trying to make sense of his divisive and confrontational approach to leading the world's most powerful country.

On another business trip, I was in the city of San Juan to see Puerto Ricans in the streets protesting the corruption in their government. The country was in turmoil. I then witnessed the celebrations when their governor stepped down in response to the protests. In all my discussions, as people reflected on these leadership stories, many were left wondering: "Is this what it means to be a leader?"

I arrived in New Zealand shortly after the tragic massacre of innocent people in Christchurch. We all witnessed the inspirational leadership of Prime Minister Jacinda Ardern as she led her country through its grief. I was struck by how her leadership resonated with so many people around the world. Many proclaimed that she was an example of the kind of leader we need in the future—one who can bring integrity, resolve, and compassion to her leadership role and do it when it mattered most. Unfortunately, in my travels, examples like Prime Minister Ardern are the exception. There have been far more stories of bad, inept, and uninspiring leadership.

I encountered other compelling leadership stories when I traveled to Chile, Germany, Italy, Panamá, Singapore, Australia, and other countries. Something interesting also happened during those trips. When people found out I was Canadian, many said how lucky I was to have Prime Minister Justin Trudeau as my political leader. It was immediately clear to me that he had made his mark on the world stage in his early days as prime minister. I was also really struck by these comments. When I asked why they thought Canadians were lucky to have him as their leader, the answer was unanimous: "Well, because he's so good looking!" Then I would respond, "What does that have to do with being a good leader?" It's important to note that when he was first elected as Canada's prime minister, he was an inspiration to many. But over time, he was involved in several scandals that left many questioning his judgment and integrity as a leader. He was fortunate to be re-elected as prime minister in the fall of 2019, but this time with only a minority government. Canadians sent him a message: They were expecting more from him as a leader. If he chooses, he now has a second chance to redefine how he leads in a way that restores the faith and hope that so many Canadians had in him when he first took office in 2015.

During all these trips I was on the ground speaking to regular people like you and me. I was there to talk about leadership accountability. It was a good thing because, given the events taking place in real time in their countries, it was the only topic people wanted to discuss. Most of the time, I felt more like a foreign correspondent for the BBC or CNN than a leadership adviser. I heard a lot about people's frustrations and disappointment with their leaders, their teams, and the cultures of their organizations. I also sensed their yearning for something better and more inspirational. It is clear to me that we are all desperate for exceptional leadership in our world and our organizations.

Is Anyone Happy?

What I have learned from all these experiences is that people are fed up. They are tired of being led by mediocre leaders, working on terrible teams, or being part of organizations with uninspiring cultures. Listening to people repeatedly vent and complain about their frustrations, I find myself asking: Is anyone happy? Are you happy?

Of course, some of us have had the good fortune to be led by great leaders. Some of us have been part of terrific teams and organizations with compelling cultures. Over my career, I have been lucky to be led by some great leaders. I have been part of some fantastic teams. I have also been in companies with inspiring cultures. Here's what these experiences have taught me. When you work for a great leader, you feel like you are at your best. When you are on a fantastic team, you feel safe and confident because everyone has your back. When you are part of an organization with an inspiring culture, you feel a powerful sense of unity and share a collective purpose. If you are lucky enough to experience all three, then your work brings you joy and meaning. It's fun, exciting, and even life-affirming.

I've also learned that these great experiences can ruin you forever. What I mean is that once you've seen what great is like, it's hard to put up with the bad, the mediocre, and the uninspiring. You've experienced good or even great, so you know that something better is indeed possible. At the same time, I've seen the price people have paid by working with a dreadful manager, being on a terrible team, or part of an organization with a toxic culture. Some of these people have never had a great experience in their professional lives. They do not even know that something better is possible. As a result, whenever I have found myself in situations that were downright awful, I worked hard to try to change them. And if I couldn't, I left the organization. Why? Simply because I have come to learn that life is too short to spend it being miserable at work.

This Is My Life's Work

I have spent close to three decades in my career, helping leaders, teams, and organizations aspire to become the best they can be. It all began when I was 27 years old and decided to start my own business. I left a large public-sector organization that did important work—it helped some of the neediest and most marginalized people in society get their lives back on track. We provided financial assistance, career development support, and access to retraining programs. The purpose of the organization was inspiring to me. Despite this, I quickly learned that the organization's culture was drab and dreadful. In my time there, I saw Zinta, a senior manager, die of lung cancer, a disease she believed was a result of the stress she endured spending her career in a highly toxic work environment.[3] This was devastating to me as Zinta was my mentor. At the time, I questioned whether her exposure to that toxic culture did indeed impact her health. Today, we know that it most likely did. In his book *Dying for a Paycheck*, Professor Jeffrey Pfeffer summarizes considerable research showing how toxic workplaces directly undermine people's health and well-being.[4] In the end, that experience with my mentor Zinta changed my life. It forced me to think hard about my career and my life's work. Over time, I discovered my passion and mission: to work with people who aspired for more from their work. I wanted to work with individuals who wanted to be exceptional leaders, lead great teams, and create inspiring cultures.

At first, I provided career counseling services to private clients who were managers and senior managers in large organizations. They told me about the challenges they faced navigating their careers. I learned firsthand the impact that lousy leaders and mediocre managers have on employees—how they undermine confidence, create stress, and erode passion and engagement.

My clients also brought me into their companies. I ran seminars for employees, managers, and senior executives to help them deal with the volume of change taking place. At that time, organizational change was a hot topic (much like it is today). In parallel to running my consulting business, I also completed two graduate degrees. I conducted research on change and leadership. When I finished my doctoral degree, I felt it was time to go back into an organization and apply everything I had learned in graduate school. I did that by joining a start-up pharmaceutical company with an amazing culture. I learned firsthand what it takes to build one, but also learned what happens when you do not focus on sustaining it over the long term.

A few years later, I returned to the world of consulting. I was part of a firm called Knightsbridge Human Capital Solutions, headquartered in Toronto. My experience allowed me to work with some fantastic clients and colleagues. I led the leadership practice within the firm. At a personal level, I worked hard to try to be a good leader, to build a great team, and to contribute to creating an inspiring culture across our organization. Our formula for success was simple: Hire amazing people dedicated to their clients, create valuable thought leadership and solutions, and establish a strong culture. We did just that and became a dominant brand in our industry.

Then in 2015, The Adecco Group and LHH (a world-leading provider of talent development and transition services) acquired Knightsbridge. A new opportunity emerged for me. Now I was part of a global Fortune 500 company, and I was given a role with clear marching orders: Take the success formula that my team and I had implemented at Knightsbridge and export it globally. We did, and due to the commitment of many exceptional colleagues, we helped leaders around the world become more accountable to drive the success of their organizations.

My career came full circle when I decided it was time to start my own company again, which I did in January 2019. I felt I needed to focus 100 percent of my energy to my lifework and mission. In many ways, I have the same sense of purpose and zeal that I had when I was 27 years old. All the experiences over my career have given me a unique perspective on leadership which I gained by consulting to C-Suite leaders, designing and delivering award winning leadership programs for my clients, conducting research, and in leading successful businesses. As I look at the leadership landscape today and over the next decade, it's clear that leadership matters more than it ever has. We need stronger leadership throughout our world. But exactly what kind of leadership do we need?

It's About Leadership Accountability

What my work with clients has taught me is that if you want to improve as a leader, a team, or a company, the quickest and most enduring way to do this is by focusing on leadership accountability. When you do, it immediately puts you on a different trajectory.

In my book *The Leadership Contract*[5] I define leadership accountability as the ability of individuals in leadership roles to step up and demonstrate personal ownership for their roles, be deliberate and decisive in the way they lead, and bring a sense of urgency, courage, and resilience to the position. They must not only demonstrate this accountability at a personal level, but they must also ensure it exists within their teams and with other leaders across their organization. They need to help inspire others to step up, take ownership, and deliver results. However, what I have discovered is that we have many people in leadership roles who simply are not accountable. They are more committed to the technical aspects of their roles—whether they are accountants, engineers, sales professionals, analysts, marketers, or investment bankers, to name a few. They do not bring the same level of personal commitment to the leadership aspects of their roles. I have come to learn many do not even define themselves as leaders, even though they have a leadership role within their company. They essentially treat leadership as a part-time job—something they do in addition to being technical experts.

I came to realize that our organizations are filled with thousands of part-time leaders. One of the primary reasons this has happened is because a lot of people get into leadership roles by accident. They excel at something technical, and organizations go to these individuals and promote them into leadership roles. The underlying assumption is that strong technical performance would translate into strong leadership performance. Sometimes that is true; but we've learned in practice that most of the time it isn't. As a result, many companies have significant leadership accountability gaps. They have people in leadership roles who simply are not stepping up or leading in a way that their company expects.

My clients asked me to help them find a way forward to resolve this problem. In my book, I positioned the critical idea of a *leadership contract* that stipulates those in leadership roles must understand they are held to a higher standard of behavior. This idea of a *leadership contract* has always existed, but we have never made it explicit with leaders. In fact, many people who are in leadership roles have treated the leadership contract like an online contract—you know, the one that comes up on your laptop or tablet with all the terms and conditions. When it does, most of us simply scroll down to the bottom of the screen and click "agree" without reading a single word. You know you are bound to something; you are not quite sure what that is. This analogy has resonated with a lot of leaders I work with. They acknowledge that they haven't been deliberate in considering what they signed up for when they took on a leadership role. Now, given the challenges that leaders will face today and over the next decade, it's critical that this idea of a leadership contract becomes explicit and that leaders appreciate what they actually signed up for in their roles.

In 2013, when the first edition of *The Leadership Contract* was released, these ideas immediately resonated in the marketplace. No matter where I went, or whom I talked to, I repeatedly heard the same thing: "This is what we've been missing. We need people in leadership roles to understand what it means to be a leader. They need to understand that they've signed up for something important, and we need them to step up and be accountable." "They can't simply be committed to only the technical parts of their roles; they need to fully commit to being accountable leaders." Those who read my book described it as a *mindset* book about leadership because it helps leaders understand how they need to think about their roles and what they must pay attention to every single day.

I believe this idea of *leadership accountability* resonated because I've come to appreciate that as humans, we expect more of people in leadership roles. We hope that they will step up and lead, create exceptional organizations, and even make the world a better place. When they succeed, we praise them, admire them, and even want to emulate them. However, when they fail, misbehave, or are simply mediocre, we feel a sense of disappointment, despair, and even disgust.

As a leader, you need to understand that you signed a *leadership contract* and that it comes with four terms and conditions (see Figure I.1). Let's explore them now.

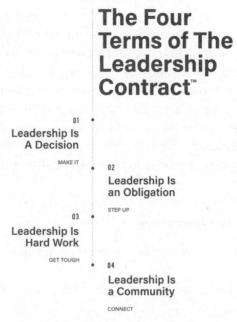

The Four Terms of The Leadership Contract™

01
Leadership Is
A Decision

MAKE IT

02
Leadership Is
an Obligation

STEP UP

03
Leadership Is
Hard Work

GET TOUGH

04
Leadership Is
a Community

CONNECT

Figure I.1   The Four Terms of The Leadership Contract

1. Leadership Is a Decision

When you are in a leadership role, you must be fully committed to your role. You must be clear on the expectations of the role and be ready to set the tone for others. You will not be successful as a leader until you are fully committed because this is what the role demands. You can't approach your leadership role lightly or be ambivalent about it. You certainly can't opt out. You must be all in, especially in today's world. The constant change, disruption, and complexity that leaders face today is considerable. If you aren't prepared to lead in this environment, then you must decide that a leadership role may not be for you and have the courage to make that decision. If, however, you decide you want to be an accountable leader, then you must fully commit.

2. Leadership Is an Obligation

Once you decide to be an accountable leader, you quickly realize that you will be held to a higher standard of behavior. We expect a lot from anyone in a leadership role today. You must also recognize that you will have obligations that go beyond yourself. It's not just about what is best for you and your career. You are obligated to your customers and employees, your organization, and the communities in which you do business. You need to create enduring value and leave things better than you found them. In this book, we will discuss your obligation to hold others accountable to be leaders, to build truly accountable teams, and to work with other leaders to establish strong leadership accountability throughout your organization.

3. Leadership Is Hard Work

Leadership isn't for the feeble—you need resilience, resolve, and determination. You will need personal tenacity to rise above the daily pressures and lead your organization into the future. You will need confidence and courage to have tough conversations and to push through barriers to strategy execution. This term of the leadership contract demands that you get tough with yourself and do the hard work that you must do as a leader. Unfortunately, too many leaders shy away from the hard work. You can't avoid or wimp out on it. If you do, it will weaken you, weaken your team, and impede your progress, and ultimately prevent you from delivering results.

4. Leadership Is a Community

The fourth term of the leadership contract demands that you connect with others to create a strong community of leaders in your organization. You need to work with your peers to create a leadership culture in which there is a sense of deep trust and mutual support, where you know everyone has your back, and where all leaders share the collective aspiration to be truly accountable. You will need to break down silos, work across departments and functions, and learn to bring a one-company perspective to your role. If you can, you will stand out as an invaluable leader in your organization.

The Ripple Effect—Accountability Breeds Accountability

Take some time to reflect on the four terms of the leadership contract. To what extent are you a truly accountable leader? Is your team as accountable as it can be? Does your organization have a culture that inspires others to step up and deliver results? If you are honest with yourself, like most leaders I work with, you will come to realize that there is an opportunity for you to be more accountable in your current role. That's one lesson I learned in my own leadership roles. As accountable as I thought I may have been, if I were honest with myself, I could see more ways to step up and be even more accountable. Here's something else I learned along the way: You can't ask anyone else to be accountable if you are not accountable yourself. You must lead by example. Why? Because accountability breeds accountability. Let me repeat that: *Accountability breeds accountability.*

If you set the right tone, most everyone will follow. It's like a ripple effect that can happen in a still pond. I'm sure you have experienced it. Once you touch the water with your finger or throw a pebble in it, you watch the ripples take form and expand throughout the entire pond. That's how accountability works in organizations. If you step up, and others see you setting an example of accountability, you create a positive ripple effect that inspires and encourages others to also step up and be accountable.

However, a ripple effect can work the other way as well—*mediocrity breeds mediocrity.* When mediocrity ripples throughout an organization, then you have a problem. I believe we have too many people in leadership roles who seem to be fine with being just okay—average or mediocre at best. No human endeavor of any significance has ever been achieved with mediocrity. Extraordinary results—whether from an athlete, an artist, a surgeon, a manager, a teacher, or a CEO—are never achieved through mediocrity.

You have a choice. What will it be for you? Accountability or mediocrity? What ripple effect are you creating in your organization?

The Dual Response to Building Strong Leadership Accountability

To me, accountability is the bedrock of truly great leadership. In *The Leadership Contract*, I suggested that a dual response is required to make it happen in an organization (see Figure I.2). First, as a leader, you must step up and be accountable at a personal level. Second, you must then build accountability across the organization as you work with your direct reports, teams, and peers. Let's explore these ideas in more detail.

The Individual Response

At an individual level, you must do your part to step up and lead in a more accountable manner. You need to set the tone by living the four terms of the leadership contract. You can't go around telling others to step up if you are not doing it yourself. To drive your personal success, you may want to review the ideas and activities in my books: *The Leadership Contract* (3rd ed.) and *The Leadership Contract Field Guide*. They include many foundational resources that will help you develop the mindset necessary to become the accountable leader your organization needs you to be. You can also go to the Apple and Google App Stores to download the Accountable Leaders App. Once you download the app, you can gain access to learning resources and courses, and be part of a community of like-minded accountable leaders committed to leading to a higher standard of behavior.

The Organizational Response

Your success will be accelerated and amplified if there is also an effective organizational response in place. By this, I mean you must go beyond yourself and strive to strengthen the leadership accountability across your entire organization. First, you must work hard to hold others accountable, build an accountable team, and help establish a strong community of leaders across your organization.

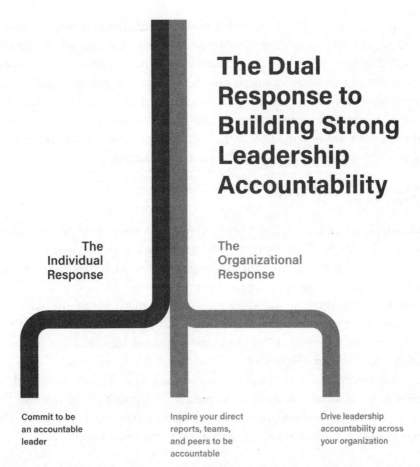

The Dual Response to Building Strong Leadership Accountability

The Individual Response

The Organizational Response

Commit to be an accountable leader

Inspire your direct reports, teams, and peers to be accountable

Drive leadership accountability across your organization

Figure I.2   The Dual Response to Build Strong Leadership Accountability

Second, as a CEO, senior executive, head of human resources, or board director, you must set the tone of strong leadership accountability for the rest of the organization. You must also put practices in place that will make leadership accountability a business priority in your organization. You must define clear leadership expectations, demonstrate resolve, and do the hard work that sustains momentum. You must also support leaders to act as a community and build a strong leadership culture.

In many ways, this book is part of what I call *The Leadership Contract* trilogy. *The Leadership Contract* (3rd ed.) presents the core ideas around leadership accountability. *The Leadership Contract Field Guide* provides 75 activities that you can use to put those ideas into action within your leadership role. This book explores what you must do as a leader to drive strong leadership accountability at an organizational level. The three books are designed to work together and provide an integrated approach for you to implement in your organization.

My Wish for You

Hundreds of organizations around the world have brought the ideas of *The Leadership Contract* to their leaders. My books and training programs are available in multiple languages. In my travels and discussions with leaders, I've seen the positive impact these ideas can have. I've seen leaders and teams take their game to a higher level of effectiveness and success. I've seen organizations build strong leadership cultures that are inspiring. I have been humbled to see this all happen. I know these ideas can work for you as well.

My sincere hope and wish for you is that you will come away with a clear sense of what you must do to be a truly accountable leader—both at an individual and an organizational level. I encourage you to reach out to me on LinkedIn or visit www.drvincemolinaro.com.

Notes

1. Brian de Haaff, "Only 30 Percent of People Believe Their Teammates Are Committed to Quality Work—Here Is How to Fix That," *Inc.*, November 21, 2018, https://www.inc.com /brian-de-haaff/only-30-percent-of-people-believe-their-teammates-are-committed-to-quality-work-here-is-how-to-fix-that .html.

2. "How Corporate Culture Affects the Bottom Line," Duke Fuqua School of Business, November 12, 2015, https://www.fuqua.duke .edu/duke-fuqua-insights/corporate-culture.

3. You can read the entire story of my colleague Zinta in Vince Molinaro, *The Leadership Contract* (3rd ed.) (John Wiley & Sons, 2018).

4. Jeffrey Pfeffer, *Dying for a Paycheck* (Harper Collins, 2018).

5. Vince Molinaro, *The Leadership Contract* (3rd ed.) (John Wiley & Sons, 2018).

PART 1
The World in Which You Lead

This section of the book has two chapters that explore the context in which you are leading.

Chapter 1: The New Game Begins Before the Old One Ends
This chapter will help you understand the future context for all leaders. We will examine the impact of several critical drivers, including the role of transformative technologies, geopolitical instability, revolutionizing work, the need to deliver on diversity, and repurposing the role of corporations in society.

Chapter 2: Why Do We Not Have Better Leadership?
This chapter examines why leadership is not as strong as it needs to be. Specifically, it examines how many leaders today are overwhelmed, disengaged, underprepared, and struggling to execute strategy. The chapter also discusses how leadership development programs must do more to help address these challenges.

CHAPTER 1

The New Game Begins Before the Old One Ends

On March 31, 2014, I was meeting a colleague for lunch at a popular restaurant in Toronto. As we sat down at our table, I looked out through the restaurant windows. "Look at what's happening up there!" I said to my colleague. I immediately pulled out my smartphone and took a photo.

Have you ever seen something happen and known right away, in your gut, that you were witnessing something significant?

In the distance, about six stories up in an adjacent building, I could see a couple of workers taking down a company's outdoor sign. The sign consisted of five giant white letters, S – E – A – R – S, atop Sears Canada's flagship store in one of the country's largest and busiest shopping centers.

Throughout our lunch, I found myself glancing out the window to track the progress of the two workers as they painstakingly pried loose each letter. As the letters came off, I could see the imprint of the company's name that remained on the brown building's façade due to decades and decades of sun exposure. These phantom letters were a sad reminder of a once-great company, one of the most enduring retail brands that the world has ever known.

What I witnessed that afternoon was more than just a sign coming down. To me, it signaled the massive unraveling taking hold in the retail industry. That's why that moment felt so important to me. That moment also underscored the kinds of challenges that leaders face today. Fast-forward to January of 2018. All the Sears stores in Canada would close. Sixteen thousand employees would lose their jobs. Their pensions would be at risk. By the end of 2018, the company in the United States would face a similar fate, only to be saved at the eleventh hour.

In many ways, the story of Sears is not unique. In the world of business, there has always been an understanding that the companies and leaders who can't adapt, can't spot opportunities, or can't change quickly enough, end up paying a severe price. The graveyard of once-great companies is full of examples of organizations that have not been able to sustain their relevance and are now long extinct. In the end, they were unable to see the need to adapt in a changing environment. Harvard Business School Professor Clay Christensen shared a terrific insight at a recent conference when he said, *"The new game begins even before you can tell anything is wrong in the old one."*[1] This is a brilliant idea that to me captures a fundamental challenge leaders must be mindful of when leading. All leaders must be accountable for leading their organizations through change, and this is what we'll explore in the rest of this chapter. To get us started, we'll examine the story of Sears in more detail to show what can happen when leaders fail to see the new game emerging.

The Story of Sears—a Once Great Company

What I find fascinating about the story of Sears is that from the time it first incorporated in 1893, the company was a disruptor. There was the Sears catalogue. Sears was one of the first department stores. Sears' amazing brands, like Craftsman tools and Kenmore appliances, inspired confidence, lasted forever, and gave consumers value for their money. The company was one of the first retailers to establish an online presence in early 2000. Sears found a way to innovate throughout most of its 125-year history. Despite all of this, the company struggled to survive in a dynamic and shifting retail landscape. This is a reality all leaders must embrace. Success doesn't last forever.

The problems for Sears, according to many industry analysts, started in 2005 when it merged with Kmart, a strategy designed to boost two struggling retailers.[2] At that time, Sears and Kmart had 3,500 stores in the United States. By 2018, they were down to just about 700 stores between the two brands.[3] That's an 80 percent erosion of the company's footprint. From 2003 to 2018, the company lost 96 percent of its value, while its key competitors doubled in value.[4] The company was missing the mark. Many argue Sears' downfall was also the result of a failure to shift to digital.[5]

The leadership angle to this story is also interesting, for at the center of it all is CEO Edward Lampert, a successful hedge-fund manager with extensive experience in the retail world. He took over management of the retail chain in 2013. He launched a series of moves designed to both modernize the company's operations and compete online while cutting overhead.

In addition to his vigorous restructuring plans, Lampert put nearly $1 billion of his own money on the line for the struggling company in loans or letters of credit. However, even that wasn't enough to spare him from widespread criticism. The media regularly chastised him about his leadership style and the way he led the company.

He rarely made personal appearances at the company's headquarters, preferring instead to do most of his work from a vast Florida estate. He would hold daily video conferences with Sears' executives toiling in the company's Illinois head office. He only traveled to the head office once a year for the annual shareholders meeting. The video conferences reportedly would get quite heated and emotional. Lampert defended his tone and approach to leadership as a way to "drive decision making and accountability at a more appropriate level." Most would agree that this was a strange way to lead a company in the throes of gut-wrenching change. In 2016, Lampert was named the most hated CEO in America based on his employee rating on Glassdoor.[6]

It would soon become clear that Sears was in a death spiral. In late 2018, Sears filed for bankruptcy protection in the United States.[7] Then in early 2019, Lampert's hedge fund bought the company for $5.2 billion, avoiding liquidation and allowing the company to keep some stores open and save an estimated 45,000 jobs. Lampert said he planned to step down as CEO, which he did.[8] About a year later, he also stepped down as chairman.

In April of 2019, the company lodged a lawsuit against Lampert and a string of its high-profile past board members for allegedly stealing billions of dollars from the once-storied retailer.[9] Unsecured creditors of Sears argued that Lampert was the cause of the company's downfall, not its savior. They asserted that Lampert, along with some of the company's most significant shareholders, unduly benefited from deals that occurred under Lampert's watch. The lawsuit alleged that Lampert caused more than $2 billion of assets to be transferred to himself and other shareholders, putting those assets beyond the reach of Sears' creditors.

Then in May 2019, Lampert asked a federal bankruptcy judge to release him from his obligation to compensate former Sears workers with an estimated $43 million in severance costs.[10] Lampert argued that the company had not lived up to its obligation to sell him most of its assets. As a result, he believed he was not obligated to pay the severance costs.

The World in Which Leaders Are Leading Today

In the end, Sears is a story of a once-great company unable to keep up with the ravages of gut-wrenching change in its industry—referred to by many as the "retail apocalypse." Sears joined hundreds of other companies facing similar struggles. Like Sears, many would be unable to adapt to the forces that have shifted the industry's landscape.

Many industry analysts assert that the claims of a retail apocalypse are overblown. While some companies have struggled and have gone bankrupt, many others are thriving in an industry that continues to grow. These analysts blame the demise of individual companies on poor leadership, not some external apocalypse. For many leaders, the world can appear to change right before their eyes. However, that isn't really the case. Signs of change and even opportunity do arise, but leaders don't always see them. Alternatively, by the time they do, it is too late. This points to the need for leaders to be both externally and future-focused to understand the world in which they lead. However, in practice, I find the opposite to be true. Many leaders are too internally focused, stuck in old thinking patterns or are simply too arrogant, believing their past success will drive future success.

Consider the example that comes from Blockbuster and Netflix. In his book *That Will Never Work*, Netflix co-founder Marc Randolph recounts the story of a meeting with Blockbuster senior brass.[11] Netflix was struggling and in debt. After months of trying to get Blockbuster's attention, they finally secured the ever-important meeting. Blockbuster could have bought Netflix for $50 million, but they chose not to. Blockbuster's CEO, John Antioco, didn't believe it was an idea worthy of consideration. You know how the story ended. Netflix went on to become widely successful. Blockbuster went bust.

As an accountable leader, leading in a time of significant change and even disruption requires you to understand what is happening in the world. How are CEOs currently thinking about the world in which they are leading? Let's look at the findings from KPMG's survey of nearly 1,300 global CEOs about their perspectives on leading their companies in today's world.[12]

- *Seventy-two percent of CEOs said that they believe the next three years will be more critical for their industry than the previous 50 years.*
- *Sixty-nine percent of CEOs are concerned about the number of mission-critical business priorities they need to tackle with no prior experience.*
- *Sixty-five percent worry about new entrants disrupting industry business models, and about half of the CEOs are concerned that their companies are not disrupting their own business models quickly enough.*

As you look at some of these high-level findings, you might say they paint a grim picture. However, CEOs also expressed a high degree of optimism about their ability to succeed. As we will see later in this book, that attitude is vital for leaders during times of change and disruption. However, leaders will need more than a good dose of optimism because leading change is hard work.

For example, McKinsey found in their research that only 26 percent of senior executives surveyed believe their organizations' efforts to transform are successful.[13] Change and churn have always been a reality in the world of business. No surprise there—however, the pace of change is unrelenting today and is also affecting corporate longevity.

Research conducted by Innosight found that in 1965, corporations stayed on the S&P 500 Index for 33 years.[14] By 1990, that number had drastically declined to 20 years, and it is forecast to shrink to 14 years by 2026. If that churn rate continues, they estimate that half of today's S&P 500 companies will cease to exist in the next decade.

It's not just companies experiencing churn. CEOs increasingly find themselves in the hot seat, and their shelf life is getting shorter and shorter. Heidrick and Struggles, a leading global search and leadership firm, found that the number of CEOs who exited from their organizations nearly tripled from 2001 to 2016.[15]

No matter where you look, the story is the same—the world in which leaders are leading is getting more challenging than ever. Leaders need to deeply appreciate the context in which they lead because it matters—I believe now more than ever.

Context Matters When It Comes to Leadership

Harvard Business School professors Anthony J. Mayo and Nitin Nohria wrote a fascinating book called *In Their Time: The Greatest Business Leaders of the Twentieth Century.*[16] In it, they chronicled the stories of some of the most successful business leaders of the twentieth century and found a close relationship between context and leadership. Based on their analysis of hundreds of leaders, they arrived at several key conclusions:

1. When it comes to leadership, context matters. In the end, long-term success comes down to awareness and sensitivity to context and business environment.
2. Leaders and companies do not fail or succeed in a vacuum. The interplay among the context, business environment, and how leaders respond is critical to success.
3. Leaders must understand their emerging context, for it impacts their ability to adapt and spot opportunities that may fuel growth and create value for shareholders and society.

These conclusions point to the need for you as a leader to take the time to understand the context in which you are leading. This is something my teams and I have always helped leaders do in our leadership development programs. Every program is rooted in the current and emerging context of the leaders we work with. We help them learn the skills they need to pay attention to their operating environment and appreciate how they need to step up and lead in times of change. The bottom line is that you need to be clear on what is coming at you, how to make sense of it, and how to lead your team or company through it all.[17]

The Emerging Context for All Leaders

In all my research and conversations with leaders like you, I've come to appreciate the key drivers that are reshaping our world. Collectively, these drivers are changing the old game and bringing about a new one. Below, I touch briefly on what I see as the top five drivers that all leaders need to pay attention to, today and tomorrow (see Figure 1.1). This is by no means an exhaustive list, but in my discussions with senior executives, these seem to be the ones they are paying attention to and even worried about.

Figure 1.1   The Emerging Context for All Leaders

1. Transformative Technologies

Klaus Schwab, the founder and executive chairman of the World Economic Forum, recently wrote: "We stand on the brink of a technological revolution that will fundamentally alter the way we live, work, and relate to one another. In its scale, scope, and complexity, the transformation will be unlike anything humankind has experienced before."[18]

Schwab nicely captures today's reality. Several technologies have emerged that will completely change our world in fundamental ways. Digital technology will continue to transform everything we do, including the way we work and learn. Big data will help organizations better predict business and people issues like nothing we've ever seen before. Artificial Intelligence (AI) will enhance decision making and complement the work of leaders and employees. For example, IBM recently announced that it developed an AI predictive attrition program that can predict which employees will leave a job with 95 percent accuracy.[19] This kind of data will become more common in the future and will assist managers to better lead their people.

In February of 2019, I gained some valuable insights into how that shaped my thinking about technological change. I took part in the Future Series (FU.SE) conference, held in Milan, Italy. The inaugural event was sponsored by Microsoft, The Boston Consulting Group, and The Adecco Group. The event brought together a broad array of business, technology, government, and policy leaders to discuss a future of work that works for everyone. I was one of the speakers, and also participated in many of the amazing sessions. Brad Smith, president and chief legal officer at Microsoft, spoke eloquently about how technology is reshaping our world and the very nature of work. He shared that technological change always follows a similar pattern. It begins slowly and gradually at first, but then change happens suddenly where the pace picks up and things take hold. He stressed that as leaders we need to not only be aware of the changes that are coming, but also be wary of the hype that typically accompanies the introduction of new technologies. We will need to have a firm grasp of new technologies and the know-how to exploit the benefits while minimizing the threats. We will also need to appreciate that in the future the way we lead will be mediated by technology, as AI will give us insights into the people we lead, what motivates them, and how to better help them succeed.

2. Geopolitical Instability

As I've traveled internationally to speak about leadership accountability, I've been surprised by the world-shaking events I've been able to experience. As I shared in the introduction to this book, it seemed that every time I landed in a country on a business trip, a big leadership story was unfolding in real time. It's become clear to me that leaders will need to be much more aware of the geopolitical dynamics in the world. Fifty-two percent of CEOs surveyed by KPMG believe the geopolitical landscape is having a more significant impact on their companies.[20] McKinsey's research[21] found that geopolitical and macroeconomic instability will create what they call *geostrategic risk,* which will have a negative impact on companies.

What's particularly concerning to me is that the vast majority of executives surveyed by McKinsey admitted to not taking active steps to address geopolitical issues. What do you believe are the risks when leaders do not actively think about geopolitical issues happening around the world? In my client work, I have seen the world of leaders turned upside down because of geopolitics. Many leaders tell me how they have had to deal with the impact of trade disputes, tariffs, and tensions between countries where they operate. These result in hundreds of millions of dollars in lost revenue. For many, it seemed to all happen in an instant. As leaders, we need to learn to be more sensitive to the world around us and try to anticipate and mitigate the risks that may emerge due to global events.

3. Revolutionizing Work

Work is a topic that has always been near and dear to my heart. Early in my working life, as a career counselor, I saw the way that meaningful work changed the lives of marginalized people. Now the future of work has taken center stage as a bona fide global obsession. Every week, I get a flood of surveys, studies, commentaries, and editorials, all talking about the future of work and jobs, many with dire and even apocalyptic headlines. I'm sure you do as well. But as I read these reports, studies, and predictions, I can't help but feel that we have been here before. This was the case for me in 1990 when I was a budding entrepreneur and starting my first consulting business. To be effective, I had to be on top of all the research on careers and the future of work. Back then, the uncertainty about the future of work, reskilling, and retraining was just as intense as it is today. We were awash in predictions about job loss, the role of technology in reshaping the workplace, and the dream of a future of leisure. What was different then was that we were only a decade away from the year 2000. If you were around then, you know that the year 2000 represented the future. That year did come, and some predictions about the future of work materialized. However, many did not.

Just like then, today there's a vast range of predictions and forecasts about the future of work. *The Guardian* recently went so far as to ask if jobs would even exist in the future.[22] The article quoted business journalist Richard Newton offering a very pessimistic view of the future: "This is either going to be very good or very bad—and either way there's not going to be much in the way of work." Oxford University recently reported that nearly half of all jobs that exist today would not be around tomorrow.[23] What do you believe?

I believe it is essential to not get caught up in the hype regarding the future of work. There are more balanced perspectives to consider. For example, a recent *Harvard Business Review* article estimated that only 5 percent of all occupations would be fully automated.[24] However, all jobs will evolve as intelligent machines take over many physical, repetitive, or basic cognitive tasks. The critical work that remains will require more technical and digital skills. It will also require more human interaction, creativity, and judgment. I completely agree. I'm all for freeing people up from mundane and repetitive work and unleashing human ingenuity and passion. Leaders must be able to unleash these capabilities in the people they lead, both today and in the future.

Work is already revolutionizing in front of our eyes. I believe leaders have a profound obligation to the people they lead to help them through the next decade. Unfortunately, some predictions about the nature of work in the future paint a grim picture of work devoid of meaning. As a result, I believe that creating an inspiring work environment in which to work will be even more critical in the future than it is today. Culture will continue to matter, and we'll need leaders who get that. I believe the debate going on is not only about jobs. It's also about the quality of the employment experience and whether leaders focus on employee well-being and creating a sense of connectedness in workplaces.

What does all this fervor about the future of work mean to you as a leader? The people you lead will be looking to you for your perspective. They are coming to work worried about whether a robot will replace them. Heck, you and I might be replaced by one as well. You need to be able to have these discussions. Your company will need to demonstrate it is taking action to support retraining and reskilling. The companies seen as leading the charge in reshaping the future of work will win in the future. Those that invest in developing their people will attract and retain the best talent. Leaders also need to focus on employee well-being, and on creating a sense of belonging, inclusiveness, and connectedness in our workplaces.

4. Delivering on Diversity, Equity, and Inclusion

One hundred seventy years. That's how long the World Economic Forum estimates it will take to realize true diversity in the workplace.[25] What?! That's not good enough. Every leader I speak to and work with agrees that diversity and gender parity are critical business issues. So why are we moving at a snail's pace? I got part of the answer to this question a while back when I had the opportunity to spend some time with Laura Liswood. She's the founder and secretary-general of the Council of Women World Leaders, a group of 72 women presidents, prime ministers, and heads of state. It's the only organization of its kind in the world. Liswood has been a strong voice for diversity for decades and even wrote a book on the topic: *The Loudest Duck: Moving Beyond Diversity While Embracing Differences to Achieve Success at Work.*[26]

In our discussion, I asked her to give me her sense of whether things were getting better when it comes to diversity. She said they are, but ever so slowly. Liswood believes how we think about diversity slows down the progress toward it. Some of us compare it to, as she calls it, Noah's Ark: "Let's just get two of everything on board, and things will be okay." This approach, however, is just too simplistic.

Liswood believes that diversity is a path to innovation for organizations and society. However, it doesn't happen by accident. First, you need to make it a priority. You need to go beyond superficialities and create a culture in which everyone's voice is heard—really heard. All people must feel included, involved, and valued—only then will they be engaged. Liswood says this is a challenge she has repeatedly seen in the corporate world. Everybody wants diversity, but they don't know what to do with it once they have it, which slows down progress. We need to take inclusion seriously. We need to go beyond all the hype and understand the mission-critical importance of this issue. We need to deliver diversity, equity, and inclusion in our organizations and in our world.

5. Repurposing Corporations

When I was doing my graduate work, I was influenced a lot by the research and thinking of Dr. Willis Harman. He headed up an organization called the World Business Academy. I was fortunate enough to spend time with him and hear his lectures. At the time, he believed that corporations were becoming the dominant institution in our society. As a result, they needed to broaden their purpose from a self-serving focus on profit and shareholder returns to making the world a better place. His ideas influenced my thinking about repurposing the role of business in society.

I've been watching this trend continue to unfold ever so slowly since those days. Recently, it seems to be gaining some momentum once again. For instance, in 2018, Larry Fink, chairman and CEO of BlackRock, wrote his annual letter to CEOs and challenged his peers not to be so single-mindedly focused on quarterly results and profits.[27] He wrote that society is looking to the private sector and expecting them to help address some of the world's biggest challenges. Fink is onto something because research conducted by the Edelman Trust Barometer reveals the public's increasing expectations of CEOs.[28] Eighty-four percent of people surveyed expect CEOs to inform conversations and policy debates on one or more pressing social issues, including jobs, the economy, automation, regulation, and globalization. They also found that 56 percent of people lose respect for CEOs who remain silent on critical social issues. The report concludes that to build trust, CEOs must lead with purpose, be authentic, and galvanize employees on the social issues that matter to them. I believe this is one of the reasons we are seeing more CEO activists—business leaders who are speaking out and taking a stand on important social and global issues like climate change, food security, poverty, domestic violence, mental health, and immigration, to name a few.

In August of 2019, the Business Roundtable, an association of CEOs of America's leading companies, released a new statement on the purpose of a corporation.[29] For a long time, the purpose of corporations was clear—create value for shareholders. The new purpose statement lays out a broader set of five commitments:

- Delivering value to customers,
- Investing in employees,
- Dealing fairly and ethically with suppliers,
- Supporting communities in which companies work, and
- Generating long-term value for shareholders.

This new purpose statement was signed by 181 prominent CEOs who committed to lead their companies for the benefit of all stakeholders: customers, employees, suppliers, communities, and shareholders. It was an exciting moment. Like many, I applauded their efforts. Now, I'm not sure whether these CEOs realized it at the time, but in creating this new purpose statement, they also established a new leadership contract for themselves. We'll see whether they will honor these commitments and if they will be genuinely accountable as they lead their organizations into the future.

Final Thoughts

I've spent my career helping leaders build great companies, led by the best leaders in their industries. When a company fails, there is considerable fallout from its demise, including the loss of shareholder value, economic prosperity, and jobs. That's why I get angry and upset when a company like Sears closes. There's a significant ripple effect on the economy, for shareholders, customers, and employees. I get outraged when a company fails. When you dig a little deeper to understand how it all fell apart, you quickly realize that it's the leaders who failed. They were not capable of stepping up when their companies needed them the most. They may not have understood the significant drivers in their context. They may not have seen the necessary changes required in their business model, or it could be that their arrogance simply blinded them. Alternatively, when they did, they reacted too slowly—or maybe it was just too late. Either way, something prevented them from responding more quickly. Whatever the reason, they failed to step up to their obligation to the people they led. They didn't appreciate the changing context in which they were leading. As a result, they were

not able to step up when it mattered most to their primary stakeholders. It is critical then that you understand the context and the world
in which you lead to be vigilant in challenging how you think about
your business and what will drive success in the future.

Gut Check for Leaders: The New Game Begins Before the Old One Ends

As you think about the ideas in this chapter, reflect on your
answers to the following Gut Check for Leaders questions:

1. How are you staying abreast of the game-changing technologies impacting your industry and your company?
2. How are you staying on top of geopolitical events taking place
   around the world?
3. To what extent are you staying on top of the trends and thinking about the future of work?
4. To what extent are you setting the tone for diversity, equity,
   and inclusion within your organization and creating a place of
   belonging for all to find meaningful work regardless of gender,
   race, sexual orientation, ability, and age?
5. What are your perspectives on the role and purpose of business
   in society, and in what way do you intend to leave your organization and our world in a better place?

Notes

1. "The New Game Begins Before the Old One Ends," Innosight
   CEO Summit Report 2017, September 2017, https://www
   .innosight.com/insight/the-new-game-begins-before-the-old
   -one-ends/.
2. Carmin Chappell, "Sears Was 'Toast' Ever Since Its 2005 Kmart
   Merger, Says Former Sears Canada CEO," *CNBC*, October 15,
   2018, https://www.cnbc.com/2018/10/15/sears-was-toast-ever
   -since-kmart-merger-former-sears-canada-ceo.html.

3. Shoshanna Delventhal, "Who Killed Sears? Fifty Years on the Road to Ruin," *Investopedia*, July 1, 2019, https://www.investopedia.com/news/downfall-of-sears/.

4. Grant Cardone, "Sears Bankruptcy Could Have Been Prevented," *The 10X Entrepreneur*, October 16, 2018, https://medium.com/the-10x-entrepreneur/sears-bankruptcy-could-have-been-prevented-530969baac5d.

5. "Sears Tanked Because the Company Failed to Shift to Digital," *Business Insider Intelligence*, August 26, 2016, https://www.businessinsider.com/sears-tanked-because-the-company-failed-to-shift-to-digital-2016-8.

6. Evan Comen, "Sears' Edward Lampert Is the Most Hated CEO in America," *24/7 Wall St.*, November 6, 2016, https://247wallst.com/retail/2016/11/06/sears-edward-lampert-is-the-most-hated-ceo-in-america/.

7. "Sears Saved by Chairman's $5.2 Billion Bid, Last-Minute Reprieve for up to 45,000 Workers," *The Financial Post*, January 17, 2019, https://business.financialpost.com/news/retail-marketing/sears-chairman-lampert-wins-bankruptcy-auction-for-retailer-with-5-2-bln-bid.

8. Soundarya J in Bengaluru, "Lampert Reveals Plans for Sears after Bankruptcy: WSJ," *Reuters*, February 13, 2019, https://www.reuters.com/article/us-sears-bankruptcy-lampert/lampert-revealsplans-for-sears-after-bankruptcy-wsj-idUSKCN1Q21D6.

9. Lauren Hirsch, "Sears Sues Former CEO Eddie Lampert, Treasury Secretary Mnuchin and Others for Alleged 'Thefts' of Billions from Retailer," *CNBC*, April 18, 2019, https://www.cnbc.com/2019/04/18/sears-sues-eddie-lampert-steven-mnuchin-others-for-alleged-thefts.html?&qsearchterm=sears%20sues%20eddie%20lampert.

10. Nathan Bomey, "Sears Buyer Eddie Lampert Wants to Avoid up to $43M in Severance Pay from Bankruptcy," *USA Today*, May 28, 2019, https://www.usatoday.com/story/money/2019/05/28/sears-worker-severance-eddie-lampert-esl-investments/1261845001/.

11. Mark Randolph, *That Will Never Work: The Birth of Netflix and the Amazing Life of an Idea* (Little, Brown and Company, 2019).

12. KPMG International, "Now or Never, 2016 Global CEO Outlook," 10, https://home.kpmg/content/dam/kpmg/pdf/2016/06/2016-global-ceo-outlook.pdf.

13. David Jacquemont, Dana Maor, and Angelika Reich, "How to Beat the Transformation Odds," McKinsey & Company, April 2015, https://www.mckinsey.com/business-functions/organization/our-insights/how-to-beat-the-transformation-odds.

14. Scott D. Anthony, S. Patrick Viguerie, and Andrew Waldeck, *Corporate Longevity: Turbulence Ahead for Large Organizations* (Innosight Executive Briefing, Spring 2016), 2, https://www.innosight.com/wp-content/uploads/2016/08/Corporate-Longevity-2016-Final.pdf.

15. "Heidrick & Struggles FTSE 350 and Global Surveys Reveal Rising CEO Churn Rate," Heidrick & Struggles, June 5, 2018, https://heidrick.mediaroom.com/2018-06-05-Heidrick-Struggles-FTSE-350-and-global-surveys-reveal-rising-CEO-churn-rate.

16. Anthony J. Mayo and Nitin Nohria, *In Their Time: The Greatest Business Leaders of the Twentieth Century* (Harvard Business School Publishing, 2005).

17. In *The Leadership Contract Field Guide*, I shared an activity that we use in all our leadership development programs to help leaders understand the world in which they are leading. You might want to have a look at it and use it in your own leadership role.

18. Klaus Schwab, "The Fourth Industrial Revolution: What It Means, How to Respond," World Economic Forum, January 14, 2016, https://www.weforum.org/agenda/2016/01/the-fourth-industrial-revolution-what-it-means-and-how-to-respond/.

19. Eric Rosenbaum, "IBM Artificial Intelligence Can Predict with 95% Accuracy Which Workers Are About to Quit Their Jobs," *CNBC*, April 3, 2019, https://www.cnbc.com/2019/04/03/ibm-ai-can-predict-with-95-percent-accuracy-which-employees-will-quit.html.

20. KPMG International, "Disrupt and Grow, 2017 Global CEO Outlook," 4, https://assets.kpmg/content/dam/kpmg/xx/pdf/2017/06/2017-global-ceo-outlook.pdf.

21. Drew Erdmann, Ezra Greenberg, and Ryan Harper, "Geostrategic Risks on the Rise," McKinsey & Company, May 2016, https://www.mckinsey.com/business-functions/strategy-and-corporate-finance/our-insights/geostrategic-risks-on-the-rise.

22. Charlotte Seager, "Will Jobs Exist in 2050?" *The Guardian*, October 13, 2016, https://www.theguardian.com/careers/2016/oct/13/will-jobs-exist-in-2050.

23. Philip Perry, "47% of Jobs Will Vanish in the Next 25 Years, Say Oxford University Researchers," *Big Think*, December 24, 2016, https://bigthink.com/philip-perry/47-of-jobs-in-the-next-25-years-will-disappear-according-to-oxford-university.

24. André Dua, Liz Hilton Segel, and Susan Lund, "It's Time for a C-level Role Dedicated to Reskilling Workers," *Harvard Business Review*, September 3, 2019, https://hbr.org/2019/09/its-time-for-a-c-level-role-dedicated-to-reskilling-workers.

25. Alan Jope, "Gender Equality Is 170 Years Away. We Cannot Wait That Long," *World Economic Forum*, January 19, 2017, https://www.weforum.org/agenda/2017/01/gender-equality-is-170-years-away-we-cannot-wait-that-long/.

26. Laura A. Liswood, *The Loudest Duck: Moving Beyond Diversity While Embracing Differences to Achieve Success at Work* (Wiley, 2009).

27. Larry Fink, "Larry Fink's 2018 Letter to CEOs: A Sense of Purpose," BlackRock, 2018, https://www.blackrock.com/corporate/investor-relations/2018-larry-fink-ceo-letter.

28. "Edelman Trust Barometer: Expectations for CEOs," Edelman, May 1, 2018, https://www.edelman.com/post/trust-barometer-expectations-for-ceos.

29. "Business Roundtable Redefines the Purpose of a Corporation to Promote 'An Economy That Serves All Americans,'" *Business Roundtable*, August 19, 2019, https://www.businessroundtable.org/business-roundtable-redefines-the-purpose-of-a-corporation-to-promote-an-economy-that-serves-all-americans.

CHAPTER 2

Why Do We Not Have Better Leadership?

In his seminal book *On Leadership,* John Gardner shared an observation: "Why do we not have better leadership? The question is asked over and over. We complain, express our disappointment, often our outrage; but no answer emerges."[1] This question is a familiar and recurring one. I'm sure you see it crop up repeatedly in the media in stories of political leaders or corporate executives embroiled in scandal, corruption, and wrongdoing. What I find interesting is that Gardner first raised this question in 1990. That was 30 years ago!

By chance, that happens to be the year I started my first company and began my journey to becoming a leadership adviser. The puzzling thing is that Gardner's question is probably even more relevant today than it was back then. I wonder what he would have to say if he were around to witness today's leadership? Consider the number of corporate scandals, the rampant sexual harassment cases that led to the #MeToo movement, the low state of employee engagement, the erosion of trust and confidence in senior leaders, and the political turmoil created by many world leaders. It has been an astonishing few years during which we have witnessed some dreadful leadership. An article in the Harvard Law School Forum on Corporate Governance and Financial Regulation cited more than 400 business executives and employees (including several prominent and high-profile CEOs) as being accused of misconduct over an 18-month period.[2] Four hundred. No, you did not misread that.

If this is not concerning enough, many of the senior executives accused of wrongdoing are rarely held accountable. For example, two CEOs of Wells Fargo left their companies unscathed, even after their organizations opened 3.5 million fake accounts, wrongly foreclosed on hundreds of homeowners, and illegally repossessed thousands of cars under their leadership.[3] How is this possible?

The World Economic Forum goes further. In *Outlook on the Global Agenda 2015,*[4] they shared findings of a survey of senior leaders that revealed 86 percent of them agreed that we have a global leadership crisis. This cry isn't new. In the 1980s, James MacGregor Burns, an American historian, presidential biographer, and leadership expert, wrote that the plight of leadership is a result of the mediocrity and irresponsibility demonstrated by many leaders. He also believed that few leaders step up and show the kind of leadership needed for the times in which they are leading.

To me, the crisis we lament isn't just about leadership, but is really about leadership accountability. Quite simply, the problem we face is that far too many leaders are not stepping up and not behaving in an accountable manner. My own research of close to 3,000 global senior business executives and human resources leaders confirms that companies around the world are facing a fundamental leadership accountability gap (see Figure 2.1).[5] We found that 72 percent of survey respondents believe leadership accountability is the critical business challenge facing their organizations, while only 31 percent of organizations are satisfied with the degree of accountability demonstrated by their leaders. We must do better! Before we explore how, we need to understand why the leadership accountability gap exists.

As discussed in the previous chapter of this book, the world in which leaders lead is getting more complex every day. Success or failure in almost every endeavor ultimately comes down to leadership. There are those who are truly accountable and able to drive extraordinary results. Then there are those with good intentions, but not able to drive success. Finally, there are leaders who are ineffective and who typically will fail.

Leadership Is Not as Strong as It Needs to Be

In *The Leadership Contract,* I explored how leadership had become disappointing, disconnected, and disgraceful. Several key themes emerged from my research and discussions with clients. First, we continue to

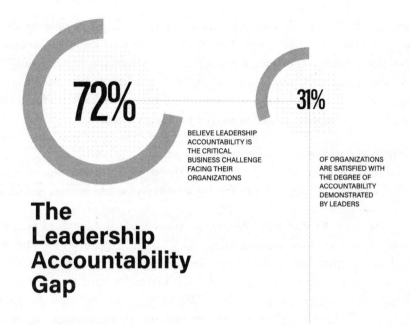

Figure 2.1   The Leadership Accountability Gap

rely on the heroic model of leadership. We glorify charismatic leaders. We also continue to promote technical superstars into leadership roles, and we have a quick-fix view of what it takes to develop leaders. As I began to write this book, I realized that not only do many of these challenges still exist, but more have emerged. We need to come to terms with these challenges because if we don't, we will never be able to make things better. Let's explore them below.

Leaders Are Overwhelmed

As we discussed in the last chapter, leaders today are facing more complexity than ever before. Many of the leaders I talk to say they feel overwhelmed and overloaded in their roles, which in turn erodes organizational performance and productivity.

Complexity Continues to Increase

According to research conducted by the Boston Consulting Group (BCG), business complexity has increased 35 times from 1955 to 2010, and organizational complexity has increased six times over the same period.[6] BCG also found that managers spend a great deal of time bogged down in their roles. For example, do you know how many levels of approvals the typical manager must obtain for any decision? If you thought seven, you would be right. Seven levels. Are you kidding me? There's no way to be accountable for your actions under those conditions. The study also found that managers spend:

- Forty percent of their time writing reports,
- Thirty to 60 percent of their time in meetings, and
- Forty to 80 percent of their time on activities that add little to no value.

These are frustrations I hear a lot from leaders. Many are bogged down by things that aren't adding value to the organization. Further evidence comes from our one-day Leadership Contract program. One exercise asks leaders to define how they make the hard work of leadership even harder for themselves. When we tally the most frequent response, we find some similar patterns globally. Leaders admit to getting in over their heads, being completely driven to distraction, and in turn, they remain stuck waiting for permission. Is this also happening to you?

Matrix Structures Create Ambiguity

The Gallup organization found that close to 84 percent of us work in a matrix structure of some kind. These structures typically establish dual reporting lines, which mean most employees end up being accountable to two different bosses. These structures are intended to create value for the organization, but in practice, they establish uncomfortable ambiguity and lack of role clarity—and erode accountability.[7]

In my own experience in matrix environments, I have often found myself in meetings with a cast of colleagues from different functions or geographies. As the conference call starts, it's clear that few know who owns the outcomes. The meeting goes on and on without any real purpose. At the height of my frustration, I'll ask, "Who is accountable for this meeting?" Awkward silence follows. It becomes clear that there is no clarity as to who owns the outcomes. Other leaders I've worked with have shared similar stories of frustration.

In the end, we haven't done a great job helping leaders learn how to lead in a matrix. We leave it to them to figure it out. Some do. However, the majority do not. Now here's the problem. When frustrations arise, leaders retreat to their silos, defeating the original purpose of matrix structures.

Leading in a Virtual World Challenges Many Leaders

Research reveals that 85 percent of global teams work and meet virtually, and 40 percent of them have never met each other face to face.[8] In the book *Can You Hear Me?*, author Nick Morgan explains that most leaders now work with colleagues from different geographies and across multiple time zones.[9] Technology can make us more productive. However, as standard as virtual work and virtual teams have become, many leaders and teams still aren't equipped to work in this virtual world. Morgan explains that everything is harder in a virtual world: how we communicate, how we make decisions, how we get work done, and how we attempt to hold each other accountable. This is the reality of leading today, and we need to support leaders to develop the capabilities they need to thrive and help their teams be successful.

All of these issues weigh heavily on leaders and employees. Workplace stress is becoming a significant challenge in many organizations. In fact, the World Health Organization recently and officially classified workplace burnout as an occupational phenomenon and revised the International Classification of Diseases.[10] They define burnout as a syndrome resulting from chronic workplace stress and defined by four factors which include: (a) feelings of exhaustion and depletion, (b) increased mental distance from one's job, (c) feelings of negativism and cynicism, and (d) reduced professional effectiveness. We must find a way to support leaders and employees so they have the capacity to be effective in their roles.

Leaders Are Disengaged

For decades, the research on engagement has remained relatively stable. At any given time, you can expect 20 to 25 percent of your employees to be fully engaged. Another 20 to 25 percent are fully disengaged—but they keep showing up to work, and you keep paying them. The rest are only moderately engaged. Many companies try to fix this problem by adding more foosball tables or improving the quality of cafeteria food, but few of these strategies have any significant impact.

Here's the other part of the problem. Your leaders are also not engaged. The Gallup organization report *The State of the American Manager*[11] found that only about 35 percent of managers are engaged in their roles. Fifty-one percent are not engaged, and 14 percent are actively disengaged. A large portion of these leaders do not care about their companies. I'm not sure how we hope to drive success if leaders don't care about customers, employees, and the company. We pay an exorbitant price for this disengagement. Gallup estimates the cost to the U.S. economy to be an estimated $319 billion to $398 billion annually.

If leaders are disengaged, it's no wonder employees are also disengaged. According to Gallup, leadership makes up an estimated 70 percent of the variance in employee engagement. Many companies have missed the boat on this issue. They have focused on superficial issues and ignored or underestimated the impact that their leaders have on employee engagement.

It's not just one's direct experience with a manager that impacts engagement. It turns out that the overall quality of a leadership culture also matters. Research reveals that when employees see their most senior leaders and other managers working well together, their sense of engagement jumps to 72 percent.[12] However, when they perceive their senior leaders and the rest of management are not working well together, engagement drops to 8 percent. Employees are always watching how their leaders work together and are forming impressions about the company and its culture.

When leadership isn't up to the task, trust declines. The research firm Edelman has been measuring and tracking trust for some time now. They have found a "staggering" lack of confidence in leadership. In a recent global survey, 63 percent of survey respondents said that CEOs are not at all or only somewhat credible.[13] The credibility of CEOs fell by 12 points in one year to just 37 percent globally.

So, if you are desperately trying to improve the engagement of your employees, the answer is clear: Fix the engagement and effectiveness of your leaders. Mediocre leadership will never drive high employee engagement.

Leaders Are Underprepared

A recent McKinsey study found that 83 percent of global leaders believe they are underprepared for their new roles.[14] Only about a third of global leaders feel that their organizations effectively support leaders assuming new roles. No wonder research also reveals that 27 to 46 percent of transitions into executive positions end in disappointment and outright failure. What are the top two barriers? Close to 70 percent of leaders attribute their inability to succeed to politics, culture, and people issues. An equal number regret that they didn't move quickly enough on changing the culture in their organizations. I have argued for a long time that organizations need to focus their energies on supporting those new to leadership roles, especially at critical turning points.

Getting leadership transitions right has a direct impact on the business. For example, the Corporate Executive Board found that when leadership transitions are not successful, team engagement erodes by 20 percent, and team performance decreases by 15 percent. When leadership transitions are successful, the team's likelihood of meeting their three-year performance goals is 90 percent and attrition goes down 13 percent.[15]

Part of the problem may be that we don't do a good enough job of helping leaders get ready for their roles. Research conducted by the Center for Creative Leadership found that 60 percent of front-line leaders never receive any training or development to help them succeed in their roles.[16] So they end up trying to figure it out on their own. Many develop bad habits that stay with them as they rise through the ranks. Much of leadership development is spent trying to reverse bad habits that leaders have developed. My team and I have seen this countless times in our client work. Every time we meet with senior executives to discuss a front-line leader training program, there is always a senior leader who admits that they need the same training. The leader then shares that they never received any development or support when they started as a leader. Imagine all these senior leaders, without really having the basic skills that all leaders need to be successful. What impact is this having on our organizations? The impact is obvious. Research estimates that only about 50 percent of managers are competent in their roles. Even worse, some feel that most managers are a disappointment, completely incompetent, mis-hired for their positions, or complete failures.[17]

Interestingly, this isn't just a manager issue. Even some CEOs struggle with feeling unprepared for their jobs. Egon Zender, a global search firm, found in a survey of 402 CEOs (from 11 countries and a cross-section of industries) that only 30 percent felt fully prepared when taking on the top job. The majority felt that the role was much harder than they expected. Part of what makes the leadership role challenging is the need for personal transformation. Close to 80 percent of the CEOs surveyed agreed that they needed the capacity to transform themselves as well as the organization. They also recognized that a commitment to personal reflection was critical to their success. About half reported that developing their senior team was much more complicated than expected. With this kind of challenge, you would think that a CEO would reach out for help and support from their boards. Unfortunately, this doesn't seem to happen very often. Only 28 percent of CEOs reportedly turn to their boards for feedback and support.

Leadership Development Is Underwhelming

A key reasons that leaders feel underprepared for their roles is because of the leadership development industry itself. It hasn't kept pace with the complexity and pressures that leaders face. It's not that companies are not investing in leadership. Not at all. According to Josh Bersin, a leading industry analyst, researcher, and educator, leadership development is an enormous industry. More than 70,000 books and videos on the topic are available. Bersin also estimates that about $14 billion is spent annually in the United States on leadership development programs alone.[18] Leadership development is big business. In recent years, spending has been increasing at a rate of 14 percent a year.[19] Companies are investing, but they're not getting results.

Several research studies paint a less-than-stellar picture of the quality of, and satisfaction with, leadership development efforts in organizations. For example, just 37 percent of leaders rated the quality of an organization's efforts as being high or very high,[20] and only 40 percent of Millennials rate leadership development programs as excellent. These findings are consistent with research done by the Brandon Hall Group that found 75 percent of leadership development to be ineffective.[21] The reasons cited include the lack of an overall leadership development strategy and the lack of an innovative approach to learning and development.

A survey conducted by Korn Ferry, a global search and leadership firm, revealed that only 17 percent of C-suite executives are confident they have the leadership talent needed to deliver on their company's strategic priorities.[22] Forty percent of respondents reported that their organizations do not review their company's leadership needs against their business strategy. In other words, there is no connection between leadership development and an organization's business strategy. From my experience, this is a huge red flag. If leadership development and business strategy are not connected, then an organization is wasting time and money. In addition, we see them pay a price in terms of their inability to execute their business strategy.

The Price We Pay—an Inability to Successfully Execute Strategy

If you are a leader who is feeling overloaded, disengaged, or underprepared for your role, it's understandable how these feelings can erode your sense of engagement. It is also understandable how this can lead one to become mediocre and unaccountable. There is also a significant price we pay for all of this, and to me it's all about the inability to execute strategy. Multiple studies have confirmed that most organizations struggle to execute their desired strategy. For example, a recent survey by the Brightline Initiative and Harvard Business Review Analytic Services found that only 20 percent of companies are successful in achieving their strategic initiatives.[23] The study also confirmed five barriers that impede strategy execution:

1. Too many strategic and change initiatives are introduced at once and overwhelm leaders.
2. Poor communication and information sharing lead to a lack of clarity.
3. Insufficient resources equate to an inability to deliver the strategy.
4. Senior leaders don't agree about the strategy and/or how to implement it.
5. The purpose of the strategic initiatives is not well communicated to the organization.

What do you notice about this list of barriers? They all have to do with leadership. If your organization has many mediocre and unaccountable leaders, they will never be able to create a compelling strategy, let alone execute one. As more companies attempt to transform themselves to be successful in the future, they need leaders ready and able to execute their strategy. The only way to overcome these barriers is to create real clarity about strategic priorities. Many senior executives assume there is clarity, when there isn't. After they have completed their road show, shot their corporate video, or completed town hall meetings, they assume everyone is clear. I can tell you from experience that most leaders are not clear. My team and I see this repeatedly in our work with leaders. Without strategic clarity, accountability won't happen, and goals won't be met.

The Faulty Assumption We Continue to Make

In all of the ideas on the current state of leadership explored above, we need to understand one more important issue. It's one that holds us back, but we may not even be aware of it. It's the prevailing and faulty assumption that many people have about leaders. What is it? I've learned that we make a faulty assumption when it comes to leadership. Mainly, we assume when someone takes on a leadership role that they will automatically step up personally and hold others accountable. We assume that when you give people manager titles, they will step up. You hope they will be accountable. But this isn't the case at all. The reality is that leaders are not good at being accountable themselves, and they're not good at holding others accountable. Writing in the *Harvard Business Review*, Overfield and Kaiser found that accountability is the single most neglected behavior among leaders globally.[24] They found that 50 percent of leaders are terrible at accountability. While we expect senior executives to be tough in holding themselves and others accountable, the sad reality is that they are not. My global research found that only 45 percent of leaders are seen as being accountable.

In the book *Results-Based Leadership*, Dave Ulrich, Jack Zenger, and Norm Smallwood write that accountability comes from discipline, which requires getting work done with rigor and consistency, meeting scheduled commitments, and following through on plans and programs to deliver promises. They also describe how accountability comes with ownership—as a person feels responsible for accomplishing work, they own the outcomes at a profoundly personal level. They write, "Leaders who foster accountability continuously improve how work gets done, deliver high-quality products and services, and ensure commitment from all employees."[25]

Final Thoughts

When I started to write this book and conduct the research for this chapter, I began feeling quite frustrated. In spite of all the efforts to build strong leadership in organizations, the reality is we still have quite a way to go. Leadership is nowhere near as strong as it needs to be.

I was reminded of the story of Sisyphus, the character from Greek mythology. If you know about him, Sisyphus was a cruel king of Corinth. He was known for his hubris and deceitful ways. Eventually, the god Hades had enough of him and condemned Sisyphus to roll a boulder up a hill for eternity. But Sisyphus was never able to reach the top. Every time he approached the summit, the boulder mysteriously rolled back down the mountain.[26] It was an endless, pointless, and fruitless task that was impossible to complete. Any job that is like this is known as a Sisyphean task.

You see, I've spent the better part of my career as an adviser to organizations around the world. I worked hard to be a strong leader myself in my corporate and entrepreneurial roles. I've worked with hundreds and hundreds of leaders and their companies. But despite all the combined efforts and investments people like me have made to build strong leadership in organizations, it feels like we haven't made much progress. Have all these efforts become one big Sisyphean task?

We need to be honest with ourselves about the current state of leadership in our organizations. Once we accept that, we need to commit to making things better. It's time to take your leadership into your own hands. You can't rely on a company or your manager to do it for you. You need to be accountable for your development as a leader. You need to be the one who inspires others to step up, own their roles, and deliver results. The rest of this book will show you how.

Gut Check for Leaders: Why Do We Not Have Better Leadership?

As you think about the ideas in this chapter, reflect on your answers to the following Gut Check for Leaders questions:

1. In what ways are you feeling overwhelmed and overloaded?
2. Are you feeling disengaged and disheartened? Why or why not?
3. Do you feel prepared and ready to take on the leadership challenges you will face in the coming years? Why or why not?
4. How has leadership development been underwhelming for you?
5. How confident are you in your ability to execute your company's strategy?

Notes

1. J. W. Gardner, *On Leadership,* p. xv (New York: The Free Press, 1990).
2. Laurie Hays Edelman, "The Board, CEO Misconduct, and Corporate Culture," *Harvard Law School on Corporate Governance and Financial Regulation*, January 12, 2019, https://corpgov.law.harvard.edu/2019/01/12/the-board-ceo-misconduct-and-corporate-culture/.
3. Cited in https://www.warren.senate.gov/imo/media/doc/2019.4.1%20Corporate%20Executive%20Accountability%20Act%20Summary.pdf.
4. *Outlook on the Global Agenda 2015,* World Economic Forum, 2015, http://reports.weforum.org/outlook-global-agenda-2015/.
5. Vince Molinaro, *The Leadership Contract* (3rd ed.) (John Wiley & Sons, 2018).
6. Yves Morieux, "Bringing Managers Back to Work," Boston Consulting Group, October 4, 2018, https://www.bcg.com/en-ca/publications/2018/bringing-managers-back-to-work.aspx.
7. Vibhas Ratanjee and Nate Dvorak, *Mastering Matrix Management in the Age of Agility* (Workplace Gallup, 2018), https://www.gallup

.com/workplace/242192/mastering-matrix-management-age-agility.aspx.

8. Jean Brittain Leslie, Margaret M. Luciano, John E. Mathieu, and Emily Hoole, "Challenge Accepted: Managing Polarities to Enhance Virtual Team Effectiveness." *People + Strategy,* 41(2), 22–40 (Spring 2018).

9. Nick Morgan, *Can you hear me?: How to Connect with People in a Virtual World* (Boston, MA: Harvard Business School Press, 2018).

10. Ashley Turner, "The World Health Organization Officially Recognizes Workplace 'Burnout' as an Occupational Phenomenon," *CNBC,* May 28, 2019, https://www.cnbc.com/2019/05/28/who-recognizes-workplace-burnout-as-an-occupational-phenomenon.html.

11. "The State of the American Manager—Analytics and Advice for Leaders" (Gallup, 2015).

12. "Effective Managers—Your Critical Link to Successful Strategy Execution" (Towers Watson, 2015).

13. Matthew Harrington, "Survey: People's Trust Has Declined in Business, Media, Government, and NGOs," *Harvard Business Review,* January 16, 2017, https://hbr.org/2017/01/survey-peoples-trust-has-declined-in-business-media-government-and-ngos.

14. Scott Keller and Mary Meaney, "Successfully Transitioning to New Leadership Roles," McKinsey & Company, May 2018, https://www.mckinsey.com/business-functions/organization/our-insights/successfully-transitioning-to-new-leadership-roles.

15. Kruti Bharucha, "The Cost of Poor Leadership Transitions," https://www.peoplematters.in/blog/change-management/the-cost-of-poor-leadership-transitions-4429?utm_source=peoplematters&utm_medium=interstitial&utm_campaign=learnings-of-the-day.

16. *Talent Reimagined: 7 Emerging Trends for Transformative Leaders* (Center for Creative Leadership, 2018).

17. William Gentry, "Derailment: How Successful Leaders Avoid It," in Elaine Biech (Ed.), *The ASTD Leadership Handbook* (Alexandria, VA: ASTD Press, 2010), pp. 311–324; William Gentry and Craig Chappelow, "Managerial Derailment: Weaknesses That Can Be

Fixed," in Robert B. Kaiser (Ed.), *The Perils of Accentuating the Positives* (Tulsa, OK: Hogan Press, 2009), pp. 97–113.

18. Josh Bersin, "Why Leadership Development Feels Broken: And How We're Fixing It," *Josh Bersin*, July 7, 2019, https://joshbersin .com/2019/07/why-leadership-development-feels-broken-and -how-were-fixing-it/.

19. Dori Meinert, "Leadership Development Spending Is Up," *SHRM*, July 22, 2014, https://www.shrm.org/hr-today/news/hr -magazine/pages/0814-execbrief.aspx.

20. *Ready-Now Leaders: 25 Findings to Meet Tomorrow's Business Challenges Global Leadership Forecast 2014|2015* (Development Dimensions International and The Conference Board, 2015).

21. Lorri Freifeld, "Survey: Leadership Programs Lack Effectiveness," *Training: The Official Publication of Training Magazine Network*, September 30, 2013, https://trainingmag.com/content/survey-leadership -programs-lack-effectiveness/.

22. "Leadership Development: CEOs' Strategic Powerhouse," *Korn Ferry* Institute, September 23, 2015, https://www.kornferry.com /institute/leadership-development-ceos-strategic-powerhouse.

23. "Testing Organizational Boundaries to Improve Strategy Execution," *Harvard Business Review*, https://s3.us-east-2.amazonaws.com/brightline -website/downloads/reports/HBR_Research-Report_Brightline .pdf?utm_source=resource-page&utm_medium=skip-link.

24. Darren Overfield and Rob Kaiser, "One Out of Every Two Managers Is Terrible at Accountability," *Harvard Business Review*, November 8, 2012, https://hbr.org/2012/11/one-out-of-every-two -managers-is-terrible-at-accountability.

25. Dave Ulrich, Jack Zenger, and Norm Smallwood, *Results-Based Leadership* (Harvard Business Review Press, 1999).

26. https://grammarist.com/usage/sisyphean-promethean-or -herculean/.

PART 2
Understanding
Leadership
Accountability

This section of the book includes four chapters that will provide an essential foundation for how to think about leadership accountability.

Chapter 3: How to Think About Leadership Accountability
This chapter discusses leadership accountability from a broader and systemic perspective and explores the role of the board, the chief executive officer, other senior executives, and the head of human resources to drive it across an organization.

Chapter 4: Leadership Accountability at the Individual Level
This chapter will help you understand how leadership accountability exists at the individual level. It first examines what mediocre leadership looks like, and then discusses what truly accountable leaders do to set themselves apart from other leaders.

Chapter 5: Leadership Accountability at the Team Level
This chapter will help you understand how leadership accountability exists at the team level. It explores how teams have transformed, and then it provides an overview of the two dimensions of truly accountable teams.

Chapter 6: Leadership Accountability at the Culture Level
This chapter will help you understand how leadership accountability exists at a cultural level. It discusses why culture is important, and then examines the ten characteristics of a strong community of leaders.

CHAPTER 3

How to Think About Leadership Accountability

If you and I met, one of the things you would immediately notice is that I always have a notebook with me. I'm always jotting down notes—from meetings with clients, internal meetings with my teams, and my latest *aha* moments. I also keep notes digitally, but my physical notebook is my go-to device. I keep all my notebooks, and when I started to conduct my research for this book, I realized that I had 15 years' worth of notebooks. As I dug into them and read each one, I discovered that I had, on average, two meetings per week with leaders from companies all over the world—that is almost 1,500 meetings in total. When I distilled the insights from these notes, it became clear to me how everything led up to my thinking about why leadership accountability matters. In the next section, I will briefly describe what I have learned from all those meetings and client projects, and how over time they've helped form the core ideas of my life's work.

The Timeline of Leadership Challenges

After analyzing my notes, I immediately saw how leadership challenges evolved and changed over time. There were five broad themes that surfaced (see Figure 3.1). Let's explore each of them in more detail.

Figure 3.1 The Timeline of Leadership Challenges

1. Leadership Becomes a Business Issue

For many years, one of the challenges I repeatedly saw in my client conversations was that senior executives were not paying attention to leadership within their companies. Some delegated it exclusively to the human resources function because it wasn't something they considered to be strategic. However, my colleagues and I began to observe several trends that would have a significant impact on organizations. The more prominent ones were the shift in workforce demographics, the increase in global competition, and the impact of new technologies. These trends were going to challenge organizations from a talent perspective—from succession management to leadership development and employee engagement. In 2005, my colleague David Weiss and I published the book *The Leadership Gap*. It served as a rallying cry to help organizations begin to think about leadership more strategically.

2. Companies Begin to Take an Integrated Approach to Leadership Development

As senior executives became more enlightened about this business issue, they began to see leadership in a more strategic way. I found that they then started to scrutinize their internal organizations' leadership development practices. Many didn't like what they saw. At the time, many organizations had fragmented offerings—coaching programs, assessment tools, succession planning, and leadership programs, all implemented in a piecemeal fashion. Everything was disconnected, and nothing aligned with the business strategy. I remember meeting with the global head of leadership for a large financial services organization. She was new to her role, and in her first three months she reviewed the company's leadership practices. She discovered that the company had amassed close to 40 different leadership models. In the end, the company had no consistent set of leadership expectations for all leaders. She said in the meeting, "I need your help to get us from 40 frameworks down to one."

Organizations needed help to learn how to think about leadership development in a more integrated manner. In 2007, we released another book, *Leadership Solutions*. My co-authors, David Weiss, Liane Davey, and I presented a unified framework called *The Leadership Pathway*. It helped companies think about all aspects of leadership development in a more integrated manner. Organizations began to have success with these ideas. Then something happened that changed everything.

3. Leaders Need Capabilities to Deal with Change and Ambiguity

In 2008, the financial crisis hit. Most companies were fighting for their very survival. They had to cut costs. Investment in leadership development slowed down or stopped entirely. Moreover, I found that some companies, especially those with a more strategic and long-term perspective, actually increased their stake in leadership development. They did so because they believed that they needed to support leaders during a tough time.

We had many organizations reach out for ideas on how to help leaders lead through a dramatic period of change, uncertainty, and ambiguity. Many clients admitted that most of their leaders had never experienced anything like this before. All they knew was leading in good times with a strong economy. Now their world was turned upside down. Many people lost their jobs. Those who remained were under tremendous pressure to deliver results under challenging circumstances. The financial crisis also put a big spotlight on corporate scandals, corruption, and bad leadership behavior. Everyone realized that leaders were not living up to high standards of behavior. The problem was pervasive in business and across society.

4. Companies Shift Their Business Models and Strategy

As things began to settle down after the financial crisis, I noticed another couple of trends start to emerge. First, the financial crisis was a huge wake-up call for many companies and their leaders. The business environment in which they operated had changed for good. The financial crisis wasn't just an economic blip but a fundamental transformation. New challenges became apparent—digital disruption, regulatory changes, competitive pressures, and increasing customer demands. Many of my clients needed to redefine their business models and strategies and take their organizations in very different directions.

I also started to see my clients realize that their shifting context had direct leadership implications. They needed their leaders to step up in significantly different ways than they had in the past. I began to hear the term *inflection point* a lot. I learned that when a company is at an inflection, everything comes under a microscope, including talent. The clients I spoke with said, "We need our leaders to be stronger than they've ever been, but they are not." More of my clients were starting to express frustration. By this time, they were all investing in leadership development again, but they didn't feel that they saw stronger leadership from their leaders. What was going on?

5. Leadership Accountability Becomes a Critical Business Challenge

As I began to see the same patterns with client after client, I knew in my gut that there was something else happening. At the same time, there were plenty of headlines suggesting a problem with leadership. Whether it was political leadership at all levels of government or corporate leadership at the most senior ranks, leadership was becoming disgraceful. Studies continued to confirm that trust and confidence in senior leaders and our institutions, in general, were in constant decline.

That's when I realized that the problem companies were facing was about leadership accountability. Organizations had too many people in leadership roles who didn't fully appreciate or understand what it meant to be a leader. All of this was quite understandable given all the changes and turmoil that companies and their leaders had faced during and after the financial crisis. However, as things settled down post-recession, we needed to do a leadership rethink.

This "re-think" led me to write *The Leadership Contract*. It came out in July of 2013, and the ideas immediately resonated. Since that time, the book has spread around the world. I've continued to have hundreds of conversations with leaders like you, hearing about the leadership accountability challenges that they face. I've learned about the frustrations people have with the disappointing leadership demonstrated by their CEOs, boards, and executive teams. In addition, many people have also expressed frustration about middle managers, often described as the "layer of clay" in organizations because they impede change and strategy execution. There were also frustrations with front-line leaders because they didn't know how to lead teams and be good managers. Then there were countless discussions about approaches to leadership development. There was widespread recognition that the traditional ways of developing leaders were becoming less and less effective, and leaders were looking for a new way forward.

What I also learned through all these discussions is that organizations approach accountability differently. Some take a direct, heavy-handed, and even fear-based approach: "YOU shall be accountable!" Of course, this is often met with resistance and resentment, especially if the senior leaders themselves do not model accountability in how they lead. In these instances, accountability becomes uninspiring and demotivating. Then mediocrity seeps into an organization, creating a more serious problem to solve.

On a personal level, I've had very different experiences with accountability. I've been lucky to work in environments where everyone is committed to stepping up, taking ownership, and working together to deliver results. When you are in this kind of environment, accountability is inspiring. You don't need your leaders to demand accountability because they demonstrate it in how they lead. It can also be vicarious—you look at how your colleagues show up, and they motivate you. You then feel an obligation to do your part to achieve success. Those who struggle or are unwilling to be accountable stick out from everyone else.

In turn, they either join in, leave, or are asked to leave. I believe this will be the key to drive stronger leadership accountability in organizations—doing it in a way that inspires people, rather than evoking fear, resentment, and animosity.

Let's continue to explore these ideas as we look next at how you need to think about leadership accountability. We will start by using the experience of Uber, during a particularly challenging six-month period in early 2017 that saw a tremendous upheaval in the company.

A Turbulent Six Months at Uber

As you may know, Travis Kalanick and Garrett Camp started a company called UberCab in 2009. They were pioneers of the new "sharing economy." Their business was built on a simple yet powerful idea—a ride-sharing company that enabled anyone to start earning an income by helping people get a ride from one destination to another.

The company quickly became a Silicon Valley darling. Everyone loved it. It was cool to be a customer. Even cooler to work there. Everything was going great until early 2017 when, almost overnight it seemed, things came to a screeching halt. A series of events unfolded that damaged the company's reputation, and eventually led to Kalanick being kicked out as its CEO and, in the process, experiencing a very public fall from grace. Let's review some of the highlights of what transpired.

In January 2017, Kalanick joined a business advisory council set up by the newly elected U.S. President Donald Trump. It would turn out to be a wildly unpopular move with Uber's young core users.[1] A few weeks later, the company was left reeling from an explosive blog post from Uber software engineer Susan Fowler.[2] Her blog post, published on February 19, 2017, was entitled "One Very, Very Strange Year at Uber." In it, she detailed a toxic culture of sexual harassment at the company. She shared her personal experiences of the inappropriate treatment and behavior of many of the male managers. When she complained to human resources, they ignored her. Fowler's blog post went viral, and Uber was justifiably under attack for its culture of sexism and toxic masculinity. The next day, Uber retained Eric Holder and Tammy Albarrán, partners in the law firm Covington & Burling LLP.[3] Their job was to conduct a thorough and objective review of the issues raised in Fowler's blog.

Maybe the mounting stress was too much for Kalanick. A few weeks later, a video surfaced where he was caught on dash cam in an argument about fares with Uber driver Fawzi Kamel.[4] Kamel was driving Kalanick and proceeded to express his frustration with Uber's fares and changing pricing policies. Kalanick maintained his composure for most of the discussion but eventually began to lose his patience. He accused the driver of not taking personal responsibility for his situation, preferring instead to blame others. Things got a little heated, and Kalanick darted out of the car. Now, under normal circumstances, this video probably would not be a big deal. However, in light of all the other issues going on with the company, it just added fuel to the fire that was already starting to burn out of control. Kalanick apologized for his behavior and treatment of Kamel. He publicly admitted that he needed help.

Unfortunately, things got worse for the company.

Other crises emerged. For example, a self-driving car crashed in Arizona, and the company temporarily suspended the experimental program.[5] A lawsuit alleged Uber had stolen trade secrets from Google in its rush to develop self-driving car technology.[6] As all these things started to come out, a downward spiral began to take hold.

In late May 2017, the company announced that it had lost $708 million in the first quarter alone. The head of finance left the company.[7] By now, industry analysts were starting to question everything about the company and its operations.

Kalanick was under tremendous scrutiny, as was Uber's culture. It became clear that under his leadership, the company had developed a toxic culture, one that was aided and abetted by executives and even HR leaders throughout the company. It wasn't just the sexism and sexual harassment either, although that alone would certainly have been toxic enough. Aggressive behavior was core to Uber's corporate values, which included phrases like "Meritocracy and toe-stepping," "Don't sacrifice truth for social cohesion," "Always be hustlin'," and "Principled Confrontation."[8] Performance reviews at the company ranked employees against one another and linked those rankings to compensation, creating a dog-eat-dog atmosphere at every level.[9]

In early June 2017, the company announced that it had hired Frances Frei, a senior associate dean for executive education at the Harvard Business School.[10] Her job was to help fix the broken culture and develop its leaders and managers. On June 13, 2017, the company released a report outlining 13 comprehensive recommendations based on the internal review conducted by Holder and Albarrán of Covington & Burling LLP. The recommendations covered a broad range of critical activities, from realigning Kalanick's responsibilities, to hiring new executives, using performance management to hold senior leaders accountable for their behavior, challenging the board to embrace more oversight of the CEO and executive team, reformulating the organization's existing values, improving diversity and inclusion practices, conducting mandatory leadership training for senior executives and other leaders and managers, and improving the HR function of the company. Then the company fired 20 employees after an internal investigation revealed 215 complaints about everything from discrimination to sexual harassment and bullying.

Also, on June 13, 2017, Kalanick announced he was taking a leave of absence from the company. Seven days later, he resigned as CEO after receiving several personal letters from board members who had revolted against him. The day-to-day management of the company was turned over to a committee. However, there were issues here as well. The *Wall Street Journal* described the culture among the senior executives as a real-life *Game of Thrones*.[11] Individuals jockeyed for status and influence while Kalanick pulled strings from behind the scenes. When this happened, senior executives were distracted with their political games and no one was left to pay attention to running the company.

Things grew even worse when the exodus started happening. A parade of senior leaders left the company.[12] It appeared as though things were out of control and the Uber house was not in order. The messy situation also meant that potential outside hires approached for the COO and CEO roles publicly withdrew their names from consideration.[13]

Arianna Huffington, a member of the Uber board, would proclaim the "new Uber" would stop hiring "brilliant jerks."[14] In late August, the company announced Dara Khosrowshahi, former CEO of Expedia Inc, as the new Uber CEO.[15] Immediately, Khosrowshahi set the tone as a more mature and measured leader, committed to transforming the culture of the organization and restoring faith in its future.

In many ways, this story came to an end in December 2019 when Kalanick severed his ties with the company he founded. He sold all his shares and stepped down from the board. He announced he was going to focus his energy on new business and philanthropic endeavors.

New York Times technology writer Mike Isaac shared an interesting reflection on the company in his book *Super Pumped: The Battle for Uber.*[16] In an interview promoting his book, Isaac explained that one of the most important purposes of the book was to show that company culture is vital from the very beginning of a start-up. He then said it needs constant attention, or things can get gnarly and out of hand, as they did at Uber.[17] To me, that's a good synopsis of the Uber story.

What did you take away from this story of Uber's remarkable six months? What were the leadership and culture issues that plagued the organization? In what ways could things have turned out differently for Uber? Let's explore some of these questions.

Leadership Accountability—Why It Matters

The story outlined above is rather dramatic, even unbelievable in many ways. The number of things that went wrong in a six- to seven-month period was staggering. In the end, Uber's challenges weren't random. They all seemed to unravel in a short period, but in reality, they had been taking hold for years. Why did this all happen, and could it have been avoided?

My intent here is not to criticize or condemn. Instead, it's to use this brief and very public period in Uber's history to draw valuable lessons for you and your organization. We will do this by taking a systemic view of the situation and considering things from the perspective of the CEO, the board, the senior executives, managers, and the HR function. Each plays a role in either enabling strong leadership accountability to take hold or impeding it from happening at all. Let's explore these ideas further.

- **The Role of the CEO.** In the case of Uber, one could easily say it's all about the leader and blame Kalanick. As the famous saying goes, "a fish rots from the head first." There is some truth to this perspective. Kalanick set the tone from the top. As a charismatic CEO and cofounder, many of his employees adored him. When he resigned, over 1,000 of them sent letters supporting him and showing their disapproval of his departure from the company. Even considering everything that unfolded, employees still admired him. To his credit, he did establish a company that disrupted an industry. He was the visionary founder of a real Silicon Valley "unicorn." The hype surrounding him and his company was considerable. However, the aggressive culture and the inappropriate behavior on the part of Uber leaders and managers were known and, in many ways, even celebrated. To say everything that happened to Uber was a result of Kalanick would be inaccurate. He needed to be more accountable at a personal level and to set the tone of accountability for the rest of the organization.

- **The Role of the Board.** Where was the leadership accountability of Uber's board in all of this? They also bear responsibility for the company's problems. How much did they know about the cultural issues at the company? Did they turn a blind eye to the bad behavior of Kalanick and the top leaders, or did they not bother to look too closely? When they saw their CEO struggle, did they support him? Did they spend time thinking about the reputational risk to the company? Did they consider the risks to Uber's investors and customers? Boards today are facing more intense scrutiny for the leadership of a company. We already see increased vigilance and action on the part of boards when CEOs or other executives misbehave. Directors will need to understand how they need to step up and be accountable as leaders and work with the CEO to set the right tone for the rest of the organization.
- **The Role of the Executive Team.** Let's now shift our focus to Uber's executive team. They must surely have seen a lot of the inappropriate behavior happening in the organization. They most likely engaged in it or condoned it. How did they support their CEO through the challenges the company was facing? If they saw all these issues play out in the months or even years leading up to 2017, where were they? Did they step up, or keep quiet and go along for the ride? The executive team needed to be accountable, and it wasn't. Did they think about the broader leadership culture of the organization? Were they supporting leaders at all levels through their development? Were they glorifying the brilliant jerks? Did they turn a blind eye to complaints about harassment and inappropriate behavior on the part of many managers? Again, it's easy to put all of this on the CEO, but the executive team also needed to bear responsibility.
- **The Role of Managers.** Let's also look at the role of managers and supervisors deeper in the organization. Many leaders don't appreciate that they also set the tone for employees. Their behaviors shape the culture every day. In Uber's case, did managers engage in bad behavior because

it's what everyone else did? Did any of them stand up to say, "This is wrong and unacceptable"? Alternatively, did they say, "We're following orders"? Did many see what was happening and choose to keep quiet?

- **The Role of Human Resources.** Uber's HR function also bore responsibility for the situation the company found itself in during 2017. In fact, in the summer of 2018, the head of HR left the company after she dismissed claims of racial discrimination from employees. Companies need to look to their HR function to set the tone for the rest of the organization. HR needs to be the conscience of the organization and challenge leaders at all levels when their behavior is causing problems. In my experience, companies often underestimate the price they pay when the HR function is weak and not doing its job. It seems this was the case at Uber.

Final Thoughts

Leadership accountability has become a critical business issue. In many ways, it is the primary leadership challenge facing organizations today. To effectively address this issue, it is crucial to think about it in a systemic manner. Many factors contribute to an organization's degree of leadership accountability. As we saw with the Uber story, when it is weak, disaster can ensue in an instant.

Gut Check for Leaders: How to Think About Leadership Accountability

As you think about the ideas in this chapter, reflect on your answers to the following Gut Check for Leaders questions:

1. What insights did you gain about the role of a CEO in driving strong leadership accountability?
2. What do you believe should be the role of the board in helping set the tone and drive strong leadership accountability?
3. How should senior executives and managers demonstrate strong leadership accountability in their roles?
4. In what ways should the HR function play a role in supporting an organization to drive strong leadership accountability?

Notes

1. Greg Bensinger, "Uber Technologies CEO Travis Kalanick Leaves President's Business Council," *The Wall Street Journal*, February 2, 2017, https://www.wsj.com/articles/uber-technologies-ceo-travis -kalanick-leaves-presidents-business-council-1486073997.

2. Susan Fowler, "Reflecting on One Very, Very Strange Year at Uber." *Susan Fowler Blog*, February 19, 2017, https://www .susanjfowler.com/blog/2017/2/19/reflecting-on-one-very -strange-year-at-uber.

3. Greg Bensinger, "Uber Fires Executive Who Shared Rape Victim's Medical Records," *The Wall Street Journal*, June 7, 2017, https:// www.wsj.com/articles/uber-fires-executive-who-shared-rape -victims-medical-records-1496891613.

4. Greg Bensinger, "Uber CEO Says He Needs 'Leadership Help' After Video Shows Him Berating Driver," *The Wall Street Journal*, March 1, 2017, https://www.wsj.com/articles/uber-ceo-says-he -needs-leadership-help-after-video-shows-him-slamming-driver -1488347091.

5. Greg Bensinger, "Uber to Let California Self-Driving-Car Permit Lapse," *The Wall Street Journal*, March 27, 2018, https://www .wsj.com/articles/uber-to-let-california-self-driving-car-permit -lapse-1522186240.

6. Tim Higgins and Jack Nicas, "Alphabet's Waymo Sues Uber Over Self-Driving Car Secrets," *The Wall Street Journal*, February 23, 2017, https://www.wsj.com/articles/alphabets-waymo-sues-uber -over-self-driving-car-secrets-1487894378.

7. Greg Bensinger, "Uber Posts $708 Million Loss as Finance Head Leaves," *The Wall Street Journal*, June 1, 2017, https://www.wsj .com/articles/uber-posts-708-million-loss-as-finance-head -leaves-1496272500.

8. Greg Bensinger, "Uber CEO Travis Kalanick Quits as Investors Revolt," *The Wall Street Journal*, June 21, 2017, https://www.wsj .com/articles/uber-ceo-travis-kalanick-resigns-1498023559.

9. Greg Bensinger and Kelsey Gee, "Leaderless Uber Scrambles to Prevent Employee Exodus," *The Wall Street Journal*, June 23, 2017,

https://www.wsj.com/articles/uber-makes-quick-workplace
-reforms-to-calm-strained-nerves-1498237561.

10. Greg Bensinger, "Uber Board to Discuss CEO Travis Kalanick's Possible Leave of Absence," *The Wall Street Journal*, June 11, 2017, https://www.wsj.com/articles/uber-board-to-discuss-ceo-travis
-kalanicks-possible-leave-of-absence-1497172226.

11. Greg Bensinger and Kelsey Gee, "Uber: 14 Bosses, One Corporate 'Game of Thrones'?" *The Wall Street Journal*, June 14, 2017, https://www.wsj.com/articles/uber-14-bosses-one-corporate
-game-of-thrones-1497468304.

12. Greg Bensinger, "Uber's President of Ride-Sharing Jeff Jones Resigns," *The Wall Street Journal*, March 20, 2017, https://www
.wsj.com/articles/uber-president-of-ride-sharing-jeff-jones-resigns
-1489961810.

13. Greg Bensinger, "Uber Chairman Says Travis Kalanick Won't Return as CEO," *The Wall Street Journal*, August 7, 2017, https://
www.wsj.com/articles/uber-chairman-says-travis-kalanick-wont
-return-as-ceo-1502141814.

14. Amanda Holpunch, "'No More Brilliant Jerks'—Arianna Huffington Ushers in the New Uber," *The Guardian*, July 30, 2017, https://www.theguardian.com/technology/2017/jul/30/uber
-ariana-huffington-travis-kalanick-ceo.

15. Greg Bensinger, "Uber Selects Expedia CEO Dara Khosrowshahi to Lead Company," *The Wall Street Journal*, August 28, 2017, https://www.wsj.com/articles/uber-selects-expedia-ceo-dara
-khosrowshahi-to-lead-company-1503881482.

16. Mike Isaac, *Super-Pumped: The Battle for Uber* (W.W. Norton and Company, 2019).

17. Brian Feldman, "'I've Never Seen a Cast of Characters That Willing to Kill Each Other': Mike Isaac on Chaos at Uber," *New York Magazine Intelligencer*, September 3, 2019, http://nymag
.com/intelligencer/2019/09/super-pumped-author-mike-isaac-on
-ubers-toxic-culture.html.

CHAPTER 4

Leadership Accountability at the Individual Level

When I was 16 years old, I got my first part-time job as a salesperson in a men's clothing retail store. Gary was the store manager who hired me. He took a big bet on me because, back then, it wasn't customary to employ 16-year-olds for that kind of role. The industry, at the time, was very traditional. The company's customers were primarily professional managers and executives.

I quickly realized that Gary had high expectations for himself and our team. It was great working for him. I learned a lot from him—specifically, how to interact with customers, how to sell, and how to maintain customer relationships. These would all be skills that would serve me well throughout my career. He was a great role model. I aspired to be like Gary. One day, he pulled me aside and said, "You know I was a little nervous hiring you because you were so young. But I'm really pleased with your performance. Thanks for doing a great job." I was so excited to receive this feedback from Gary. Now I felt even more motivated to excel further in my job.

About a year into my job, Gary got a big promotion to manage the company's flagship store, and in came Stephen as our new store manager. Initially, he seemed like a decent person. However, as my colleagues and I got to know him, we quickly realized he was quite different from Gary. He was much more self-absorbed. He told us, *"Don't do as I do; do as I say."* I remember getting so frustrated whenever he said that, and he said it a lot. It communicated to us that he saw himself as being separate from our team and that he had a different set of standards for himself than for us. Stephen would often leave the store for hours on end. When he returned, he would not tell us where he had been. He would typically show up late and leave early most days. In team meetings, he could be dismissive of colleagues. It was pretty clear to all of us that it was his way or no way.

What surprised me about the contrast between the two leadership styles was how differently Gary and Stephen made me feel as an employee. I wanted to give Gary everything I had. I tried to live up to his high expectations, so I worked hard.

Stephen, however, didn't motivate us in the same way. The store had a completely different feeling when he ran it. It wasn't as fun, nor was it positive or inspiring. My job didn't change at all. It was the same— essentially to serve customers, sell clothes, clean up the store, and balance the books at the end of each day. However, we were led differently by Stephen, and it served to decrease my motivation and my desire to perform at a high level.

I didn't realize it until many years later, but that experience with those two managers triggered in me a keen interest in the topic of leadership. Over time, I became what I call *a leadership geek*. Leadership was my passion and focus of interest, which has driven my life's work for over two decades. When I reflect on the two styles of these managers, I would have to say that Gary was truly accountable and Stephen was mediocre.

It's Time to Pay Attention to Mediocre Leaders

In *The Leadership Contract Field Guide*, I wrote about mediocre leaders. I shared a definition of the word *mediocre* I found in *Webster's Dictionary*, which defines it as something of low quality, value, ability, or performance. Little did I know that this word "mediocre" and its connection to leadership would generate so much discussion and debate in my conversations with leaders around the world.

For example, in April 2018, I was the opening keynote speaker at a Conference Board event on leadership development in New York City. About 200 heads of leadership development from many

Fortune 500 companies filled the room. During my presentation on leadership accountability, I shared some of my preliminary thinking and research about mediocre leaders. When participants engaged in tabletop conversations, I could sense a buzz in the room. The topic was generating a lot of meaningful discussions among the delegates. When I opened up the floor to a large group debriefing, I heard the reactions. It became clear that these companies struggled to deal with their mediocre leaders. At one level, this wasn't a surprise to me. My global research shows that organizations believe about 55 percent of their leaders are mediocre.[1] Also, 80 percent of organizations do not know how to address the problem. What was surprising to me was that these conference delegates were from some of the biggest and most successful companies in the world. They were heading up the leadership function, and they realized they needed to do much better when it came to this problem.

I came away from that conference with a real sense of clarity that we needed to conduct more research to better understand why mediocre leaders exist and how we can help them be better. First, we began to take pulse surveys at other conferences where I was a keynote speaker. We built a database of the top 10 worst kinds of leadership behavior, and then asked the people in my audiences to acknowledge whether any of those characteristics described their leaders. We then expanded our research with various online surveys (distributed through my website and among LHH clients) that reached out to hundreds of leaders in North and South America. In total, we gathered over 1,800 responses from C-level leaders, VPs, middle-level and front-line managers, and employees. My team and I then validated our findings through conversations with executives.

The Top Five Characteristics of Mediocre Leaders

Overall, the surveys had some very compelling findings. First, there was a high degree of alignment between respondents in North and South America. Also, we didn't see any significant differences in the responses, regardless of whether they came from CEOs, VP-level executives, middle and front-line managers, or employees. To me, this suggests that we all define mediocre leaders in similar ways. It also gives me confidence that the top five characteristics described below are a meaningful way of understanding how mediocre leaders show up every day (see Figure 4.1). Let's discuss these in more detail.

The Top Five Characteristics of Mediocre Leaders

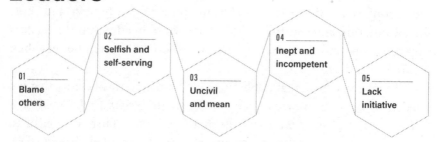

Figure 4.1   The Top Five Characteristics of Mediocre Leaders

1. **Blame Others.** The first characteristic of mediocre leaders is that they tend to blame others. If something goes wrong, they immediately point the finger at someone else. They never personally acknowledge their role or contribution to any mistake or failure. The blaming nature of their behavior typically also brings negative energy to a team or a company. The negativity can influence others and become a habit that is hard to break. If you see this behavior occurring frequently in someone in a leadership role, it's a sure sign that they are unaccountable.

2. **Selfish and Self-Serving.** Mediocre leaders also tend to be profoundly selfish. They act out of self-interest. They bring a sense of entitlement to their roles. Some described how those leaders don't appear to care about the company, its customers, or the employees they lead. It's always about "ME, ME, ME!" If your direct leader is like this, you must accept the fact that you will never grow and develop under their leadership. These leaders won't invest in you because, ultimately, they only care about themselves.

3. **Uncivil and Mean.** The third characteristic is that some medio-cre leaders can be rude and disrespectful in how they relate to oth-ers. It's a tell-tale sign of a lousy boss. You know these leaders—the ones who regularly and routinely mistreat, demean, and insult oth-ers, usually in public. They are bullies. They're dreadful to work for, and they create tremendous personal stress for those they lead. One study found that 63 percent of workplace bullies are bosses.[2] It also found that one in five employees experience bullying, while 61 per-cent of employees are aware of abusive conduct. Close to three out of four bullies are men, and 60 percent of the targets are women. These findings are unacceptable, and we need to address this prob-lem within our organizations.

4. **Inept and Incompetent.** Many mediocre leaders are seen as being inept and incompetent. They don't have the right instincts for leadership. They make bad decisions and leave a trail of disaster behind them. The worst ones are those who are inept but think they are great. No one can understand how these people were ever able to get into a leadership role in the first place. It's important to determine whether these individuals actually want to be in a leadership role. Typically, I find if someone is inept or incompetent as a leader, they know it. They could ask for help, but egos prevent them from address-ing the issue. They may be better suited for another role that doesn't require them to be honest with themselves. They do whatever they can to hang on to their roles, which isn't a good thing for anyone.

5. **Lack Initiative.** Mediocre leaders are lazy and unwilling to work hard. They look for the easy way out of any situation. They deflect responsibility, or they always play under the radar, never to be seen or heard. When their teams need help, they don't step in. They wait for permission and always defer decisions to others or avoid making them entirely.

What is your reaction to these characteristics? What has been your experience in working with mediocre leaders? What is it about them that drives you crazy? At the same time, we need to be open to be self-critical of ourselves as leaders. Are you or have you become a mediocre leader? Do you demonstrate some of the five characteristics describe above?

Now, if a leader demonstrates one or two of these characteristics from time to time, then it may not be considered a big deal. It could be temporary. It could also be a reaction to stress and a heavy workload. However, if a leader demonstrates most of these characteristics, every day—I mean full-on mediocrity—on a consistent basis, then it needs to be addressed. The impact of doing nothing is considerable.

The Impact of Mediocre Leaders

My findings from my global research also confirmed a fear I have long held—that mediocre leaders are everywhere, and they have a significantly negative impact on the people they lead. Survey respondents from my research provided hundreds and hundreds of open-ended comments describing how mediocre leaders affect them and make them feel. They were all emotional responses that, quite frankly, bordered on despair. Before I present some direct quotes from survey respondents, I'd like you to pause and remember a time when you worked with a manager or leader you'd describe as mediocre. How did that leader make you feel?

Let's see how your reactions compare to what we found in our survey. The figure presents some of the most impactful comments shared by survey respondents (see Figure 4.2).

The quotes in the figure describe employees whose sense of commitment is eroding. As we've already seen, leadership is estimated to account for up to 70 percent of the variance in employee engagement. Mediocre leaders destroy engagement. They do not unleash the discretionary effort of their employees. I'm not sure that our organizations are fully aware of the price they pay when they tolerate mediocrity. For example, a survey of human resources practitioners found that 73 percent of them have to spend a significant part of their time dealing with problems that arise from ineffective managers.[3] One in three also acknowledged that their organizations tolerate just about anything from a problem manager who achieves results, which perpetuates the problem.

The picture is even worse when you consider the amount of time wasted on dealing with the unnecessary drama created by mediocre managers and leaders. Some research reveals that employees spend up to 2.5 hours per day on workplace drama.[4] Weak leaders perpetuate workplace drama. They either create it directly or, because of their ineffectiveness, create the conditions where everyone else spends

"Slowly but surely I feel like I'm dying a little at a time in my job—it's soul destroying."

"It's such a struggle to come to work every day—they suck the life out of my job."

"You can't learn from them, you can't admire them, so you start thinking about looking for another job."

"My manager makes me feel frustrated, anxious, and even depressed most days at work."

"It feels like I'm hitting my head against a wall and now I don't even feel any pain."

"Mediocre leaders suck the very energy, drive and 'can do' spirit out of you."

"When I see poor leaders, it demotivates me to do my job."

"Mediocrity does not inspire people to do their best work, or go above and beyond what they already do."

"When leaders ignore their best people and ideas, maintain the status quo … is easiest for them."

"After a while, I feel like I'm just treading water to get by."

Figure 4.2   The Impact of Mediocre Leaders

time caught up in gossiping, complaining, and whining about poor leadership in the company. Imagine if your people were free from the distraction of workplace drama and were able to focus on driving business results.

The question I frequently ask myself is: Why? Why do people put up with mediocre managers? When I have asked this question of others, the typical responses are that their work is personally meaningful and that it compensates for a lousy boss. Others cite the positive relationships with their colleagues and team members, which can also compensate for an ineffective leadership experience. It seems that mediocre managers can bring a team closer together as they support one another through their collective misery. Finally, for others, the overall purpose and culture of the organization are so inspiring that it helps them pay less attention to the negative experience created by their manager. While a meaningful job, cohesive team, or inspiring culture can compensate for a mediocre leader, to me it still means that people are not able to perform at their highest level.

In the introduction to this book, I spoke of the ripple effect of leadership. Great and accountable leaders create a positive ripple across an organization. Mediocre ones create a negative ripple across an organization. This means, whether good or bad, leadership can be contagious. Research conducted by Jack Zenger and Joe Folkman found that inadequate and mediocre leadership spreads lousy leadership, while good leadership spreads good leadership. In both cases, there is what they call a trickle-down effect.[5] These findings most likely confirm what you already know from your own experience. When you work with a lousy leader or mediocre manager, you don't feel like you are at your best. Your level of engagement is weak, and you may, as a result, fail to set a positive example for others.

Remember, mediocrity breeds mediocrity. Lousy leaders or mediocre managers will never hire the best talent. Their insecurity will prevent them from doing so. Alternatively, they may be incapable of even recognizing great talent when they see it. Also remember that leadership is contagious. It has a ripple effect. What is rippling throughout your company? Mediocrity or accountability?

Mediocrity Is the Ultimate Enemy

In his book *Good to Great* Jim Collins said that good is the enemy of great and that's the reason we so rarely achieve greatness.[6] People settle for good and don't strive for greatness. I would extend his ideas further to say that mediocrity is the enemy of excellence. To be a great leader, a genuinely accountable one, doesn't happen by accident. It takes commitment and much hard work. I find too many leaders underestimate what's required or aren't prepared to work that hard, nor are they committed to aspiring to greatness. Senior leaders and organizations have enabled this to happen in many ways. We have tolerated bad and mediocre leadership for far too long. As we have already seen, we've also paid a high price (and will continue to pay a high price) as a result of not addressing mediocrity in our organizations.

When I talk to leaders who admit they have become mediocre, they cite some barriers or reasons that keep them where they are. Here are some of the most frequent reasons I've heard:

- Some say that their organizations haven't made leadership expectations clear.
- Many say there aren't great role models that they can look up to, admire, or even emulate.
- Others say they are afraid of stepping up in case they fail. The challenge is that their organizations have little tolerance for failure and people pay heavily for mistakes.
- Some say they couldn't say no to a leadership role; they had to accept it, even if they didn't want it or didn't feel ready.
- Others talk about being overloaded with roles that have too many priorities and too many people to lead.
- Some are worn down and give up after years of working at cross-purposes with colleagues in other departments or functions.
- Others complain that they are not empowered to be accountable, where senior leaders micromanage and control all decision making.
- Finally, others cite little investment by the company in their development. They feel they were thrown into the deep end of a leadership role and had to figure things out for themselves.

Can you relate to any of these points?

Now depending on your perspective, you may read this list and say these are legitimate barriers that impede leadership accountability. Others may say it's merely a list of excuses. Accountable leaders overcome these barriers regardless of their situation. I believe the truth is somewhere in the middle—this is both an individual and organizational issue. At the individual level, leaders need to be honest with themselves to see whether they have let themselves become mediocre. At the same time, organizations need to appreciate how their systems, processes, and structures drive good and well-meaning managers and leaders to become mediocre. One of the most insightful ideas that Peter Senge shared in his book, *The Fifth Discipline*, is that if you put good people in poor systems, you'll get bad results.[7]

When an organization keeps mediocre leaders around and does nothing to help them, it signals to everyone that the company will tolerate mediocrity, which is a dangerous thing. It's vitally important to help develop truly accountable leaders. Let's now shift our focus to understand what accountable leaders do that sets them apart from the rest.

How Do Truly Accountable Leaders Set Themselves Apart?

In *The Leadership Contract*, I presented my global research on leadership accountability. My team and I found that among industry-leading companies, accountable leaders consistently demonstrate a set of five behaviors that set them apart from others (see Figure 4.3).

1. Hold Others Accountable for High Standards of Performance

Amazon CEO Jeff Bezos's letters to shareholders are major news events each year. People both inside and outside the company are keen to hear the latest musings from the leader of one of the world's most successful companies.

In 2018, Bezos tackled the idea of the need for leaders to set high standards. A big part of Amazon's success is due to Bezos's relentless drive to meet ever-increasing customer expectations. In short, successful leaders not only set high standards, but they also hold the people they lead to account for their ability to meet those standards.

In his 2018 letter to shareholders, Bezos explored the topic of standards and expectations. He discussed whether the drive to set high standards is intrinsic, or whether you can teach it to others. My sense is that Bezos believes it's a little of both. He says it helps to hire "high standards" people—those predisposed and wired to set the bar high for themselves and others. It's also essential to create a culture that encourages people to strive for high standards in everything that they do. Bezos

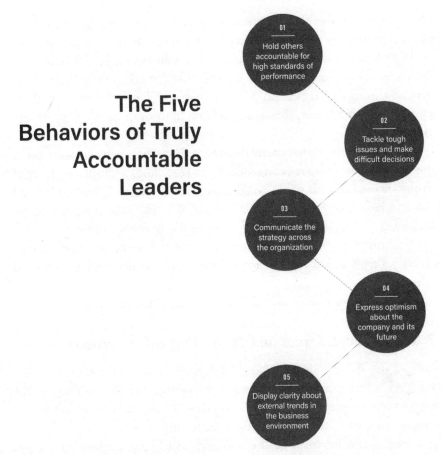

The Five Behaviors of Truly Accountable Leaders

01 Hold others accountable for high standards of performance

02 Tackle tough issues and make difficult decisions

03 Communicate the strategy across the organization

04 Express optimism about the company and its future

05 Display clarity about external trends in the business environment

Figure 4.3 The Five Behaviors of Truly Accountable Leaders

believes high standards are contagious. If you bring someone onto a team where high standards are the norm, that person will be more likely to adopt the same standards as part of a commitment to supporting the success of the team. Bezos concluded his letter by highlighting some other benefits that accrue from building a culture of high standards.

First, high standards allow you to build better products and services for your customers. Second, high standards attract and retain the best talent in your industry. Third, a culture of high standards helps to cultivate what Bezos refers to as "invisible work," or the extra effort people put in when the leaders are not around. He believes it is an indication that your people think that doing great work is a reward in and of itself.

Finally, Bezos insists that high standards can be fun, and that once people accept them as part of their day-to-day work, there's no going back.

The letter closely relates to experiences in my career. Whenever I felt I was at my personal best, it was because I worked for a leader or as part of a team that strived to achieve high standards. Sometimes, these standards even felt unrealistic, but aiming high motivated me to do my very best.

Unfortunately, far too many leaders go about their work on auto-pilot, going from meeting to meeting, deadline to deadline, without any thought about setting high standards. Maybe they are overloaded or even burned out and have lost passion for their work. Whatever the reason, when a leader fails to set and live up to high standards, everyone suffers.

It is no surprise that my research found this to be the first characteristic of truly accountable leaders. High performance begins with high standards.

Have you set high standards for yourself and your team?

2. Tackle Tough Issues and Make Difficult Decisions

One of my favorite quotes about leadership comes from Alibaba CEO Jack Ma, a billionaire who has built one of the world's most successful e-commerce companies. He believes that if you want your life to be simple, then you shouldn't take on a leadership role.

Inherent in his message is the reality that being a leader isn't easy. There is considerable hard work, and you will be called upon to tackle many difficult decisions. As I discuss in *The Leadership Contract*, many leaders struggle with this. Too many avoid the hard work, and that undermines their leadership and accountability. It's no surprise, then, that my research reveals this is something that accountable leaders pay attention to and even excel at, relative to other leaders. These leaders understand Ma's point of view and ensure they have the resilience, determination, and deep sense of personal resolve they need to be effective.

This topic generates much interest in my discussions with leaders. Many say this one behavior is the defining characteristic of an accountable leader. At the same time, it was also the behavior most glaringly absent among more mediocre leaders.

Do you tackle tough issues and make difficult decisions when required?

3. Communicate the Strategy Across the Organization

Accountable leaders effectively communicate their company's strategy to the people they lead. This behavior is crucial. It helps teams understand how their work contributes to making the company successful, in turn, making each task more meaningful and rewarding. A clear vision of the strategy helps every team member "buy in" and stay motivated in their roles. In the end, it's foundational for establishing accountability. If, for example, I'm personally clear on expectations, what I must do, and how it's connected to advancing the strategy, then there's a higher likelihood I'll be successful.

At the same time, if I'm unclear, off course, and my performance is lagging, then there should be a mechanism to discuss it, refocus attention and energy, and hold people accountable for the results they must deliver. It all starts with clarity on the strategy. Unfortunately, many studies show that leaders and employees are usually unclear about their company's strategic objectives. One study found that only 29 percent of employees can describe their organization's strategy.[8] That's just one in three. Another survey of chief financial officers reveals that strategic ambiguity is one of the issues they worry about the most.[9] They defined strategic ambiguity as the uncertainty that arises when an organization can't effectively:

- Define the strategy,
- Communicate it to internal and external stakeholders,
- Align the required resources to implement the strategy, and
- Execute it to achieve desired outcomes.

Accountable leaders focus their energy on bringing strategic clarity to the people they lead. A great example comes from Dr. Lisa Su, CEO of Advanced Micro Devices. When she took over the company, it was losing money and in significant debt. Her human resources team recommended the company engage in a process to create new mission, vision, and value statements. Su knew she didn't have the time for a long, drawn-out process. Instead, she focused on bringing strategic clarity to the organization. How? By communicating the three most important priorities: "to build great products, deepen customer relationships, and simplify everything we do."[10] These three priorities became the focus of the company and guided leaders and employees to make effective decisions in real time. That focus on strategic clarity allowed Su to turn around a company that was on the brink of extinction.

Are you clear on your company's strategy and confident that you can communicate it to others?

4. Express Optimism About the Company and Its Future

Another behavior that accountable leaders consistently demon-strate is their ability to express optimism about the company and the future. Leaders viewed as unaccountable seem to merely go through the motions in their day-to-day work without personal investment in the direction of the team. Many appear disengaged or unenthusiastic, which undermines the ability of the company to fully engage employ-ees. As one client said, "If leaders are not excited about what we are trying to do as a company, then our employees will never be."

Bill Taylor, a co-founder of *Fast Company Magazine*, wrote about the importance of optimism in the *Harvard Business Review*. He said, "In a time of wrenching disruptions and exhilarating breakthroughs, of unrelenting turmoil and unlimited promise, you can't create a better future for your organization and your colleagues unless you first believe in the future."[11] John Gardner, a well-known leadership thinker, also wrote about the need for leaders to be *tough-minded optimists*.[12]

As so many companies are attempting to transform themselves in the face of change and disruption, optimism will be even more critical. Many efforts to lead transformation stall because leaders do not buy into the change. They may also not be passionate or excited about the future. Some may try to fake it, but everyone around them can tell that they are not genuine.

Are you excited and optimistic about the future of your company?

5. Display Clarity About External Trends in the Business Environment

A while back, I was conducting a pre-interview with a CEO of a com-pany to kick off a project. The purpose of the interview was to under-stand her company's business context and strategy. I typically begin these discussions with an outside-in approach. We first explore the external forces facing the organization. Then we discuss the business strategy. We then conclude by reflecting on the changing expectations for leaders and how they must step up to help drive the success of the company.

The discussion started well, as the CEO began to identify some external challenges. Her industry was facing tremendous disruption and change. Then I noticed something: She would quickly shift her responses from external to internal issues. I kept bringing her back to her external context, but she always automatically went back to her internal operational challenges.

After about 10 minutes of this, I stopped and said to her, "Do you notice what is happening?" When I brought it to her attention, she hadn't even realized it. She was utterly shocked at how absorbed she had become by all the internal challenges she was facing. It was understandable given the transformation she was leading. However, she realized this was something she needed to address. If as the CEO she was absorbed by internal issues, then chances were good that the rest of her leaders were doing the same. At that moment, she also recognized the risk inherent in the fact that no one was looking externally to spot potential risks and opportunities.

This CEO is not the only one I've met who is struggling with the same issue. Organizations, both big and small, have a lot going on, and it's easy to get caught up in all that internal stuff. This is amplified when an organization is attempting to transform itself. The problem is that if all the senior leaders are in the weeds and dealing with internal challenges, they cannot spot opportunities and potential threats in the external world.

In my experience, many leaders fall prey to this fixation on internal issues—at times to the exclusion of external forces. As we already discussed in Chapter 1, as a leader you need to continually challenge yourself to see whether you are too internally focused or have your head stuck in the sand. Accountable leaders proactively assess their environment to spot opportunities and identify threats and risks they can manage. This proactive approach contributes to stronger accountability overall.

Are you clear about external trends in your business environment?

Final Thoughts

When leaders step up at the individual level, they demonstrate very different behaviors from those who are struggling in their roles or seen to be mediocre. It's incumbent upon all leaders to steer away from mediocrity and embrace real accountability in how they show up every day.

Gut Check for Leaders: Leadership Accountability at the Individual Level

As you think about the ideas in this chapter, reflect on your answers to the following Gut Check for Leaders questions:

1. Do you demonstrate any of the five characteristics of mediocre leaders?
2. Do you set high standards for yourself and those you lead?
3. Do you have the courage to tackle the hard work and make difficult decisions?
4. To what extent do you bring strategic clarity to the people you lead?
5. Would the people you lead describe you as being optimistic and excited about your company's future?
6. Are you clear on the trends in your external business environment?

Notes

1. Vince Molinaro, *The Leadership Contract Field Guide* (3rd ed.) (John Wiley & Sons, 2018).
2. Gary Namie, "2017 WBI U.S. Workplace Bullying Survey," Workplace Bullying Institute, June 2017, https://www.workplace bullying.org/wbiresearch/wbi-2017-survey/.
3. Wallace Immen, "Bad Managers Prove Headache for HR Department," *The Globe and Mail*, April 30, 2018, https://www .theglobeandmail.com/report-on-business/careers/career -advice/bad-managers-prove-a-headache-for-hr-department /article562752/.
4. Cy Wakeman, "Drama Researcher Explains How to Avoid Drama at Work," *Quartz at Work*, October 18, 2017, https://qz.com /work/1101863/a-psychologist-explains-how-to-stop-wasting -time-on-work-drama/.

5. Jack Zenger and Joseph Folkman, "The Trickle-Down Effect of Good (and Bad) Leadership," *Harvard Business Review*, April 2016, https://hbr .org/2016/01/the-trickle-down-effect-of-good-and-bad-leadership.

6. Jim Collins, *Good to Great* (HarperCollins, 2001)

7. Peter M. Senge, *The Fifth Discipline* (Doubleday/Currency, 1990).

8. "When CEOs Talk Strategy, Is Anyone Listening?" *Harvard Business Review*, June 2013, https://hbr.org/2013/06/when -ceos-talk-strategy-is-anyone-listening.

9. "Turning Strategic Ambiguity into Strategic Clarity," *The Wall Street Journal*, June 20, 2013, https://deloitte.wsj.com /cfo/2013/06/20/turning-strategic-ambiguity-into-strategic -clarity-2/.

10. Lydia Dishman, "How This CEO Avoided the Glass Cliff and Turned Around an 'Uninvestable' Company," *Fast Company*, September 11, 2018, https://www.fastcompany.com/90229663/ how-amds-ceo-lisa-su-managed-to-turn-the-tech-company -around.

11. Bill Taylor, "Why the Future Belongs to Tough-Minded Optimists," *Harvard Business Review*, March 3, 2016, https://hbr .org/2016/03/why-the-future-belongs-to-tough-minded-optimists.

12. John Gardner, *John Gardner's Writings "Personal Renewal"* (Phoenix, AZ: PBS, Delivered to McKinsey & Company, 1990), http://www .pbs.org/johngardner/sections/writings_speech_1.html.

CHAPTER 5

Leadership Accountability at the Team Level

Take a moment and recall the best team experience you have ever had. Remember what it felt like to be part of that team. Now recall the worst team experience: What did it feel like being part of that team? What differences do you notice between the two experiences? When I've asked these questions of other leaders, here are some of the most common responses. In the great team experiences:

- Everyone was clear and aligned with what needed to get done.
- Each team member was accountable, pulled their weight, and went to great lengths to support one another.
- Everyone felt safe challenging one another and confronting issues head-on without fear.
- Team members leveraged the unique capabilities of everyone.
- Everyone worked hard but also managed to have fun and celebrate success.

In contrast, terrible team experiences are likely to be ones where:

- Team members are misaligned and work at cross-purposes to one another.
- Everyone works in isolation and demonstrates little support or trust.

- The team avoids critical conversations because no one feels safe enough to speak up or cares about the team's success.
- Not everyone pulls their weight, creating frustration and resentment.
- Everyone is cynical and negative, thereby creating conflict and tension on the team.

While we desire to work on great teams, most people I talk to admit that they have had more experience working on terrible and dreadful teams. We must do better. Now here's the challenge we face—all of us are spending more time on teams than ever before. It stands to reason that we need to figure out how to make these team experiences more positive.

A recent article by Microsoft on the changing nature of work reported that most employees are on twice as many teams as they were just five years ago.[1] Other research suggests that expectations of collaboration in organizations increased 50 percent in the past few years alone.[2] One of the challenges we also face is that many leaders I've worked with admit to never really learning how to lead teams effectively. Many learned on the job, often by trial and error. Many also didn't have great role models to emulate. The good news is that this chapter will help you understand what it takes to build a truly accountable team and create an inspiring experience for those you lead.

Teams Have Transformed

In recent years, teams have taken on greater importance in organizations. Customers are demanding more value and innovation. In turn, this means that companies must bring different capabilities and areas of expertise together to generate value to meet increasing customer expectations. The implication is that we are working with colleagues across departments, functions, and geographies. As organizations have become more global and matrixed, so have teams. The way we work is also much more virtual in nature. Your day-to-day interactions with teammates are most likely via a conference call, video chat, or a collaboration app versus an in-person meeting. Remote teams rule the day. You may work with team members you have never even met face-to-face. Given the global nature of work, your colleagues are also more diverse than ever before.

What's also different today is that some of your team members aren't even employees of your company. You are working with others who are strategic partners, vendors, suppliers, freelancers, and consultants. As more companies have shifted to agile methodology, teams today are also more fluid—they are formed, disbanded, and rebuilt continually. As a result, you may be participating on several teams at once, either as the leader or as a team member. A few studies have revealed that today, 81 to 95 percent of us are working on multiple teams at any given time.[3] The research also suggests this increases the stress and pressure that people feel when it comes to managing the expectations and workload of being on numerous teams.[4]

We are also trying to navigate the many collaborative project management and social apps implemented in companies. These are all designed to leverage technology and drive team performance. However, I speak to leaders who are overwhelmed by the number of apps and passwords they need to keep track of in their work.

I suspect none of this is new to you, as it probably reflects your current reality. However, we must come to terms with the fact that as organizations rely more and more on teams, our satisfaction with their performance is underwhelming. For example, a few years back my team did a research project in partnership with the Human Capital Institute.[5] The survey found that 92 percent of respondents said that teams were essential to their organization's success; however, only 23 percent said they were satisfied with the performance of their teams. We clearly have work ahead to improve the effectiveness of teams.

Teams and Accountability—the Critical Connection

My colleagues and I have had many experiences working with teams over the years. It's typically a natural extension of our leadership development work. We've had extensive experience working with:

- New teams coming together for the first time with a significant mandate to deliver for their organization;
- Executive teams that are struggling, mired in conflict, dysfunction, or outright hostility toward one another;

- Cross-functional teams where leaders from across an organization come together to work on a mission-critical priority; and
- Teams made up of leaders from different organizations, such as public-private partnerships or strategic alliances. Sorting out who is accountable in these teams is, at times, a challenge.

Regardless of the type of team, their purpose remains the same: *to create a whole that is greater than the sum of its parts.*[6] That's the ultimate promise of teams, but it is one that many fail to achieve. Interestingly, many of these clients began to see an important connection between the ideas of the leadership contract and their application to teams. As a result, we started to pay more attention to teams through the lens of leadership accountability. As we looked to the research in the area, we found some interesting insights on teams and accountability. For example, Katzenbach and Smith, two pioneers in the area of teams and teamwork, found in their work that we do not understand how accountability plays out in teams. They believe that no group ever becomes a team until it can hold itself accountable as a team.[7]

In his book *The Five Dysfunctions of a Team*, Patrick Lencioni found that avoiding accountability was a common challenge for many teams.[8] A recent article by Joseph Grenny in the *Harvard Business Review* found that the weakest teams demonstrate little to no accountability. In weak teams, the team leader is the source of all accountability.[9] In the strongest teams, the team members manage most issues and performance problems among themselves. That's the telltale sign of an accountable team. Based on these insights, it's clear we have much work to do to understand how teams can be more accountable and thereby more successful. These insights are important, as they shed light on what is really required to build and sustain high-performing teams—accountability.

Now it's important to understand that when many think about teams and accountability in teams, they believe it's all about the team leader holding the team accountable. That's certainly part of it, but it's even more powerful when team members learn to hold each other accountable and have the courage to hold the team leader accountable as well. I believe this is the ideal end state, and we need to create truly accountable teams where each team member is accountable at an individual level and mutually accountable to one another. So how do we make this happen? We need to start by understanding the characteristics of truly accountable teams.

The Core Characteristics of Truly Accountable Teams

Through our client work with many teams, we began to glean important ideas and develop a deeper appreciation of the core characteristics that define what it means to be a truly accountable team.

The first insight we had is that accountable teams balance an interplay between individual and collective accountability. If team members are not accountable at an individual level, then it will require significant work, time, and energy to cultivate and sustain mutual accountability at a team level. I can't tell you how many times we've been asked to work with a team in trouble, only to see that their issues are not team issues, but individual leadership accountability issues. Some of the team members were not stepping up individually, not being accountable, and thereby undermining the success of the team. The other team members couldn't count on them.

The second insight we gained was that truly accountable teams demonstrate two critical dimensions: team clarity and team commitment. The figure below further defines each of these two dimensions (see Figure 5.1).

As a leader, these two dimensions are invaluable as a way of thinking about driving mutual accountability and sustaining high team performance

TEAM CLARITY	TEAM COMMITMENT
Clarity to the business context in which they operate, anticipating external trends	Commitment about the team's mandate
Clarity of the strategy of their organization	Commitment to work with key stakeholders
Clarity of expectations of stakeholders, understanding their interdependencies with other teams	Commitment to lead the team
Clarity of the priorities of the team itself	Commitment to each other and having each other's backs

Figure 5.1   Team Clarity and Team Commitment

over the long term. It doesn't matter what kind of team you are leading, or how many teams you are leading—these two dimensions are critical.

Team Clarity

Accountable teams need to have clarity about the business context in which they operate. They demonstrate this clarity in four specific ways.

1. *They anticipate external trends and understand their business context.* When a team excels at this, you will find that they are clear on the patterns and drivers in their external business environment and industry, the needs of external customers/consumers, as well as changes and issues impacting their organization. They also work to bring a strong level of clarity to others on the broader team or business unit.

2. *They have clarity on the strategy and purpose of their organization.* Accountable teams demonstrate this through shared accountability to understand the purpose and direction of their organization. When a team is strong in this area, they are clear on the links between the strategy, external market trends, customer expectations, the team's mandate and how it aligns to organizational strategic priorities, and the primary obligation of the team to deliver results. They also commit to regularly communicate and cascade the progress against objectives to others.

3. *They have clarity on the expectations of their stakeholders and the interdependencies that exist with other parts of the organization.* When teams excel at this, they demonstrate clarity on the issues that matter to their key stakeholders. They understand the specific stakeholder relationships needed to drive success and have a game plan to drive the strategic priorities of the organization. These teams also demonstrate a keen understanding of how to align work across the organization.

4. *They demonstrate internal clarity in terms of what needs to get done and how it will get done.* When teams are strong in this area, they demonstrate clarity on their collective goals and priorities, an understanding of how to execute their priorities, and a reasonable degree of knowledge. These teams also demonstrate a keen sense of their strengths and gaps as a team and the kind of leadership culture required to succeed.

Team Commitment

Accountable teams also demonstrate a high degree of commitment needed to deliver results. They demonstrate their commitment in the following four ways.

1. *They have a deep sense of commitment to driving success.* You can tell when a team has this in spades because you see team members being passionate and excited about the future. They step up and take personal ownership for executing the strategy and set high standards of performance for everyone on the team. They also consistently show up in an aligned manner and with a united front to the rest of the organization.
2. *They invest time in working across the organization and with key stakeholders.* Those who excel at this find ways to break down silos to drive collaboration with other teams. They demonstrate the courage to tackle difficult issues with stakeholders. They invest time to build good relationships with key stakeholders and work to minimize unhealthy politics in their relationships with them.
3. *They work to make their team as strong as it can be.* Accountable teams achieve this by sharing high aspirations to be truly accountable leaders, supporting each other's development, tackling tough issues, and having resilience and resolve. They also come together in the face of adversity when the team is tested.
4. *They show a deep commitment to one another.* When this is particularly strong, you will find team members holding each other accountable and calling out unproductive leadership behavior. They will genuinely care about one another and demonstrate high trust by having each other's backs. They will also make a commitment to spend time together to get to know each other on a personal level.

Accountable Teams—What the Research Reveals

To better understand the dimensions of team clarity and team commitment, we conducted a focused study.[10] We deployed several data collection strategies. First, we surveyed close to 100 companies of various sizes from different industries on the state of teams in their organizations. Second, we conducted in-depth semi-structured interviews with several chief human resources officers. Finally, we analyzed the data from a diagnostic assessment tool and interviews we used when working with executive teams. The research revealed five key findings:

1. We found that the vast majority of teams are seen to be mediocre.
2. We were able to assess team clarity and team commitment and determine the strengths and gaps that currently exist among most teams.
3. We found that the dimensions of team clarity and team commitment are positively correlated, and if you increase clarity, you automatically increase commitment.
4. We found that high-performing companies have more accountable teams compared to those identified as average- and poor-performing ones.
5. Finally, we found that teams in high-performing companies score consistently higher on all behaviors of accountable teams compared to those on average- and poor-performing companies.

1. The Vast Majority of Teams Are Mediocre

Respondents identified that 80 percent of teams in their companies are mediocre or weak (see Figure 5.2). They also reported that 19 percent of teams in their organizations as being good. Only 1 percent of teams were seen as being truly accountable.

These findings are sobering and quite concerning. Given the importance of teamwork in organizations today, it is clear we need to do a much better job of building truly accountable teams. Let's continue.

2. Team Clarity and Team Commitment—a Current Snapshot

In the survey, we asked respondents to rate 32 behaviors on a 5-point scale (1 = strongly disagree and 5 = strongly agree). We found several behaviors across all types of teams that were rated higher compared to other behaviors for both the team clarity and team commitment dimensions.

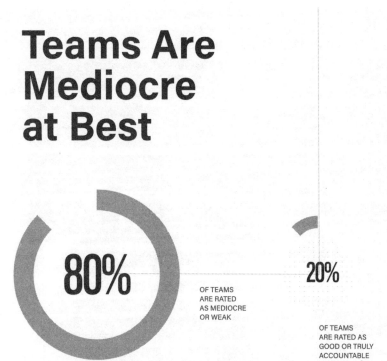

Teams Are Mediocre at Best

80% OF TEAMS ARE RATED AS MEDIOCRE OR WEAK

20% OF TEAMS ARE RATED AS GOOD OR TRULY ACCOUNTABLE

Figure 5.2   Teams Are Mediocre at Best

Team Clarity—Highest- to Lowest-Rated Items

Figure 5.3 presents the highest- to lowest-rated items for the team clarity dimension.

As you can see, the top three highest-rated items on the team clarity dimension include clarity on the needs of customers, clarity on the collective goals of the team, and clarity on the primary obligation of the team to drive success. As we look at the bottom three lowest-rated items, we see teams struggling with their ability to influence key stakeholders, understanding where they stand as a team, and how to align work across the organization.

It seems that teams focus their energies on gaining clarity on what they must do to be successful. Yet, they may struggle in how they must go about achieving their objectives, especially as this seems to be a particular challenge when working with other teams and key stakeholders across the organization.

Figure 5.3 Team Clarity—the Highest- to Lowest-Rated Items

Team Commitment—Highest- to Lowest-Rated Items

Figure 5.4 presents the highest- to lowest-rated items for the team commitment dimension.

As you can see, the highest-rated items reveal that teams are passionate about the future of their organization, genuinely care about one another, and set high standards for the team. These are good strengths for any team to have. However, when we look at the lowest-rated items, it shows that teams struggle to tackle tough issues and have difficult

Figure 5.4 Team Commitment—the Highest- to Lowest-Rated Items

conversations. They don't drive collaboration, nor can they break down silos across the organization. Finally, they have a difficult time holding one another accountable.

These findings suggest we have teams that have the best intentions to be passionate, to care for each other, and to aspire to high standards of performance. However, they struggle with some of the hard work that is required to build a truly accountable team, especially as it pertains to difficult work they must do as a team.

The other important insight in looking at the findings from both dimensions is that there is a tremendous opportunity for teams to get stronger. A rating of 3.8 out of 5 is okay, but most likely not strong enough for teams to perform at their best and drive extraordinary results.

3. Team Clarity and Team Commitment Are Positively Correlated

Another important finding from the research is that a positive correlation exists between the dimensions of team clarity and team commitment. Teams that demonstrate a high degree of clarity will also demonstrate a high degree of commitment. This finding provides us with a valuable insight on what it takes to build a truly accountable team. Essentially, if you as a leader can focus your energy on driving higher levels of team clarity with your team, you will invariably increase the team's level of commitment. As one of the leaders we interviewed said, "We talk about it as shared outcomes—shared values around a shared purpose. I think that's an amazing motivator for people. Also, the more emotionally connected you get, the more accountable you become to the team."

We have also seen the opposite in practice. When team members do not have a collective understanding of their strategy, nor appreciate how everyone's work contributes to the execution of the team strategy, then their commitment erodes. Another leader we interviewed shared, "An accountable team starts with leadership. The leader needs to drive a clear mandate. It can be collaborative, but in the end, it has to be crystal clear where you're headed."

4. High-Performing Companies Have More Accountable Teams

In our study, we asked survey respondents to self-identify if their company's performance was industry-leading, average, or below average relative to competitors. When we analyzed the data against these three groups, some compelling patterns emerged.

The findings revealed that industry-leading organizations scored much higher than average to poor-performing organizations on both dimensions of team clarity and team commitment. Furthermore, respondents in average-performing companies were also consistently higher on these measures than the respondents in poor-performing ones. There is a clear connection between truly accountable teams and company performance. If you have many accountable teams in your company, it will translate into higher company performance. At the same time, if you have only a few accountable teams or none at all, then your company's performance will suffer.

These findings also align closely with the global leadership accountability research I presented earlier in this book. It all makes sense. If you have leadership accountability issues at an individual level, you're going to have them at the team level. Now if you have leadership accountability issues at the individual and also the team level, then your organization's performance will suffer. The critical insight to take away is that building truly accountable teams will enhance your ability to drive stronger company performance. Poor or mediocre teams will never be able to drive high performance.

5. Teams in High-Performing Companies Outpace Teams in Average- and Poor-Performing Companies

Another consistent finding was that teams in high-performing companies scored substantially higher on all items in the survey compared to teams in average- and poor-performing companies. Interestingly, teams in average-performing companies also scored higher than teams in poor-performing companies.

Team Clarity and Company Performance

As you can see in Figure 5.5, in the high-performing companies, accountable teams were rated higher in all four sub-scales of having high clarity on their business context, strategy, stakeholder expectations, and having clarity within the team.

You will also see that teams in average-performing companies score higher than teams in poor-performing companies. Again, this reveals the connection between strong team performance and company performance.

Team Clarity Behaviors and Company Performance

We also explored the net difference by company performance for each of the 32 behaviors in the survey. We found five items in particular in

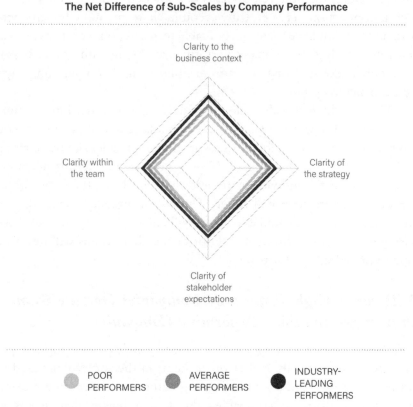

Figure 5.5 **Team Clarity—the Net Difference of Sub-Scales by Company Performance**

the team clarity dimension, where the net difference was the greatest (see Figure 5.6).

These results paint a clear picture of what matters most to teams when driving high team clarity. A team needs to be clear on its collective goals. It must understand how its mandate aligns with the organization's overall priorities. It needs to be clear on the changes across the organization. It also needs to understand the leadership culture the team needs to succeed. Finally, it needs to be clear on how to align work across the organization. We will come back to these points later in the book.

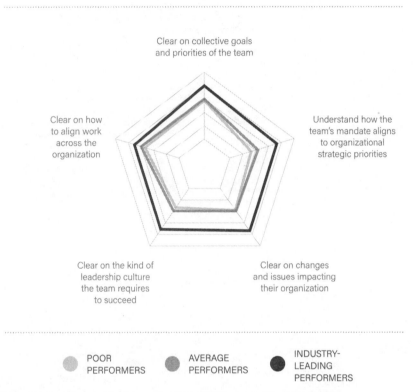

TEAM CLARITY
The Net Difference by Company Performance

Clear on collective goals
and priorities of the team

Clear on how
to align work
across the
organization

Understand how the
team's mandate aligns
to organizational
strategic priorities

Clear on the kind of
leadership culture
the team requires
to succeed

Clear on changes
and issues impacting
their organization

POOR
PERFORMERS

AVERAGE
PERFORMERS

INDUSTRY-
LEADING
PERFORMERS

Figure 5.6 Team Clarity—the Net Difference by Company Performance

Team Commitment Sub-Scales and Company Performance

Figure 5.7 shows the differences between company performance and the sub-scales of the team commitment dimension.

Once again, we see that accountable teams in industry-leading companies were stronger in each of the four sub-scales.

Team Commitment Behaviors and Company Performance

Figure 5.8 shows the team commitment behaviors where we saw the largest net difference between the industry-leading and average- and poor-performing companies.

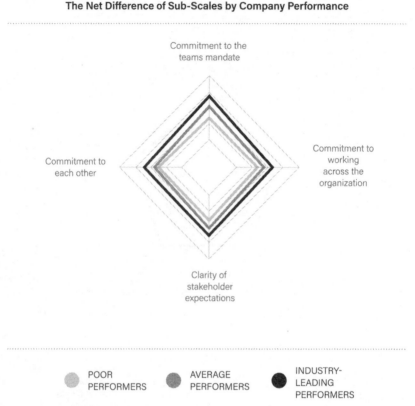

TEAM COMMITMENT
The Net Difference of Sub-Scales by Company Performance

Commitment to the
teams mandate

Commitment to
each other

Commitment to
working
across the
organization

Clarity of
stakeholder
expectations

POOR
PERFORMERS

AVERAGE
PERFORMERS

INDUSTRY-
LEADING
PERFORMERS

Figure 5.7   Team Commitment—the Net Difference of Sub-Scales by Company Performance

The most important aspect of commitment is that team members are passionate about the future of the organization. They then demonstrate accountability for executing the organization's strategic priorities. They support each other's development as leaders. They work together to break down silos and drive collaboration across the organization. Finally, they hold each other accountable and call out unproductive leadership behavior when it arises on the team.

These findings suggest what behaviors set truly accountable teams apart from others and how this difference contributes to delivering results.

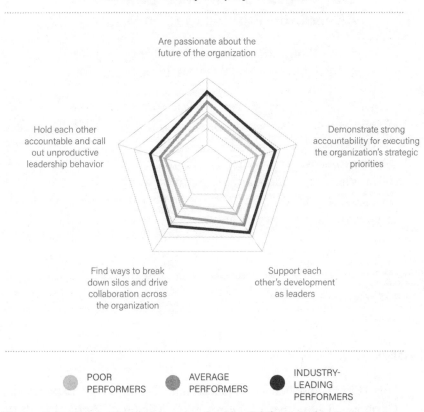

TEAM COMMITMENT BEHAVIOURS
The Net Difference by Company Performance

Are passionate about the future of the organization

Hold each other accountable and call out unproductive leadership behavior

Demonstrate strong accountability for executing the organization's strategic priorities

Find ways to break down silos and drive collaboration across the organization

Support each other's development as leaders

POOR PERFORMERS

AVERAGE PERFORMERS

INDUSTRY-LEADING PERFORMERS

Figure 5.8 Team Commitment—the Net Difference by Company Performance

Final Thoughts

Although teams have always been essential, there's a clear sense from the leaders and organizations I work with that teams matter more today than ever before. Whether it's an executive team, departmental team, cross-functional project team, or even a team established with external partners and suppliers, organizations have higher expectations of teams. Unfortunately, at a time when we are increasingly relying on teams, it's clear they are not stepping up to meet these increasing expectations. You are being counted on to build strong and truly accountable teams.

Gut Check for Leaders: Leadership Accountability at the Team Level

As you think about the ideas in this chapter, reflect on your answers to the following Gut Check for Leaders questions:

1. What has been your experience with teams?
2. Would you say have you spent more time on terrible teams or terrific ones?
3. Do you believe you currently are part of a truly accountable team where team members are mutually accountable?
4. To what extent do your team members demonstrate mutual accountability toward one another?
5. How satisfied are you with the performance of the teams you lead?
6. What insights did you gain about the dimensions of team clarity and team commitment?

Notes

1. Lori Wright and Natalie McCullough, "New Survey Explores the Changing Landscape of Teamwork," Microsoft, April 19, 2019, https://www.microsoft.com/en-us/microsoft-365/blog/2018/04/19 /new-survey-explores-the-changing-landscape-of-teamwork/.

2. Rob Cross, Reb Rebele, and Adam Grant, "Collaborative Overload," *Harvard Business Review*, January–February, 2016, https://hbr.org/2016/01/collaborative-overload.

3. Andre Martin and Vidula Bal, "The State of Teams," Centre for Creative Leadership, 2015, http://www.ccl.org/wp-content /uploads/2015/04/StateOfTeams.pdf.

4. Troy Smith, Bradley Kirkman, Gilad Chen, and G. James Lemoine, "Research: When Employees Work on Multiple Teams, Good Bosses Can Have Ripple Effects," *Harvard Business Review*, September 26, 2018, https://hbr.org/2018/09/research-when-employees-work-on -multiple-teams-good-bosses-can-have-ripple-effects.

5. Aubrey K. Wiete, "The New Organizational Currency: Designing Effective Teams," Human Capital Institute, January 2014, https://www.hci.org/research/new-organizational-currency-designing-effective-teams-0.

6. David Weiss and Vince Molinaro, *The Leadership Gap* (John Wiley & Sons, 2005).

7. Jon R. Katzenbach and Douglas K. Smith, *The Wisdom of Teams* (Harvard Business Review Press, 2015).

8. Patrick Lencioni, *The Five Dysfunctions of a Team* (Jossey-Bass, 2002).

9. Joseph Grenny, "The Best Teams Hold Themselves Accountable," *Harvard Business Review*, May 30, 2014, https://hbr.org/2014/05/the-best-teams-hold-themselves-accountable.

10. In our survey, respondents were asked to rate the teams in their organizations along 32 described behaviors. In total, 16 of the statements assessed the team clarity dimension, while the other 16 statements assessed the team commitment dimension. One hundred respondents were from among LHH clients. The distribution by role of the survey respondents was nicely balanced: C-suite executive leaders (18 percent), VP-level leaders (24 percent), director level/senior managers (34 percent), and middle managers (23 percent). We also interviewed CHROs from various companies. In addition, in-depth analysis of our diagnostic survey used with intact teams was also conducted. You can access the full report at: https://theleadershipcontract.com/2018/04/20/gut-check-are-you-building-a-truly-accountable-team/.

CHAPTER 6

Leadership Accountability at the Culture Level

"Things were even worse than I expected." This admission came from a new CEO at a financial services organization who was hired to transform her organization. Going in, she knew she was taking over a company that needed to change. She was aware of the organizational and cultural challenges she and her executive team would have to overcome. Even with her eyes wide open going in, she was still surprised at the severity of her organization's problems.

After a recent series of meetings with leaders at the middle and frontline levels of her organization, she realized they lacked clarity around the organization's new strategy. She knew she needed to align leaders with a new set of leadership expectations, create real accountability, and drive a one-company mindset across the leader population.

Unfortunately, in open and frank discussions with her leaders, she heard that her new company was leagues away from achieving those goals. Her leaders told her they were stuck in silos and were unclear on how to navigate in a more complex business environment. Of more significant concern, they had no opportunities to work with colleagues across the organization to execute on shared priorities.

I could sense her frustration and anguish. As we continued our discussion, it became clear to both of us that leadership culture was going to be her number one priority. If she didn't make it stronger, she and her executive team wouldn't be successful.

Culture: The Number One Asset and Number One Liability

The story above would not be a disturbing one if it were rare. However, this CEO's story is not that different from many other conversations I have had with other C-suite leaders who realize the critical importance of culture. The good news is that many CEOs today understand that it is critical. For example, Ginni Rometty, CEO of IBM, believes that culture is a company's number one asset.[1] In 2011, before she even became CEO of Big Blue, she spoke at a Yale CEO Summit. She told the audience that culture is a defining issue that will distinguish the most successful businesses from the rest of the pack.

Since then, I've seen the topic become more and more prominent. For example, in 2014, *Merriam-Webster*, the dictionary and reference book company, proclaimed "culture" as their word of the year.[2] They did so because they saw a significant spike in people going to their website to search for the definition.

I bet a lot of those searching for the definition were CEOs because, as the Gartner Group found in its research, the use of the word has increased on earning calls.[3] Since 2010, when they started tracking it, culture has been the most frequently discussed talent issue among CEOs. Mentions of culture have been increasing by 12 percent annually. Gartner also found that many CEOs expect their heads of HR to both invest in and deliver on culture initiatives. However, here's the problem: only 31 percent of the CHROs surveyed by Gartner are confident that their companies have the culture needed to drive future success.

While culture can be the number one asset for a company, it can also be a liability. For example, recent high-profile stories from companies, such as Wells Fargo, Uber, and Volkswagen, point to the price that is paid when cultures are weak and even dysfunctional. For example, in September 2015, the Environmental Protection Agency (EPA) in the United States issued a notice of violation of the *Clean Air* Act to Volkswagen, the German automaker. The agency found that the company had intentionally programmed diesel engines to only activate emission controls during laboratory emission testing. This resulted in no emission outputs of nitrogen oxide during testing, but up to 40 times in real-world driving. The scandal became known as Dieselgate, when it was confirmed that the company had essentially rigged emission tests on its diesel vehicles to qualify them for sale in the United States. Within the first few days of the scandal becoming public, the company's stock dropped by 30 percent. Martin Winterkorn, the company's CEO, was at the center of the storm. Although he apologized for his company's actions, Winterkorn claimed he did not have any direct knowledge of what happened. He vowed to find out who was responsible.

Then stories began to emerge about Winterkorn's leadership style.[4] He was an extremely demanding leader who put considerable pressure on his managers. Both outsiders and insiders suggested that Winterkorn may have encouraged his people to cut corners and falsify results. In April 2019, German prosecutors charged former Volkswagen CEO Martin Winterkorn with fraud. Business writers and industry analysts immediately connected the company's actions to its culture. An article in the *Financial Times* said that the Volkswagen scandal showed the world how much corporate culture matters.[5] In a recent LinkedIn article, Google's former head of human resources, Laszlo Bock, went further by saying that failures in culture have been the single biggest destroyer of value among many companies.[6]

Many astute leaders are devoting more attention to gaining a better understanding of corporate culture and how to create a great one. Research conducted by Deloitte confirms this in their "Global Human Capital Trends 2016" report. They reported that 82 percent of CEOs and HR leaders surveyed believe that culture is a critical potential source of competitive advantage.[7] The report also shared that culture isn't merely an HR issue—the CEO and senior executive team should take responsibility for their organization's culture.

So senior leaders are taking culture seriously. That's good. However, here's the bad news: only 28 percent of the survey respondents believe they understand what culture even is, and only 19 percent believe they have the right culture in place. These findings suggest that there is significant work ahead for all of us as leaders. So let's get started on this important work right now.

What Exactly Is Culture?

In my work with leaders, I find that while many understand the importance of culture, few understand it tangibly. Most business leaders see culture as an amorphous thing. Many CEOs I've worked with describe it as "Jell-O"—something jiggly and gooey that they struggle to grasp.

One common definition of culture is "the way things are done around here." However, that definition is incomplete. In the book *The Leadership Gap*, my co-author and I defined culture as the distinguishing features—the specific values, behaviors, and ways of doing things that are unique from one organization to another. An organization's culture should differentiate it from other organizations.[8] It is also important to understand that culture connects to values, which represent what is fundamentally critical to an organization. Values guide behaviors and decision making and, in turn, those behaviors, repeatedly reinforced through action, create culture. Culture is about expectations, what an organization values, and what it condones.

Leaders Create Culture

Let's get more specific: It is *leaders* who create culture. This idea originated with Professor Edgar H. Schein, who wrote about culture decades ago in his book *Organizational Culture and Leadership*. He believed that leaders are the ones who create culture based on how they behave. His work convinced me that leadership and culture are deeply connected. It is those repeated behaviors demonstrated consistently *by leaders* that set the tone for everyone else in the organization.

A client of mine, an EVP of business development based in Singapore, really summed up this point nicely when she said, "The senior leaders create the culture and set the tone for the organization. It's imperative that they drive the set of behaviors which influence the behaviors of the next line leaders and the rest of our employees." What all this suggests to me is that as a leader, you must be deliberate about the leadership culture you need to drive the success of your organization. If you are not intentional, then you will get a weak culture by default.

Three Weak Leadership Cultures

In *The Leadership Contract*, I describe three kinds of leadership cultures that can take hold in a company if you are not deliberate and intentional in creating a strong one. Once entrenched, a weak culture will be hard to change, so it's important to be aware of them. Let's review them below so you can spot them before they take hold. As you read through this section, think about your own experiences. Have you worked in these types of leadership cultures before? What impact do you recall they had on you?

1. A Rotting of Zombies

I'm sure at some point in your life you've seen a zombie movie or an episode of *The Walking Dead*. Most feature the aftermath of a zombie apocalypse, and a few remaining human beings are fighting for their lives to avoid a zombie attack. Unfortunately, a zombie apocalypse isn't merely a fantasy found in movies and TV shows; it's a reality in many organizations.

Imagine a leadership culture where leaders and employees show up every day like zombies—wandering without purpose Monday to Friday. Apathy runs rampant. It can be demoralizing and soul-destroying. What happens when a zombie bites a person? The person becomes a zombie. The same thing happens to employees in zombie cultures. Once bitten, they become zombies and don't even realize it. It's scary.

2. A League of Superheroes

This type of leadership culture is often rooted in the dominant personality of one leader—usually the charismatic founder or CEO. If the superhero is a decent individual—one with integrity, who cares for employees and treats them well—then a good culture can take hold. However, if that superhero has a dark side, then the organization will have problems. Some superhero leaders can be highly paternalistic and loyal to their long-serving employees. On the surface this may look like a good thing, but in practice it isn't. Often, employees are kept in the company years and years after they've stopped adding value. This creates significant frustration and even animosity among high-performing individuals. The real risk with these leaders is an over-reliance on one person's leadership. Little is done to build the leadership of others in the organization. When the superhero leader leaves, nothing sustainable is left behind. The organization will struggle to move forward.

3. A Stable of Thoroughbreds

Imagine horses at a racetrack just before the bell rings—in their starting gates, pawing the ground, snorting, full of restrained energy. The starting bell rings and the horses are off, each determined to reach the finish line first. Now imagine that each horse represents a function, department, or line of business in your company. Everyone is competing against everyone else. They all have blinders on and single-mindedly focus on their objectives and priorities. The internal competition is fierce. Everyone may also be working at cross-purposes. Protecting turf becomes a primary focus and silos compete with one another. Conflict is rampant, and frustration is high. Getting anything done feels next to impossible. These are harsh cultures to be in, and difficult to survive in and be successful over the long term. The only people who thrive in them are the sociopaths among us.

I've worked with some organizations that have all three types of weak cultures at the same time in different departments. This is a difficult scenario to turn around. It's possible, but not without significant work. In the end, the best strategy is to try to stay clear of these weak cultures if you can. It's much better to be deliberate and intentional about creating a strong leadership culture.

What Kind of Leadership Culture Would Enable You to Be at Your Best?

Take a moment and think of your answer to this question: What kind of leadership culture would you require for you to be at your best and make your fullest contribution as a leader? I've asked this question hundreds of times around the world. It's fascinating that the answers are pretty much the same, whether I'm in Hong Kong, Zürich, Boston, Montréal, Lima, Singapore, Auckland, or Frankfurt. The same themes keep coming up repeatedly.

First off, no one has ever said to me, "Vince, I would be at my best in an environment of apathy—surround me with a group of zombies and watch me soar." It seems a rotting of zombies doesn't bring out the best in people. I've also never heard, "Vince, I want to work for a self-absorbed, narcissistic leader who is a control freak and micro-manager." No one, it seems, thrives working for this kind of superhero leader. Finally, no one has ever said, "Vince, I would be at my best in a hypercompetitive cut-throat culture, where every day I can count on my colleagues to be there to stab me in the back, sabotage me, or throw me under the bus." It seems a stable of thoroughbreds doesn't inspire us, either. Do you know what people do say? Here are the top three answers:

- "I will be at my best in a climate where leaders have real clarity about the value they must bring."
- "I will be at my best when there's a deep commitment to the organization and to being the best possible leaders we can be."
- "I will be at my best in a climate where there is high trust and mutual support among leaders."

After years of asking the question repeatedly and getting the same answer from leaders in all sectors, at all levels, and in different countries, it seems we already know what a strong leadership culture looks like. People want to be part of what I call *a community of leaders*. And it's no surprise we crave community at work—we are hardwired for it as humans.

In *The Leadership Contract*, I introduced 10 characteristics of *a community of leaders*. Leaders often ask me for the origin of these characteristics. Well, they emerged in hundreds of conversations with leaders like you and are grounded and validated in my client work. Initially, I began with a much longer list. But as I continued to discuss, reflect, and test out this list with senior executives, the original list became more focused. The image below (see Figure 6.1) presents the top 10 characteristics of a strong community of leaders.

Imagine for a moment what it would be like if you were part of *a community of leaders* with these 10 characteristics. Imagine you and your fellow leaders were all genuinely aligned to the vision and strategy of

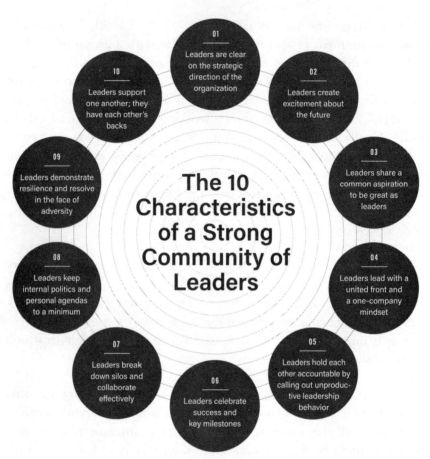

Figure 6.1 The 10 Characteristics of a Strong Community of Leaders

your organization, with no one working at cross-purposes. Imagine if there was a real sense of collaboration that enabled innovation to flourish. What if all the leaders in your organization showed up every day fully committed to being the best leaders they could be? What if leaders supported one another to achieve higher levels of personal and collective performance? All of this would be a game-changer for you, your colleagues, and your company. I believe a community of leaders is the real missed opportunity in organizations today. If there is anything I know for sure after a couple of decades at this work, it is this: *If you can create a strong community of leaders in your organization, it will become your company's ultimate differentiator.*

There are some essential reasons why we need a community of leaders right now. As we explored earlier in the book, the world in which you are leading will continue to become more complex. No one person will have all the answers. You will need to be good at tapping into the experience and expertise of people from across your organization. You will need to be even better at coming together to build teams, get important work done with people from around the world, and deliver extraordinary results.

Companies desperately need communities of leaders who create a strong leadership culture. At the same time, people desperately want to be part of strong communities of leaders. Many leaders I talk to struggle with the isolation and loneliness of their roles. They feel disconnected. They aspire for something more—a greater sense of connection and community.

Gina Bianchini, founder and CEO of Mighty Networks, brings an interesting perspective based on her years in creating online communities. Her company is a technology leader in ushering a new era of creative business built on community. My team and I participated in one of her company's community design courses a while back. During one session, Bianchini spoke passionately about what all thriving communities have in common. First, there is a joy that comes from being part of something bigger than yourself. You do not feel isolated or lonely; you feel connected to something truly meaningful and important. Second, when pursuing a common goal with others, we can take on work challenges and overcome obstacles that others cannot do on their own. Third, there is also the joy that comes from building skills, getting better every day. Finally, successful communities provide their members with permission to be vulnerable as they navigate challenges together.

Dr. Henry Mintzberg of McGill University has also written about the need for community at work.[9] In an article in the *Harvard Business Review*, Mintzberg wrote:

> Individualism is a fine idea. It provides incentive, promotes leadership, and encourages development—but not on its own. We are social animals who cannot function effectively without a social system that is larger than ourselves. This is what is meant by "community"—the social glue that binds us together for the greater good.

He continued by saying that community means caring about one's work and one's colleagues, and then being inspired by this caring.

The research supports the idea that having a strong community of leaders will be critical. Earlier in this book, I shared findings from a study done by consulting firm Willis Towers Watson. It's worth repeating here briefly. They found that when employees perceive managers and senior leaders as working well together, in an aligned and supportive manner, their personal engagement jumps to 72 percent.[10] However, when employees don't see managers and their senior leaders aligned and working well together, their sense of personal engagement drops to 8 percent. How your leaders show up, not just at an individual level, but collectively, really matters. It shapes culture by driving the engagement of employees.

Glassdoor, in a survey of 615,000 users, found that although compensation is a driver of employee satisfaction, two other factors are critical to consider: workplace culture and values, and the quality of senior management.[11] Once again, we see the connection between culture and leadership emerging. When it is strong, employees feel it.

Let's keep going and explore each of the 10 characteristics of a community of leaders in more depth.

A Community of Leaders—the Current State

A few years ago, I learned through my global research on leadership accountability the troubling fact that only 27 percent of the organizations surveyed believed that they had a strong leadership culture in place. Fewer than one in three. Since that time, I've conducted other research to get a sense of the current state of organizations and their communities of leaders.[12]

The first question we asked was: *How important is having a strong leadership culture to the success of your organization?* Respondents were asked to rate the question with the following scale, where 1 = not at all important and 5 = critically important. Take a moment and give your organization a rating.

Organizations Are Not Confident They Have the Leadership Culture They Need

We found that 89 percent of respondents said that having a strong leadership culture was critically important. When we combined the 4 and 5 ratings, the overall average jumped to 96 percent. This essentially means that pretty much all organizations believe that having a strong

89%

SAY THAT HAVING A
STRONG LEADERSHIP
CULTURE IS CRITICALLY
IMPORTANT TO THEIR
ORGANIZATION

33%

SAY THAT THEY
ARE CONFIDENT
OR EXTREMELY
CONFIDENT
THAT THEIR
ORGANIZATION
CURRENTLY HAS
A STRONG
LEADERSHIP
CULTURE

The Current State of Leadership Cultures

Figure 6.2   The Current State of Leadership Cultures

leadership culture is critical to their success. The second question we asked was: *How confident are you that your organization currently has a strong leadership culture in place?* This time respondents were asked to rate the question using the scale 1 = not at all confident to 5 = extremely confident. Once again, how would you rate this question for your own organization? Only 7 percent of survey respondents said they were extremely confident. When we combined 4 and 5 ratings together, that number jumped to 33 percent. Either way, confidence levels are low and suggest that organizations must do more to build strong leadership cultures in their organizations (see Figure 6.2).

A Community of Leaders—a Snapshot of the 10 Characteristics

We then asked respondents to rate each of the 10 characteristics of a community of leaders on another five-point scale, 1 = extremely weak to 5 = extremely strong. Here's what we found (see Figure 6.3).

Figure 6.3   An Assessment of the 10 Characteristics of a Community of Leaders

Let's spend some time discussing each of these characteristics, in order of strength, as they appear in Figure 6.3. I'll share comments that have most frequently emerged in my discussions with leaders to provide more in-depth insights.

1. **Leaders demonstrate resilience and resolve in the face of adversity.** When discussing this item with leaders, they often speak with pride. Whenever there is a crisis, they seem to be able to put

their differences aside and come together to lead. But many astute leaders see this not as a strength, but rather as a sign of weak leadership. Their rationale is that if leaders only come together in times of crisis, then they aren't leading. If your leaders need a crisis to lead, then you do not have a genuine community of leaders.

2. **Leaders are clear on the strategic direction of the organization.** It's so vital for leaders to be clear on the strategic direction of their companies. We already explored this earlier in this book. Without that clarity, nothing happens. But there's more—leaders must not only be clear themselves, but they must also bring clarity to the people they lead. In this regard, organizations are less confident. Most leaders I've talked to also shared that a 3.67 out of five isn't a strong result at all. One CEO said, "To me, this number needs to be a 4.5 or greater."

3. **Leaders celebrate success and key milestones.** This characteristic always gets a tremendous reaction from leaders. Some have commented that many leaders spend too much time celebrating and not enough time delivering results. Others have said that this is a big missed opportunity within their companies because they do not do enough of it. This characteristic connects closely to employees' level of engagement. If employees don't have opportunities to pause, see when the company is winning, and celebrate those wins, their engagement is eroded.

4. **Leaders create excitement about the future.** This characteristic is an increasingly important expectation that CEOs and other executives have for their leaders. They understand it's their role to create excitement, but they need to be able to rely on other leaders and managers in the organization to do the same. What was clear in my discussions is that this can't be an artificial or fake type of excitement, but a fundamental sense of optimism about the company and its future. This is how leaders inspire others. If you are excited about the future, then chances are your team will be, too. Again, given the mediocre rating, leaders see a lot of opportunities to be better in this area.

5. **Leaders support one another; they have each other's backs.** All leaders believed that this item is critical to their success, and while they see some strength in their organizations, it's uneven and

unbalanced. It was clear from my discussions on how pivotal the executive team is in setting the tone for the rest of the organization. If they support one another and genuinely have each other's backs, then everyone will see it and model it. Few executive teams can set the right tone in this regard. They don't typically have each other's backs; this is both a challenge and a significant opportunity for senior teams.

6. **Leaders share a common aspiration to be great as leaders.** Given how many people said their companies had a large gap here, I would have expected a lower rating. Nonetheless, it seems companies can still be much stronger in setting clear expectations of their leaders and holding them to higher standards of behavior. Companies must decide to build the best leaders in their industry.

7. **Leaders keep internal politics and personal agendas to a minimum.** Of all 10 characteristics, this one had the most significant divergence in perspectives. Some companies believed that internal politics and personal agendas consumed most of their leaders' time. Others (albeit a small number) thought they had built a culture in which leaders prioritized what's best for the company ahead of their self-interest.

8. **Leaders lead with a united front and a one-company mindset.** Many CEOs I talk to desperately want to see strength in this characteristic. Unfortunately, they often do not. They say that too many of their leaders focus their energy on their silos, whether that's a function, department, line of business, or division. Sometimes they do so at the expense of the company's broader goals.

9. **Leaders break down silos and collaborate effectively.** Again, it is clear that many leaders are heads-down, stuck in silos. They are building walls rather than tearing them down. Collaboration doesn't happen, or if it does, it is downright painful. A McKinsey survey found that 83 percent of CEOs believe their organizations have silos and 97 percent state that silos have a negative impact.[13] Gillian Tett, the author of the book *The Silo Effect*, says that silos can create a kind of tunnel vision that causes people to do stupid things and make bad decisions.[14] Silos are a significant barrier to building a strong leadership culture where leaders work together to drive results.

10. **Leaders hold each other accountable by calling out unproductive leadership behavior.** This last characteristic is the lowest-rated item. What's fascinating is that it was also the lowest-rated item in my global leadership accountability survey. Moreover, in all the discussions, leaders said this was going to be critical in the future. It seems leaders do a better job of holding others accountable in a boss-employee relationship. However, employee-to-boss feedback is lacking. The largest gap that exists is in peer-to-peer feedback, a real challenge. I have learned that this rarely happens in most organizations. Given the degree of teamwork, collaboration, and cross-functional projects leaders will need to accomplish in the future, we will all need to be stronger at being open to feedback and demonstrating courage to hold one another accountable.

Look back over this list of the 10 characteristics of a strong leadership culture. How does your organization measure up? How much more could you accomplish if your organization scored high on all 10 of these characteristics?

Final Thoughts

When I find myself in a big city during a business trip, I engage in a little practice. I take a few minutes to look up and see what's around me. Sometimes, I see skyscrapers in the central business district of a major city. Other times, I see a building in an industrial park or a large manufacturing plant. I always wonder about the people inside and consider what world they have created for themselves. Are their days filled with constant drama, infighting, and petty politics? Or have they created a fantastic culture where everyone is fully committed to driving extraordinary results? The interesting thing is, whatever the answer is, I know that they have created their own worlds. We need to understand this about leadership culture—we can create it. We do not have to settle for a weak, poor, or even dysfunctional culture. We can have the aspiration to create a great one and set an inspiring tone for all employees.

**Gut Check for Leaders: Leadership
Accountability and Culture**

As you think about the ideas in this chapter, reflect on your answers to the following Gut Check for Leaders questions:

1. How do you define culture?
2. What leadership culture would enable you to be at your best as a leader?
3. What has been your experience working in weak or dysfunctional cultures? What price have you paid? Your colleagues? What price has your organization paid?
4. Does your organization currently have a strong community of leaders in place?

Notes

1. Patricia Sellers, "IBM Exec: Culture Is Your Company's No. 1 Asset," *Fortune*, March 10, 2011, http://fortune.com/2011/03/10 /ibm-exec-culture-is-your-companys-no-1-asset/.
2. "2014 Word of the Year: Culture," Merriam-Webster Company, 2014, https://www.merriam-webster.com/words-at -play/2014-word-of-the-year/culture.
3. "Top Insights for the World's Leading Executives. 2017– 2018 Annual Edition," Gartner, 2017, https://emtemp.gcom .cloud/ngw/globalassets/en/human-resources/documents/top -insights-hr-2017-18.pdf.
4. "Fear and Respect: VW's Culture under Winterkorn," Reuters, October 11, 2015, https://www.cnbc.com/2015/10/11/emissions -scandal-vws-demanding-culture-under-winterkorn-led-to-crisis .html.
5. Robert Armstrong, "The Volkswagen Scandal Shows That Corporate Culture Matters," *Financial Times*, January 13, 2017,

https://www.ft.com/content/263c811c-d8e4-11e6-944b-e7eb37a6aa8e.

6. Laszlo Bock (linkedin.com/in/laszlobock), "Your Culture Will Make or Break Your Business, June 4, 2019, https://www.linkedin.com/pulse/your-culture-make-break-business-laszlo-bock/

7. "Global Human Capital Trends 2016," Deloitte, 2016, https://www2.deloitte.com/insights/us/en/focus/human-capital-trends/2016.html.

8. David S. Weiss and Vince Molinaro, *The Leadership Gap* (John Wiley & Sons, 2005).

9. Henry Mintzberg, "Rebuilding Companies as Communities," *Harvard Business Review*, July/August, 2009, https://hbr.org/2009/07/rebuilding-companies-as-communities.

10. "Effective Managers: Your Critical Link to Successful Strategy Execution," Willis Towers Watson, 2015.

11. Andrew Chamberlain, "What Matters More to Your Workforce than Money," *Harvard Business Review*, January 17, 2017, https://hbr.org/2017/01/what-matters-more-to-your-workforce-than-money.

12. To understand the current state of organizations' views on community of leaders, we conducted a small research project. The data collection strategy included a global online survey, surveys conducted at keynote presentations, and surveys within organizations. We also held several customer events to discuss the issues emerging from the research. Our surveys were held during off-site sessions. In total, there were 2,220 responses to the survey. Eighteen percent were from C-suite leaders, 18 percent from executive-level leaders, 38 percent from director/middle-management level leaders, 12 percent from front-line leaders, and 15 percent from individual contributors. A total of 51 percent of responses came from North America, 21 percent from South America, 11 percent from Australia/New Zealand, 8 percent from Europe, and 2 percent from the Middle East. There was representation from 22 industries, with the top five being manufacturing, finance and insurance, technology, healthcare, and professional services.

13. "Call Your Broker," *McKinsey Quarterly*, https://www.mckinsey.com/business-functions/organization/our-insights/five-fifty-call-your-broker.

14. Gillian Tett, *The Silo Effect: The Peril of Expertise and the Promise of Breaking Down Barriers* (Simon & Schuster, 2015).

PART 3
The Organizational
Response—for All Leaders

This section explores how you can inspire accountability among your direct reports, teams, and peers.

Chapter 7: How to Hold Others Accountable for Being Leaders

This chapter presents the four strategies that leaders can use to hold their direct reports accountable for being leaders. Specifically, it examines how to make leadership accountability a priority, how to define leadership expectations, how to build the resilience and resolve of those you lead, and how to help others succeed across the broader organization.

Chapter 8: How to Build an Accountable Team

This chapter presents the four strategies that leaders can use to build a truly accountable team. Specifically, this chapter presents strategies on how to make leadership accountability a priority with your team, how to define team obligations, how to increase the resilience and resolve of your team, and how to be one team.

Chapter 9: How to Be a Community Builder

This chapter presents the four strategies that all leaders can implement to help create a strong leadership culture across their organizations. Specifically, the chapter presents strategies on how to commit to be a community builder, how to think and act in a one-company way, how to create the foundation to tackle the hard work of leadership, and being deliberate in how you build relationships with peers and colleagues.

The Dual Response to Building Strong Leadership Accountability

The Individual Response

The Organizational Response

Commit to be an accountable leader

Inspire your direct reports, teams, and peers to be accountable

Drive leadership accountability across your organization

Leadership is a decision

MAKE IT

Hold others accountable to be leaders

Make leadership accountability a critical business issue

Leadership is an obligation

STEP UP

Build a truly accountable team

Define and embed clear leadership expectations

Leadership is hard work

GET TOUGH

Be a community builder

Do the hard work to sustain momentum

Leadership is a community

CONNECT

Foster a community of leaders across your organization

CHAPTER 7

How to Hold Others Accountable for Being Leaders

I was speaking with the head of the human resources (HR) department at an investment firm that was a big fan of *The Leadership Contract*. Over several years, all leaders at the firm had experienced our training programs. The senior executive team spent considerable time learning the concepts themselves and ensuring they were effective role models for the rest of the organization. During our conversation, I asked this head of HR about some of the most tangible outcomes. She shared that leaders at all levels were stepping up in more significant ways. They were demonstrating more ownership for their roles. They were taking the initiative to work across the company on priorities with peers and colleagues. Then I asked her what she felt was the most significant impact. She immediately responded, "Our leaders are doing a much better job of holding other leaders accountable for being leaders."

She couldn't have had a better answer. As a leader, you are expected to hold others accountable for their performance. Many leaders also struggle to hold others accountable. Now you may think it's just junior leaders with little experience who struggle. Well, some CEOs struggle as well. Studies show that close to 20 percent of CEOs cite holding others accountable as their biggest weakness and another 15 percent struggle with dealing with an underperformer.[1]

As a leader, you need to address these issues with those you lead. As we discussed earlier in the book, you may find many are accountable and committed to the technical parts of their roles. However, they may be less committed to being accountable leaders. This is where you must apply your focus. The real end state you want to achieve is one where individuals step up and are fully committed to being accountable leaders. No opting out. No coasting. No flying under the radar. You need to set the expectation for your direct reports to own it, step up, and demonstrate real accountability every day. If you succeed, you will elevate your ability to lead to the right level. You will also eliminate the inordinate amount of time you spend dealing with accountability issues on your teams. You will also create a ripple effect of accountability across your organization.

This chapter will provide you with the strategies you need. We will explore how you can use the four terms of the leadership contract to guide your efforts to hold others accountable to be leaders (see Figure 7.1 below).

The Four Strategies to Hold Others Accountable

01
Leadership Is a Decision
Make leadership accountabilty a priority in how you lead

02
Leadership Is an Obligation
Define the leadership expectations you have for the people you lead

03
Leadership Is Hard Work
Support your direct reports by increasing their resilience and resolve to tackle the hard work they must do as leaders

04
Leadership Is a Community
Help your direct reports build strong reputations so they can succeed across the broader organization

Figure 7.1   The Four Strategies to Hold Others Accountable

Make Leadership Accountability a Priority in How You Lead

Do you know with certainty which of your direct reports are truly accountable and which are mediocre? When I ask leaders this question, many have a response, often based on a gut reaction rather than analysis.

The first step to holding others accountable for being leaders is knowing where they stand. Taking stock of your direct reports from a leadership accountability perspective can be incredibly valuable. We will do this by completing a quick assessment based on the four terms of the leadership contract.

To start, I'd like you to identify a direct report and think about how they are showing up currently as a leader. Now read each of the 20 statements in Figure 7.2 and check off whether the statement is strong or weak for the individual.

Understanding Your Assessment of Your Direct Report

What insights did you gain from your quick assessment of your direct report? Let's have a closer look. First, if you found that you predominately checked off the 20 statements as strengths, then you can conclude you have a direct report who is an accountable leader. This is great. You must keep nurturing the person's development and ensure they act as a role model for others on your team. The more leaders you have who set the tone of accountability, the more others will step up. Remember, accountability breeds accountability.

Second, if you found you had direct reports who had an equal amount of strengths and weaknesses, then you need to focus your attention on helping them be stronger. The strategies in the rest of this chapter will help you do just that. You may also want to review *The Leadership Contract Field Guide*. It contains 75 valuable activities that can help your leaders become stronger and more accountable.

Finally, if you have a direct report who is weak in most areas, this person needs your immediate attention. You will need to have a meaningful conversation with that individual to share your insights. Learn how they see themselves and determine what might be getting

LEADERSHIP IS A DECISION	DIRECT REPORT	
	STRONG	WEAK
01 Demonstrate personal ownership for being truly accountable leaders		
02 Are clear about what is expected of them in their leadership role		
03 Fully embrace the challenges and difficulties that come with being a leader		
04 Are excited about the organization and its future		
05 Hold themselves accountable to high standards of performance		

LEADERSHIP IS AN OBLIGATION	DIRECT REPORT	
	STRONG	WEAK
06 Are committed to living up to their personal obligations as a leader		
07 Put what is best for the organization ahead of what's best for them personally		
08 Effectively communicate the organization's strategy to the people and teams that they lead		
09 Are clear about what their stakeholders value and expect of them		
10 Understand the business and organizational context in which they lead		

LEADERSHIP IS HARD WORK	DIRECT REPORT	
	STRONG	WEAK
11 Effectively handle the pressures and scrutiny of their leadership role		
12 View the challenges they face as a leader as opportunities to grow and develop		
13 Directly tackle tough conversations with others in the organization		
14 Never shy away from making important decisions that may be difficult or unpopular		
15 Continuously work on developing their personal resilience and resolve as a leader		

LEADERSHIP IS A COMMUNITY	DIRECT REPORT	
	STRONG	WEAK
16 Actively look for ways to collaborate with peers from across the organization		
17 Lead with a one-company mindset		
18 Build high trust relationships with colleagues and peers		
19 Ask for help and reach out to others for advice and support when required		
20 Are known as a leader who has other people's backs		

Figure 7.2   Assessing Leadership Accountability

in the way. You can ask the person to do a self-assessment on the 20 statements. See what that reveals. Perhaps you haven't been clear on your leadership expectations. Perhaps the person is committed to the technical parts of the role but hasn't spent time thinking about being a truly accountable leader. Alternatively, the person may have good intentions to be accountable, but is struggling to create value and have impact. No matter what the issue, an open and transparent conversation is an excellent place to start.

Do You Have a Mediocre Leader on Your Hands?

If you rate a direct report as having many weak areas, you may also need to ask yourself whether they are mediocre leaders. Go a little deeper in your analysis by looking at the top five characteristics of mediocre leaders that we explored earlier in the book. The questions below will be helpful:

1. **Blame others.** Do you see this leader regularly point the figure at someone else? Do they struggle to accept personal responsibility when things go wrong?
2. **Selfish and self-serving.** Does this leader focus only on their own priorities? Do they not care about other colleagues?
3. **Uncivil and mean.** Does this leader regularly and routinely mistreat, disrespect, and demean others? Is the individual known to bully others?
4. **Inept and incompetent.** Does the person not seem right for a leadership role?
5. **Lack of initiative.** Does this person rarely appear as a self-starter? Do you need to provide direction on every priority?

If you find yourself saying yes to any of these questions, then chances are you have a mediocre leader on your hands. You will need to act. Begin by having a direct and open conversation. Gauge how the individual reacts to your feedback: Do they respond positively? Do they accept your feedback? Or do they react with defensiveness and anger? You may also need to reevaluate whether these individuals are in the right role. Maybe they need to be moved into a more technically oriented position. Perhaps there is a culture fit issue. Regardless of what is going on, it would help if you took action to help these individuals. If you don't, you will inadvertently send a message that you are a leader who tolerates mediocrity. You wouldn't want to do that, would you?

Define Your Leadership Expectations

One of the most important obligations you have as a leader is to set clear leadership expectations for your direct reports. Surprisingly, few leaders do this. I believe it's the most significant missed opportunity for you to drive stronger leadership accountability among your direct reports. You see, without clear leadership expectations, you do not have clarity nor the foundation to hold others accountable to be leaders. By not making your expectations clear, you also leave it to others to decide what is important. Don't make this a guessing game: Be clear with your leadership expectations. If you recall the findings from my global research on leadership accountability, only 49 percent of companies surveyed claim to have set clear leadership expectations.

Take a few minutes now to start thinking about the leadership expectations that you have for your leaders. Here are some ideas to get you started:

1. If your organization has already created a set of leadership expectations for all leaders, make sure you use these as your inspiration with your own team. If your organization hasn't set clear leadership expectations, then use the remaining steps below.
2. Reflect on your current business context and strategy. What does that tell you about how your leaders will need to step up and be truly accountable?
3. Identify a set of five to seven critical behaviors that they will need to demonstrate consistently to drive the success of your team.
4. If your organization has a leadership model or framework, make sure you use that as your inspiration.
5. Articulate your expectations in simple and clear language.
6. Test out your ideas with a few of your leaders to get their feedback and ensure your expectations are clear.
7. Communicate and reinforce them on a regular basis.

8. Communicate your leadership expectations frequently.
9. Acknowledge when leaders are stepping up to your leadership expectations.

Once you have identified the leadership expectations for your team, you should see a greater sense of clarity from your leaders. You will also see a more aligned and consistent approach to how your team members lead. I certainly learned this a few years back. I was leading a senior team driving a significant change in our business strategy. My team and I were having a two-day offsite. Before this meeting, I sent an email to stimulate their thinking. In it I told them how excited I was about the journey we would be taking together. I also expressed that my expectations of them were changing. I reinforced how important accountability was to me, how I wanted to create a team where we had each other's backs. I expressed the need for us to practice what we preached to our clients. I also reinforced that our leadership culture would begin with us, so we had to set the right tone for the rest of our team. I wanted our collective leadership experience to be one of the best career experiences they would ever have. I also told them we would have some challenging work ahead—changes in talent, changes in how we approached our business, and so on.

A few of my team members immediately responded to my email saying they appreciated the clarity. They also admitted to feeling a little scared about where the bar was being set. I was, too. The challenge was enormous. These ideas inspired the conversation during our two-day meeting. They added their perspectives, and we developed an aligned set of leadership expectations for ourselves and our team.

1. *United front.* We wanted to be seen as a unified team to our clients and our internal stakeholders.
2. *Above the belt and in the ring.* When conflict came up, we wanted to be direct with one another, rather than gossiping, and have transparent conversations.
3. *Be the leader.* We wanted to set the expectation that everyone was expected to lead, and that there were going to be no passengers or bystanders.

4. *Accountability for results.* We expected an unrelenting focus on results and would support one another to achieving them.
5. *Bring a sense of urgency.* We would be responsive and take the initiative in everything we did.
6. *Win as a team.* We defined success as our collective success, and it was everyone's responsibility to ensure everyone was winning.

We communicated these expectations to our entire team. They became a foundation for how we behaved and how we led.

You can take this one step further by using your leadership expectations to create your own leadership contract for everyone to sign, including yourself. In my book *The Leadership Contract,* I provide a sample leadership contract for the reader to sign. That sample leadership contract is tied specifically to each of the four terms. So if this idea appeals to you, you may want to check it out.

In the end, there is power in setting clear leadership expectations. It's an essential step to building accountable leaders. However, once you have implemented this step, you must reinforce the expectations regularly. This is what we will explore next.

Reinforce Leadership Expectations Through Regular Check-Ins

I worked with an energy company a while back. Their chief human resources officer said that the board chair of the company was a big proponent of leadership accountability. He often said that, to drive and sustain it, a leader must apply *constant warm intensity.* By *constant,* he meant that as a leader you need to be deliberate and always setting the expectation of accountability. By *warm,* he indicated that people should sweat a little and feel the heat of being held accountable. If they don't, then you aren't challenging them enough. However, if you are too forceful and apply too much heat, they may not respond adequately. Finally, *intensity* means that you need to be focused and bring an energy that communicates the importance of the leadership expectations you set.

How do you react to these three words: *constant, warm, intensity*?

Once you have set your leadership expectations, you need to embed them in how you and others lead. Many leaders set expectations, but don't do enough follow-up. Over time, clarity dissipates and accountability wanes. Old leadership behaviors resurface, making change difficult. About 20 years ago, I had an interesting insight into how this can happen. My wife and I were growing our family and decided to buy a larger home. To save a bit of money, we moved our kitchen appliances from our old house to our new home. There was just one problem. The layout in our old kitchen meant that our refrigerator door opened from the left-hand side. In the new home, the refrigerator door needed to open from the right side.

No worries, I thought. I popped open a few plastic covers and removed some bolts and pins. In about 20 minutes, I got the door handle moved from the left to the right side of the refrigerator. Easy, right? Not so. For weeks afterward, I approached the refrigerator and instinctively reached for the handle on the left side of the door. This happened again and again. I would be looking at the door handle on the right side of the refrigerator, but my arm and hand would be reaching to the left side. Eventually, we all adapted to the new configuration, but it was surprising how long it took me.

Now, you might be asking what an old refrigerator has to do with being an accountable leader? Well, any change requires us to discontinue old behaviors and replace them with new ones needed for success. All of us have muscle memory for aspects of our roles—habits that have served us well, or at least not gotten us into trouble. We cannot evolve and grow if we don't change. Change also requires us to understand that there may be a new set of leadership expectations we need to embrace. Therefore, as a leader, you need to be unrelenting in holding those you lead accountable for being leaders. If you don't, their muscle memory will have them reverting to old patterns of behavior.

A useful way to sustain momentum is by having regular check-ins or conversations, say two or three times per year. Use these discussions to provide an open forum to have your direct reports discuss their own leadership. These check-ins are not intended to replace regular performance or coaching conversations, but rather to ensure you have time set aside throughout the year to focus on discussing leadership accountability. Use the check-ins to reinforce what is working well and provide feedback on areas that can be stronger.

Here are some questions you can explore in your check-in conversations. Send them out to your direct reports before you meet, and then review the responses together.

- In what specific ways did you step up to our leadership expectations?
- What were some of the critical leadership decisions that you made?
- How did you increase the value you created for the organization?
- What hard work did you tackle? What was the impact?
- What hard work did you avoid? Why? What got in your way?
- How did you strengthen the sense of community among leaders on our team or across our organization?
- Looking ahead to the next few months, how will you continue to put the four terms of our leadership contract into expectations?

Clarify Leadership Expectations at Critical Leadership Turning Points

In *The Leadership Contract*, I wrote a lot about what I called *leadership turning points*. These are moments when an individual assumes a new leadership role that brings a new set of expectations and a higher degree of responsibility, scrutiny, and pressure. In my team's work with thousands of leaders over the years, we have defined four critical leadership turning points. At each one, you must sit down with your direct report to discuss what your expectations will be going forward. It's a great habit to establish, and an even better way to embed your leadership expectations with those you lead. It's also crucial because, as we already discussed in Chapter 2 of this book, many leaders struggle and even fail to integrate into new leadership roles. Don't let this happen to you and your leaders. Let's quickly explore the four critical leadership turning points:

- **Individual Contributor/Emerging Leader.** The first turning point occurs when you tap on someone's shoulder and tell the person you see leadership potential. I'm sure this probably happened to you at some point in your career. It's quite the moment.
- **Front-Line Leader.** The second critical turning point occurs when an individual takes on his or her first supervisory or front-line

management role. It represents a significant shift from focusing on one's performance as a measure of success to being measured on the performance of others. Some front-line leaders are stepping into a leadership role on a team where they used to be members. Learning to lead former colleagues isn't easy. You can play a crucial role in supporting your direct report through this experience.

- **Mid-Level or Senior Leader.** The third critical leadership turning point is when one assumes a mid-level or senior management role. The demands of leadership change considerably, and how one sees oneself must change. At this level, the leader is most likely managing other leaders. The individual is also thrust into a world of working with other leaders from other departments and functions from across your organization. The new leader needs to have a strong reputation because influence is vital at this level.
- **Executive Leader.** The final critical turning point of leadership occurs when one assumes an executive role. Expectations are even higher. Leaders are expected to not only understand their part of the business, but also be ambassadors for the whole organization.

Each turning point represents a significant shift in leadership expectations. Not only does the role change, but the leader must also change at a personal level by developing a new mindset aligned with the new leadership expectations. You must help your leaders understand these expectations, as well as how they need to step up and demonstrate strong accountability. You can't just be putting someone into a role, hoping for the best. No matter how enthusiastic the individual may be, it's better to pause and have an explicit conversation about the changing demands and expectations of the role.

Below is a set of questions you can use when a direct report takes on a new leadership role. Begin by explaining your leadership expectations, then engage in a discussion that addresses these questions:

1. What does strong leadership accountability look like when you are entirely successful in your role?
2. What are the specific expectations, demands, and pressures that you believe you will face in your new role?
3. What excites you about this role? What concerns you?

4. What is the deliberate leadership decision you need to make to be successful in this role?
5. How do you need to think about your leadership obligations?
6. What is the specific hard work that you know you need to tackle to be successful in your role?
7. What critical relationships with peers and colleagues will you need to rely on to help you be a more accountable leader?

The more you can support your direct reports at leadership turning points, the more successful you'll be in helping them continue to step up and be accountable.

Increase the Resilience and Resolve of Your Direct Reports

Once you lead others, you realize that part of your role is helping them build their own personal resilience and resolve as leaders. As you know from your personal experience, leadership is hard work. The position is demanding, and many leaders don't fully appreciate this until they are in the role. You can help your leaders become more self-aware about how they respond to adversity, scrutiny, and the pressure of a leadership role.

I remember one direct report I led years ago who was relatively new in a leadership role. He was a great performer, but whenever something would go wrong, he would become quite unsettled. One day, we had an issue crop up on a project he was overseeing. His workstation was just outside my office. I had my door open, and I could sense him fidgeting and getting distracted. It was early in the morning, so a lot of our team wasn't in the office yet. I peeked out of my office door and asked him to come in for a chat. As soon as we sat down, he started to vent. He was frustrated with how things had quickly gotten out of control, creating an issue with the project. He continued to vent. I listened.

When he paused, I asked him, "Are you planning on letting this ruin your entire day?" He was surprised by my question. We discussed that stuff happens, but as leaders, we must be able to respond, reframe, and move on. Given how he was reacting, he was on the path to letting this problem interfere with his entire day as well as his judgment. Had he not paused, he would not have been at his best to deal with any other issues that came his way.

We discussed his game plan to fix the problem. He thanked me for the conversation, and his mood and tone changed immediately.

It's helpful to understand the resilience and resolve of your leaders. Here are some things you can look out for, so you can better help them:

- Do they see the hard work in their leadership role as an opportunity to grow?
- Do they remain optimistic in the face of adversity?
- How do they respond to criticism and scrutiny?
- How do they self-regulate their emotions and reactions to stressful events?
- Are they able to get back on track after a setback or disappointment?
- Do they manage their personal energy to maintain their performance?
- Do you observe them asking for help and drawing on the support of others?

As you review the seven questions above and think about your direct reports, what insights jump out at you? Where do you need to focus your attention?

If you can help your direct reports strengthen their resilience and resolve, you will provide tremendous value to them both professionally and personally.

We need to become more transparent and open in discussing the hard work of leadership. It's one of the most valuable things that happens in our leadership contract programs. Leaders open up about their struggles and provide support to one another. An essential part is of all of this is being able to be vulnerable with others. Dr. Brené Brown has eloquently written about this in her books.[2] She describes vulnerability as the uncertainty, risk, and emotional exposure that we feel when we open up and talk about something outside of our comfort zone.

If you let your direct reports know you are available to lend some support and help them reframe a situation, particularly when they are having a rough day, you will be valued and admired. If you are the leader people know they can be vulnerable in front of and feel safe with you will have a tremendous impact on their lives. Be that kind of leader!

Help Your Leaders Succeed Within the Broader Organization

As organizations continue to drive more collaboration and innovation across their enterprises, all leaders will need to know how to work across departments and divisions. Working in this way may be new to many leaders. You can help them navigate these uncharted waters by positioning them strongly and helping them build relationships with peers and colleagues. Here are some ideas to consider:

- **Help build the credibility and positive reputations of your leaders.** When everyone on your team has strong personal credibility and is viewed in a positive light, that's a winning formula. Your job becomes much more manageable because not everything hinges on you. Your team's reputation and positive word-of-mouth can create the ideal conditions for getting important work done across a company. If your team members do not have that credibility, they run the risk of being marginalized, ignored, or bypassed for opportunities. If their credibility is weak, others will avoid them, or do workarounds to not engage them on important projects. Ensure that you are doing your best to build your leaders' reputations.
- **Connect your leaders to key stakeholders and influencers.** Do you spend time introducing your leaders to others in the organization? Many times, leaders can get stuck in their silos and don't reach out to build relationships. You can leverage your internal network to help them establish relationships. This will lead to better collaboration and innovation and better outcomes for your organization as a whole.
- **Showcase the talent and impact of your leaders.** One of the best things that leaders I've worked with have done for me is to tell others about my work and accomplishments. That's why I routinely do this with my direct reports. Often, the impact that a leader has may go unnoticed, especially among senior leaders. That's why it's important for you to routinely showcase your team members and

communicate their accomplishments to others. To what extent do you do this for the leaders you lead?

Final Thoughts

In this chapter, we focused on what you can do to better hold others accountable for being leaders. There is a real opportunity for you to be the leader in your organization who helps others succeed. The side benefit is that you will also develop a reputation as a builder of truly accountable leaders. Top talent will seek you out and ask to work for you, because they know they will become better with your support and leadership.

Gut Check for Leaders: How to Hold Others Accountable for Being Leaders

As you think about the ideas in this chapter, reflect on your answers to the following Gut Check for Leaders questions:

1. To what extent do you make leadership accountability a priority in how you lead others?
2. Have you invested time in defining and articulating clear leadership expectations of those you lead?
3. In what ways can you work to increase the resilience and resolve of the people you lead?
4. To what extent do you help your direct reports succeed across the broader organization?

Notes

1. Shannon Howard, "Holding Employees Accountable: Where Most Leaders Fail," *The Predictive Index*, March 21, 2019, https://www.predictiveindex.com/blog/holding-employees-accountable/.
2. Brené Brown, *Daring Greatly: How the Courage to Be Vulnerable Transforms the Way We Live, Love, Parent, and Lead* (Penguin Books, 2012).

CHAPTER 8

How to Build an Accountable Team

As we explored in Chapter 5, teams are critical to the success of organizations. However, based on the research presented, most teams are seen as being mediocre. You therefore have a tremendous opportunity to set yourself apart by committing to build a team that demonstrates accountability and sets the tone for other teams in your organization. The good news is there are some proven steps you can take to drive success. Once again, we will use the four terms of the leadership contract to guide your efforts in building a truly accountable team (see Figure 8.1).

Make Leadership Accountability a Priority with Your Team

A good starting point to make leadership accountability a priority with your team is to have a good sense of where the team stands. Conducting a team assessment will provide a baseline measure, confirm current strengths, and pinpoint gaps where the team must be stronger. Take a few minutes now to evaluate your team against the dimensions of team clarity and team commitment. Read each statement and check off whether you see it as strong or weak (see Figures 8.2 and Figure 8.3).

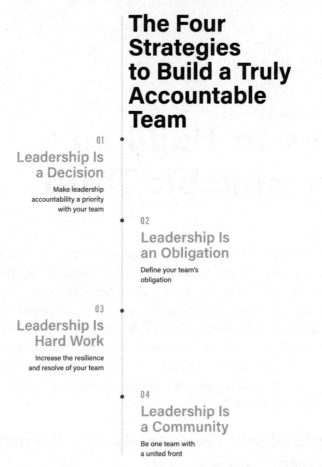

The Four Strategies to Build a Truly Accountable Team

01

Leadership Is a Decision

Make leadership accountability a priority with your team

02

Leadership Is an Obligation

Define your team's obligation

03

Leadership Is Hard Work

Increase the resilience and resolve of your team

04

Leadership Is a Community

Be one team with a united front

Figure 8.1　The Four Strategies to Build a Truly Accountable Team

Making Sense of Your Assessment of Your Team

What insights did you gain from your quick assessment of your team? What strengths did you see? What weaknesses or gaps did you see? Let's analyze your assessment a little further.

- **A Truly Accountable Team.** If you checked mostly "strong" boxes, this suggests that you have a team that demonstrates a high degree of accountability. Congratulations. All of this should be translating into extraordinarily strong performance and results. The challenge for you and your team is to maintain this high level of

TEAM CLARITY DIMENSION

CLARITY OF THE BUSINESS CONTEXT The team demonstrates the accountability for anticipating external trends and understanding their business context	STRONG	WEAK
01 Team members are clear on the trends and drivers in their external business environment and industry		
02 Team members are clear on the needs of external customers/consumers		
03 Team members are clear on changes and issues impacting their organization		
04 Team members provide clarity on the business context to others on the team		
CLARITY OF THE STRATEGY The team demonstrates the accountability for understanding the purpose and strategy of their organization	STRONG	WEAK
05 Team members are clear on the links between the strategy and external market trends and customer expectations		
06 Team members understand how the team's mandate aligns to organizational strategic priorities		
07 Team members are clear on the primary obligation of the team in driving the success of the organization		
08 Team members regularly communicate and cascade the strategy to others		
CLARITY OF STAKEHOLDER EXPECTATIONS The team demonstrates the accountability to understand the interdependencies that exist with other parts of the organization	STRONG	WEAK
09 Team members are clear on what matters to their key stakeholders		
10 Team members are clear on the stakeholder relationships needed to drive success at the organizational level		
11 Team members are clear on how to influence key stakeholders to drive the strategic priorities of the organization		
12 Team members are clear on how to align work across the organization		
CLARITY WITHIN THE TEAM The team demonstrates the accountability to understand its priorities and plans, and the efforts needed to ensure the successful attainment of business results	STRONG	WEAK
13 Team members are clear on the collective goals and priorities of the team		
14 Team members are clear on how to execute the team's strategy and priorities		
15 Team members are clear on where they stand as a team (current strengths and gap areas)		
16 Team members are clear on the kind of leadership culture the team requires to succeed		

Figure 8.2   Assess the Team Clarity Dimension of Your Team

TEAM COMMITMENT DIMENSION

COMMITMENT TO TEAM'S MANDATE The team demonstrates the accountability to build a deep sense of commitment to driving its success	STRONG	WEAK
17 Team members are passionate about the future of the organization		
18 Team members demonstrate strong accountability for executing the organization's strategic priorities		
19 Team members set high standards of performance for the team		
20 Team members consistently demonstrate an aligned and united front		
COMMITMENT TO WORKING ACROSS THE ORGANIZATION The team demonstrates the accountability to effectively work with key stakeholders across the organization to drive positive business outcomes	STRONG	WEAK
21 Team members find ways to break down silos and drive collaboration across the organization		
22 Team members demonstrate the courage to tackle difficult issues with stakeholders		
23 Team members invest time to build productive relationships with key stakeholders		
24 Team members minimize unhealthy politics and work with stakeholders in the interest of the whole organization		
COMMITMENT TO LEADING THE TEAM The team demonstrates the accountability to work together and are committed to making the team as strong as it can possible be	STRONG	WEAK
25 Team members share high aspirations to be truly accountable leaders		
26 Team members support each other's development as leaders		
27 Team members demonstrate the courage to tackle tough issues and have difficult conversations with each other		
28 Team members demonstrate resilience and resolve in the face of adversity		
COMMITMENT TO EACH OTHER The team demonstrates the accountability to be deeply committed to each other	STRONG	WEAK
29 Team members hold each other accountable and call out unproductive leadership behavior		
30 Team members deeply care about each other		
31 Team members demonstrate high trust and have each other's backs		
32 Team members regularly commit to spending time to get to know each other on a personal level		

Figure 8.3   Assess the Team Commitment Dimension of Your Team

accountability and performance over the long term. The strategies outlined below will help you to continue to maintain strong momentum on your team.

- **A Driven Team.** If you have many strength areas in the team clarity dimension but very few in the team commitment dimension, then you may have a highly driven team. These teams tend to demonstrate a real focus on driving results, which is a good thing. However, you will need to determine whether the performance is coming solely from strong individual efforts rather than collective efforts. You may also need to determine whether the team values are cohesive. Many driven teams don't care about this and want to focus on their work and tasks they need to accomplish. You may need to consider whether the lack of cohesion acts as a barrier to a team's growth.

- **A Supportive Team.** In contrast, if you find you have more strength areas in the team commitment dimension, then you may have a supportive team. This team typically has a positive intention to work as a team but may lack a purposeful direction. The team experience is excellent—everyone gets along and has fun. But, and it's a big "but," the lack of clarity may mean the team doesn't deliver expected results. If the team can improve its sense of clarity, it can work toward becoming a truly accountable team.

- **A Weak or Mediocre Team.** If you find many gaps checked off on both the team clarity and team commitment dimensions, your team is weak and possibly even mediocre. You need to take action because a team like this just will not cut it in today's organizations. I would encourage you to implement all the strategies discussed in the rest of this chapter.

You might also want to go back to Chapter 5 and review your assessment of your team against the research data I presented. You may find it valuable to compare your results with the results from the teams in the industry-leading companies. Now that you have a good grasp of where your team stands on team clarity and team commitment, you may also find it useful to have your entire team complete the survey to gain a shared understanding of where the team sees itself.[1]

Define Your Team's Obligation

Once you have a sense of where your team stands, then the next critical work to be done is to define your team's obligation and then create an explicit leadership contract for your team. You will find that these steps will immediately improve both team clarity and team commitment.

It's always powerful to see a team that has taken the time to define its team obligation. You immediately gain an increased sense of focus, alignment, and commitment to one another. It's incredible to witness. And yet, very few teams take the time to do this. That's unfortunate because they are neglecting a simple, yet compelling way to improve their team performance and experience.

Below I present a series of questions for you to reflect on. I always encourage team leaders to work through these questions first on their own before engaging with the team. Defining the team's obligation is a team task, but I find it valuable for the team leader to think this through beforehand.

To respond to the questions below, think about a point in time in the future, say two or three years out. Imagine that by this date your team is truly accountable and wildly successful in driving extraordinary results. Imagine also that your team has set a positive tone for other teams in your organization. With this ideal vision in mind, now respond to the questions below:

- What enduring value did your team create?
- In what specific ways did this team leave your organization in better shape than you found it?
- What did your customers say about your impact?
- What did your key stakeholders say about what it was like to work with your team? In what specific ways did you create value for them?
- What did other employees within your team or across your organization say about the tone your team set for the organization?
- How did senior management view your team's impact? What specific things did they say to acknowledge your contribution?
- What is one statement that best captures your team's primary leadership obligation?

Your answer (and your team's answer) to the last question is the most critical; it defines what your team is all about. When teams establish a leadership obligation statement, they reap several benefits. First, it gives teams immediate focus. There is no confusion about what the team is there to do. Second, it inspires the team. Third, it helps the team come together to support one another to achieve success.

Create a Leadership Contract for Your Team

A team's leadership obligation statement identifies the "what" of a team. Creating a team leadership contract defines the "how" of a team by clearly spelling out the specific ways the team intends to behave and work together. Research shows there are many benefits to establishing a team contract:[2]

- First, it makes explicit how team members will interact with one another.
- Second, it identifies and reinforces desired team behaviors, and thereby helps the team avoid less-productive or even dysfunctional behaviors.
- Third, it drives a sense of responsibility and trust among the team members.

The process of creating one is straightforward. Simply use the four terms of the leadership contract as a guide to articulate expectations and commitments for your team. Before you begin, let's see how a team did this work and created their own team leadership contract.

The Senior Executive Team of an Investment Management Firm

My team worked with the senior executives of a full-service investment firm providing investment management, wealth management, and financial planning to their clients. The senior team represented all the top executives from the critical functions of the company. Traditionally, they had been working independently of one another, but as the company grew significantly, they started to experience growing pains. They needed to lead the company not as a group of isolated functions, but as a truly aligned senior executive team. My team worked with them to develop a team leadership contract. It then became the foundation for each executive to work with his or her functional leadership teams to establish consistency and alignment across the organization.

The executives signed their team's leadership contract. They communicated the terms of their contract to their teams. They also used it as a living document to guide the way they worked together, both during meetings and when working on cross-functional initiatives. The teams also devoted some time every quarter to assessing their progress. Here's the leadership contract that they created (see Figure 8.4). As you read this team's leadership contract, identify what stands out for you and may be relevant for your own team.

You can see how detailed they are in identifying key behaviors and expectations. The more specific and explicit you can be, the better and easier it will be for your team to step up, be accountable, and hold each other to account. Many other teams have created team leadership contracts as well. While they adhere to a similar structure, they are also highly unique from one another. The sample in Figure 8.4 has a lot of specific behaviors the team agrees to live up to; other teams have fewer. You can decide what will work for your team.

Now it's your turn. Think about some of the themes coming from the team assessment you completed earlier in this chapter. Then review your ideas about defining your team's leadership obligation. Now think about how your team needs to show up. What expectations and commitments must they live up to? Use the worksheet in Figure 8.5 as a guideline.

Once you have created a draft of your team's leadership contract, you must discuss the consequences of not living up to it. Ensure your team members are clear on how they intend to hold one another accountable for living up to the expectations you set together. What will be the consequences if team members do not step up?

Increase the Resilience and Resolve of Your Team

You can employ several strategies to help ensure your team does the hard work of leadership. A big part of this is helping your team build

We understand that The Leadership Contract represents a deep and personal
commitment to be the best leadership team that we can be—the leadership team
our organization needs us to be.

By signing it, we are making a collective commitment to each other. In turn, we will
no longer settle for mediocrity. We will not simply go through the motions as a
leadership team. We will be an accountable leadership team.

—01

Leadership Is a Decison

MAKE IT

- We commit to finding a collaborative solution and supporting that resolution to its conclusion.

- We won't be afraid to ask for help from each other and to accept it without any judgment.

- We will lead with the why and provide context for everything that we do.

- We will debrief and recap every meeting and action items from the agendas and add them to our team portal.

—02

Leadership Is an Obligation

STEP UP

- We will set lofty and attainable objectives and deliver on them.

- We will set behavior expectations, model them, and promptly address behaviors inconsistent with our values, no exceptions.

- We will communicate our strategy, listen for and consider feedback, and evaluate our priorities.

- We will consider all stakeholders, work toward consensus, and make decisions that are good for our clients, our employees, and the firm.

- We will develop our people and foster a culture of leaders providing experience, opportunities, mentoring, and programs to prepare for the future of the firm.

—03

Leadership Is Hard Work

GET TOUGH

- We will declare what we can and cannot do. Once we declare we can do it, we will own it and call out scope creep.

- We will be open to feedback and will assume a positive intent when giving it and receiving it. We will have any tough conversations in a safe, non-defensive environment.

- We will own our missteps and know when to recalibrate and refocus.

- We will manage expectations and communicate with each other in a timely manner. "I'm too busy" is not an answer, but it can be a call for assistance.

—04

Leadership Is a Community

CONNECT

- We will engage and communicate formally and informally with everyone in the firm.

- We will be open, honest, and vulnerable with each other.

- We will commit to spending time together and celebrate success—team and firm wide.

- We are committed to supporting community and firm events.

- We will be approachable and accountable as ambassadors of the firm.

We agree to the four terms of The Leadership Contract set out above and will demonstrate our commitment by signing below.

Figure 8.4 A Sample Leadership Contract for Senior Executive Team

Opening Statement
Summarize your team's leadership obligation

....

Leadership Is a Decision
(Identify 3 to 4 behavioral statements that you believe are important for your team to demonstrate):

• _____

• _____

• _____

....

Leadership Is an Obligation
(Identify 3 to 4 behavioral statements that you believe are important for your team to demonstrate):

• _____

• _____

• _____

....

Leadership Is Hard Work
(Identify 3 to 4 behavioral statements that you believe are important for your team to demonstrate):

• _____

• _____

• _____

....

Leadership Is a Community
(Identify 3 to 4 behavioral statements that you believe are important for your team to demonstrate):

• _____

• _____

• _____

....

Team Members Sign Below

_____   _____

_____

Figure 8.5   Create Your Team's Leadership Contract

the resilience and resolve it will need to lead effectively as an account-able team. Below I describe several practical strategies for you to consider.

Help Your Team Tackle the Hard Work

In *The Leadership Contract*, I described the Hard Work Rule of Leadership. It says that as a leader, if you avoid the hard work in your role, you will become weak. However, if you demonstrate the courage to tackle the hard work, you will become strong. The same rule applies to teams. Many teams avoid the hard work of leadership; when they do, they weaken themselves. As the team leader, you need to ensure your team doesn't fall into this trap.

What kind of hard work do teams avoid? There are two catego-ries: (1) the hard work within the team itself, and (2) the hard work outside of the team. Here are some common challenges that happen within teams:

- A divided team is misaligned and not arriving at a good business decision.
- A team member is not pulling their weight and is bringing down the performance of the entire team.
- A team member misbehaves and violates the terms of your team's leadership contract.
- There is underlying or overt conflict within the team.
- Team members are behaving as mavericks, unwilling to sacrifice for the benefit of their colleagues.

The second category is the hard work involving interactions (or altercations) with teams in other departments or functions across your organization. Here are some common examples:

- A team in another department is bad-mouthing your team.
- A team isn't living up to its commitment to supporting your team.
- Another team is not transparent or isn't playing nicely with you.
- Another team is dismissive and marginalizing your team.
- A poor-performing team is letting you down and undermining your own team's ability to perform at a high level.

If you do not address the hard work within your team and outside of it, you will find it harder and harder to build a truly accountable team. Take a few minutes to reflect on these two questions:

- What is the hard work of leadership that you and your team are avoiding within your team?
- What is the hard work of leadership that you and your team are avoiding outside of your team?

When your team members and colleagues know that you won't shy away from any of the hard work that comes your way, it sets a powerful tone for everyone. Be the leader with the courage to tackle the hard work you will face as a team.

Increase Your Team's Ability to Have Tough Conversations

One of the critical capabilities that truly accountable teams have is their ability to call each other out when necessary and have direct and honest conversations on important issues. You must help your team develop this capability. You can do a lot by setting the right tone and having tough conversations at a one-to-one and team level; but your team also needs to step up. The research also shows one essential ingredient that you will need to have in place.

According to Dr. Amy Edmondson, professor at the Harvard Business School, teams that feel safe perform better. In her book *The Fearless Organization: Creating Psychological Safety in the Workplace for Learning, Innovation, and Growth*, Edmondson says that creating psychological safety isn't about being nice; it's about having the courage to have candid conversations, give direct feedback, and admit when one has made a mistake. If you can create this sense of safety on your team, your ability to have tough conversations will increase dramatically.[3]

How you have tough conversations also matters. In *The Leadership Contract Field Guide*, I provide steps that leaders can take in having tough conversations. You can also use these steps with your team. Here's a quick summary of the most critical steps for you to consider:

- **Focus on how much you care.** Begin by helping your team to focus on how much it cares about the person, the other team, your company, and your collective success. When teams begin here, I find that having a tough conversation is a little easier, most likely because a sense of safety is established. If I know you are coming from a good place and that you care about me, then I will be much more willing to engage in a tough conversation.

- **Determine whether the team is ready to have the conversation.** Sometimes your team is working hard, under the gun on a deadline, and may not be in the ideal headspace to have a tough conversation. If that's the case, schedule another time when the team is ready.
- **Be direct and factual.** All team members should strive to be straightforward during tough conversations. Some team members may react emotionally, which is perfectly fine. But keep a focus on the known facts.
- **Show the impact of their behavior.** Sometimes when conversations get heated, team members may lose sight of the impact of not addressing the hard work. Explain how the team's behavior is undermining the collective success, credibility, and reputation of the team.
- **Encourage an honest response.** Strive to create a climate in which you are open to disagreement and debate. Support others when they react defensively or with anger. As the team leader, stay calm.
- **Reaffirm your positive intention.** At the end of your tough conversation, reassure your team that you appreciate the courage it took to engage in this conversation. Identify lessons that can carry over to the next tough conversation the team will have.

In my experience, I find that teams that don't have tough conversations are much less effective. When issues arise and are not addressed, the pent-up emotion, anger, and even resentment can build. These emotions become a hidden barrier to your team's success. Over time, team members can feel weighed down by carrying the stress of the unresolved issues. Don't let this happen to your team. Have the courage to have the tough conversations and build a safe climate for doing so.

Develop Your Team's Resilience and Resolve

In my experience, when a team faces real adversity, one of two things can happen: either they come together, or the team collapses. If the team collapses, everyone turns on each other and starts the blaming, and fighting ensues. When teams come together, they support one another and deal with the adversity from a place of strength.

This is why it's vital for a leader to regularly gauge their team's collective resilience and resolve. The CEO of a hospital that I worked with excelled at this. She would routinely walk the hospital floors and have informal conversations with staff. Through those chats, she would gauge their mood, sense of optimism, and reserve power. When I talked to her about this strategy, she said: "We are trying to get a lot done with scarce resources. It's important work caring for our patients. I need to know whether my team has the resilience to handle their current workload and know when they can take on more. If I push them too much, then we won't succeed. So I'm constantly connecting with them to see how they are doing." Are you as connected with your team as this CEO?

Here are some strategies to consider that will help you manage your team's resilience and resolve:

- **Reach out.** Just like the CEO above, make a habit of reaching out to your team members regularly, not to have a performance discussion but to see how they are doing. This is particularly key if you are leading a virtual team. A phone call or Skype discussion with no agenda other than a check-in is a good idea.
- **Watch out for uncharacteristic behavior.** Sometimes a team member may be overreacting or getting emotional. If it is uncharacteristic behavior, this could be a telltale sign that something is wrong. It could be a personal issue. Some team members will be open enough to tell you; others may not. You need to ensure that you communicate your support at these moments. This simple gesture is often appreciated and helps the team member cope with a stressful experience.
- **Provide recognition and show appreciation.** I find this to be the most undervalued and under-used leadership strategy. Few leaders do it and do it well. We don't always appreciate how recognition and appreciation can foster resilience and resolve, especially when you show how you value your team and their contributions. Recognition also means noticing the often-unnoticed things that employees do to make their organizations successful. The surprising

thing is that many managers rarely provide recognition to the people they lead. It's such a missed opportunity. Don't let it be for you.

- **Make resilience and resolve a meeting topic.** Make resilience and resolve a topic of discussion during your team meetings. This is an important practice as it communicates to others that you take these ideas seriously, and it helps your team not only gauge where they are personally, but also where their colleagues are.

Be One Team with a United Front

You know you have a truly accountable team when the team presents a united front. In the end, this is all about a sense of community, and when you achieve it, your team sustains its momentum and high performance over the long term. Some leaders may feel that this is a soft concept. However, you'd be surprised how often this sense of community surfaces in my work with leaders. Here are some strategies for building a sense of community and connection on your team:

- **Help the team get to know each other.** It is surprising to me how often teams say that they don't know their teammates on a personal level, and many desire to do so. This is especially true of executive teams. Encourage your team members to get to know one another. A simple and powerful way to do this is the Leadership Timeline Activity that I included in *The Leadership Contract Field Guide*. It's an activity whereby individuals reflect on their lives and careers to identify the experiences that have shaped them. Have your team members complete the activity and share their timelines. Even after years of doing this activity with thousands of leaders, I'm always amazed at how effective it is. There is no faster way for leaders to get to know each other and develop a greater appreciation of their diverse backgrounds and unique value.
- **Take time to have fun as a team.** As the team leader, you need to keep driving high levels of performance. That's a given. However, you also need to find times where the team can relax a little. Now I'm not talking about formal team-building sessions—just times to connect, strengthen relationships, and enjoy each other's company. This

is ideally done face to face, but it can also happen virtually. I've seen some teams get creative with having fun, even over conference calls. Maybe they begin a team meeting with fun personal facts about each team member. Others begin team calls with positive shout-outs to acknowledge significant contributions to the team's success.

- **Encourage your team members to meet without you.** This is something I've always done. I want to make sure that my teams have strong relationships without me being a mediator. The simplest way to do this is to remove yourself and encourage them to step up and connect with one another.
- **Build relationships with other teams.** No team is an island in today's organizations. Reach out and build strong relationships with other teams you work with. Look for ways to meet and learn about what each team does. You may find other teams have things figured out that can be of value for you. Of course, the reverse is also true. Engage in joint planning and problem solving.
- **Fix strained or poor relationships.** Getting into the habit of building relationships is key, but it's also important to fix strained or poor relationships with other teams. You should probably start by having a conversation with the team leader of the other team. Maybe the issue is just between the two of you. If you let these relationships remain as they are, they will only worsen and prevent both teams from being truly successful.

Final Thoughts

Teams are the future of organizations. Let me restate that. Accountable teams are the future of organizations. As we've seen from the research, most teams are seen as being weak and mediocre. We need leaders who can create much stronger teams and team experiences for the people they lead. You can be the leader who sets the tone for others. Commit to putting the ideas in this chapter into practice, and you will develop an excellent reputation as a builder of effective and accountable teams that demonstrate clarity and commitment.

Gut Check for Leaders: How to Build an Accountable Team

As you think about the ideas in this chapter, reflect on your answers to the following Gut Check for Leaders questions:

1. Do you make leadership accountability a priority with your teams?
2. To what extent are you clear about your team's obligations?
3. Have you created a leadership contract for your team?
4. To what extent does your team demonstrate resilience and resolve?
5. Have you established a safe climate so your team can hold each other accountable and have tough conversations?
6. Does your team present as a united front and a cohesive group to the rest of the organization?

Notes

1. Go to my website at www.drvincemolinaro.com, where you can access information on conducting a complete team assessment and session with your own team.
2. Christine M. Riordan and Kevin O'Brien, "For Great Teamwork, Start with a Social Contract," *Harvard Business Review*, April 17, 2012, https://hbr.org/2012/04/to-ensure-great-teamwork-start.
3. Amy C. Edmondson, *The Fearless Organization: Creating Psychological Safety in the Workplace for Learning, Innovation, and Growth* (John Wiley & Sons, 2019).

CHAPTER 9

How to Be a Community Builder

As we discussed earlier in the book, if you and your colleagues can build a strong community of leaders in your organization, it will become the ultimate differentiator. Your culture will help you stand apart from your competitors. Your employees, customers, suppliers, and other stakeholders will know you are building something extraordinary. But building a strong culture is not easy. It's not something just for the CEO and executive team to pay attention to. All leaders must play their part, and you will need to step up in new ways. You will need to become a community builder. The four strategies in this chapter will show you how, and they will each connect back to the four terms of the leadership contract (see Figure 9.1).

Commit to Being a Community Builder

Why is it so essential to be a community builder?

Many companies today have more integrated business strategies. They are driving greater collaboration across departments and functions. They also recognize the competitive advantage that can come from having a strong leadership culture in place. Now some leaders may think that these ideas are naïve or too soft. Some think the ideas are about all your leaders holding hands and singing "Kumbaya." Far from it. You will need a deep sense of commitment, resilience, and resolve because this is really hard work. It's about having tough conversations. It's about

Figure 9.1   The Four Strategies to Be a Community Builder

confronting the harsh reality of what is not working. It's about breaking down silos rather than building walls. It's about reaching out to help colleagues who need help. It's about raising your hand and asking for help when you and your team need it.

Unfortunately, most of us have been conditioned to work and lead in a way that is pretty much the opposite of how community builders operate.

Understand the Journey Ahead

If you are like most leaders, you probably spend most of your time thinking about your performance or that of your team, function, or division. You also spend considerable time in silos or dealing with "us versus them" dynamics in your organization. Working in highly individualistic, hyper-competitive, dog-eat-dog cultures wears people down. As a result, you have learned to protect your turf, keep your cards close to your chest, and be a bystander in your organization, all of which impedes your company's ability to execute its strategy and create enduring value.

Here's a little secret: *Your peers and colleagues are fed up with working at cross-purposes, staying stuck in silos, fighting with one another, and leading in uninspiring cultures.*

All of this is weighing down on them, too. I once worked with the COO of a global professional services organization. In our first conversation, he said, "Our organization has been set up to frustrate people and impede progress. It's exhausting. We need to find a way to break through."

Most leaders I talk to want to be in an environment where there is real clarity, alignment, commitment, and mutual support. We want it desperately because we know intuitively that this is the environment that will help us be our best. That's what a community of leaders is all about. Your organization needs your help to create one.

The good news is that you can help from wherever you are in your organization. You don't need the permission of your CEO or manager. You can build a community anywhere. It just takes an accountable leader to want it and make it happen. Are you up for it? Does the vision of creating a strong community of leaders excite you? I hope you said yes to both questions. Let's continue.

Are You Wired to Be a Community Builder?

Leaders who are naturals at this kind of stuff are, at their core, selfless. These leaders rarely put themselves or their agendas first. They lead with a higher purpose in mind. Robert K. Greenleaf called this *servant leadership*.

Reflect on the following questions to determine whether you are wired to be a community builder.

The first question you need to think about is: Are you selfish or selfless? Many of us as leaders have been conditioned to place self-interest above all else. We are always thinking: "What's in it for me?" Interestingly, everyone else you work with can spot a selfish leader. They know everything is all about you, and it erodes their trust and their willingness to work with you.

The next questions you need to reflect on are: Do you have a propensity to use your power not only to promote your career but also to hold others down? Do you take advantage of your position to make decisions and orchestrate outcomes so that you will personally gain in the end? Do you withhold information from others because it gives you an advantage? This kind of behavior doesn't build community.

Another set of questions to explore is: How much of your energy is spent protecting your turf? Are you locked in battles over resources with peers and colleagues? This is a classic challenge in many organizations. We set up a zero-sum game where, if you win, you do so at the expense of a colleague, and if others win, they do so at your cost. So you are eternally locked in a battle. Also, you most likely make decisions and take actions only through a personal lens, rather than doing what's best for your entire company. If you're worried only about your department, budget, and resources, you'll never build a genuine sense of community.

Another question to consider is: Do you typically act as a bystander in your organization? Think about how you respond when you see others struggle, whether they are individuals, teams, or departments. You see their pain, their anguish as they try to drive success but run into problems. How do you respond? Are you a good Samaritan who offers help? Do you stand there and watch, perhaps even relish in the misfortune of others?

A final set of questions to consider is: Are you a political animal? Do you spend all your time caught up in the ongoing drama of your organization and workplace? Do you spend more time scheming and planning your next career move than you do leading and driving business results?

What does this quick assessment tell you about yourself? If you answered yes to even a few of the questions above, then you have some serious work to do to develop the mindset of a community builder.

Think One-Company and Act in the Best Interest of Your Organization

Community builders focus on two critical strategies. The first is that they develop a one-company mindset. The second is that they act in the best interest of the organization.

Develop a One-Company Mindset

To be an effective community builder requires a one-company mindset. While you may be primarily accountable for driving the success of a team, function, department, or line of business, the way you do it matters. Do you approach that task with a single-minded focus, or do you approach it with a broader perspective?

Unfortunately, the research I shared earlier in the book revealed that a one-company mindset is one of the lowest-rated leadership behaviors. I believe part of the reason is that it hasn't been an expectation of leaders at all. You have most likely developed a more functional mindset from years of being entrenched in silos. In the end, this creates a sort of rigidity in how leaders approach their work. You become much more "inward-looking," focused primarily on your team, function, or department and unable or unwilling to work outside these boundaries.

Reflect on this for yourself: How much time do you spend focused (or preoccupied) on leading inside your team, functional, or business unit? If you are like most leaders, the answer is *a lot*.

A leader who participated in one of our leadership programs shared a strategy for developing a one-company mindset that worked for her. She held quarterly "big-picture" lunch meetings, where she invited some of her peers from across the company. Over lunch, they would discuss broad business issues they faced. These meetings yielded very positive results for the organization. First, the group developed a one-company mindset as they learned to appreciate their colleagues' issues. Second, they identified areas where they could work more effectively together.

Finally, they spearheaded initiatives to bring greater alignment and engagement in their work together. They did this all on their own. No senior executive was telling them to do it. That's real leadership accountability.

Another leader shared an even more straightforward tactic. She developed the practice of taking a walk around her office building once a day. Each day she would take about 15 or 20 minutes, venture to a different floor at the headquarters, and drop by the office of a colleague to chat for a few minutes. At first, some of her colleagues did not know how to take this strange behavior. However, she persisted. During these conversations, she asked about what her colleagues were working on currently, the challenges they were facing, and the possible ways they could work together. The practice was personally beneficial to this senior leader because she developed an excellent understanding of how the organization operated as a whole. It also helped her to lead her division more effectively with the interests of the entire organization at heart.

In what ways can you develop a one-company mindset? I believe this will become increasingly important in organizations because many of them are striving to operate more as "one-company."

Act in the Interest of the Whole Organization

I recently worked with an organization in the insurance industry. The CEO asked the senior leaders who reported into the executive team to solve a complicated and thorny business problem. The solution wasn't readily apparent. The top leaders met several times, and the discussions did not go well—mainly because all of them came into those meetings with their elbows high, fists in the air, ready to fight. No one conceded in any way for fear of looking like they had lost. The discussions kept going around and around—no one budged.

Finally, one leader proposed that she would be prepared to give up resources to support another colleague. Suddenly, the tone of the conversation changed. Another leader offered to help a colleague. Soon the solution they had spent hours trying to find emerged, almost with no effort. They went from being solely fixated on their self-interests to acting more broadly in the interest of the entire organization.

I was in a Leadership Contract session with those leaders several weeks after this significant breakthrough. As they told me the story, I asked them what led them to the change in their approach. They said that as soon as that one leader offered to help another colleague, the energy in the room changed from hostility to collegiality and mutual support. I asked that leader what led to her decision. She said she stood back and thought about what was best for the organization as a whole to resolve the issue. The very moment she had that thought, the solution was right in front of her. She knew what she had to do.

Interestingly, in some organizations, that one leader's behavior would have been perceived as a sign of weakness. Not in this organization. Her colleagues saw her as a leader with real courage and strength. Another leader summarized the entire experience by saying, "We stopped behaving like small-minded managers, and started to behave as accountable leaders for this entire company." I love it when this happens. I also know it has fueled these leaders to go after even more chronic problems that have been holding them back.

This example shows the value when leaders act in the best interest of the whole organization. As you reflect on your role, where can you be doing the same? What opportunities exist for you to demonstrate that you act in the best interest of your entire company?

Create the Foundation to Tackle the Hard Work

Earlier in the book, we discussed research findings that suggested two areas where leaders struggle. First, in their ability to hold one another accountable, and second, in breaking down silos to better drive collaboration. These are two critical areas of leadership that community builders focus on. It isn't easy work, but they have the perseverance and resolve to tackle it.

Cultivate Credibility and Trust

When you are trying to build a community, you quickly begin to realize how important it is to have credibility and build trust with your colleagues. Others will not want to engage with you if they don't believe you are someone they can trust. Many leaders assume that authority and power come from one's position and title. However, in today's organizations, a title alone will not get you very far. Increasingly, you are working with peers and colleagues over whom you have no formal authority. You may not be their boss or manager. If you want to get something done, the only currency you have is your credibility and track record.

I've seen too many leaders become marginalized within their organizations because they don't have the credibility they need. It could be because they are mediocre and weak performers, or because they are bullies and not team players. Often, "workarounds" emerge as people try to avoid interacting with these individuals altogether.

Typically, when a leader has a negative reputation, this perception extends to the team he or she leads as well. As a result, you need to be deliberate in understanding the state of your personal credibility and the extent to which you have built trust with peers and colleagues.

In the book *The Leadership Gap*, my co-author David Weiss and I presented a simple way to think about the stages of trust that help build credibility.

- **Are you competent?** The first stage is where people trust you because of your competence. Quite simply, this means that you are good at what you do. You are reliable, responsive, and deliver high-quality work. Your colleagues can trust you to deliver on what you say you will deliver and do so at a high standard. If you can't fulfill this first stage—in other words, if you are inept or mediocre as a leader—it's hard to build credibility with others.

- **Are you honest and forthright?** The second stage is the extent to which others can trust you to be honest and forthright. People need to know they can trust what you say. It's also about the alignment between what you say and what you do. When you get it right, the people you work with perceive you as being honest and forthright. This stage of trust reflects the degree to which there is close alignment between what you say you will do and what you deliver. Many times trust is broken by unfulfilled promises which creates a sense of you being dishonest. If something doesn't work out, do you have the courage and honesty to admit your mistake, apologize, and repair the relationship?

- **Can you be counted on to have my back?** The last stage of trust comes when people know that if they are vulnerable, they can count on you to support them. You will not take advantage of them in any way. For example, if you see someone talking badly about another colleague, what do you do? Do you join in, or do you challenge the person to stop the bad-mouthing? When colleagues are struggling and going through a tough time, are you there for them? Or do you walk away? If you hear something in the corporate grapevine that suggests a colleague's project is in trouble, do you share that information with them? Or do you keep it to yourself and watch them crash and burn?

Building your credibility and trusting relationships is critical to leading in organizations today. However, there is another crucial benefit. When you have credibility and trusting relationships with peers and colleagues, it becomes so much easier to confront difficult issues and have tough conversations with them. It creates the necessary foundation for you to tackle the hard work with your colleagues.

I believe one of the primary reasons leaders struggle to have tough conversations with one another is because they attempt to have them in the absence of a trusting relationship. Think about this for a moment. Imagine that you and I were colleagues, but we didn't invest any time in our relationship. Now imagine I came to you one day, challenging you on an issue. Your immediate response might be, "Who the heck does Vince think he is? How dare he challenge the work of my team and me!" You can imagine where the conversation would go next. We would most likely engage in a heated discussion that would further erode our working relationship.

Let's imagine a different scenario—one where you and I spent time getting to know one another. We have built mutual credibility and trust. When I come to challenge you, or you come to challenge me, and we need to have a tough conversation, it will go very differently, mainly because you will understand me, my motives, and what I'm trying to achieve.

How would you evaluate the current state of your credibility with your peers? Have you built trusting relationships? Does the absence of both make it harder for you to have tough conversations with these peers?

Break Down Mental Silos

I was getting ready to lead a half-day session on The Leadership Contract with the top 80 leaders of a health care organization. As soon as the CEO walked into the training room, she said, "I hate this pillar!" She pointed to the large pillar right in the middle of the room. It was about three feet wide on each of the four sides. It was there to provide structural support, of course, but it was smack dab in the middle of the room. As a result, we had half the chairs organized on one side of the pillar and half on the other side.

Later in the session, the topic of organizational silos came up. I told the group what the CEO said about the pillar. Then I said, "Let's talk a little bit about what this pillar does." Many in the group chimed in: "It provides structure. Without it, the ceiling would fall on us." Then I said, "The pillar has value. But there are some unintended consequences. Can you name some?" Several answers immediately emerged. "It's dividing the group into two," said one leader. Another shared, "It's blocking my view. I can't even see some of the others in the room." Finally, another leader said, "It makes having a large group discussion difficult because we have to constantly move to see who is talking."

Then I said, "The pillar is like the silos we create in an organization. They do serve some purpose, mainly to organize and structure people; but they also have unintended consequences." One of the things silos do is govern behavior. We start making assumptions about what we can and cannot do. We feel we can't cross the room to talk to colleagues. We compete with one another. We imagine one silo is better than another. In the end, a lot of drama can ensue.

I explained that the biggest silos are not physical, but in our heads. As leaders, we must do the hard work of breaking down these "mental silos."

We then evolved the discussion to explore the barriers that were getting in their way as senior leaders. We even discovered that many of the leaders in the room didn't talk to one another because it wasn't customary for leaders from different departments to do that. They didn't involve each other in planning departmental priorities that had an organization-wide impact because they never thought they could. They revealed that they had developed what they called a "mail it in" habit, where a team would put a minimal amount of effort into supporting another team's project. They'd just "mail it in" without really owning their part. They knew this wasn't the right thing to do, but no one challenged the habit.

It was a great discussion, and those leaders left that room with a much greater awareness of the mental silos that were getting in their way and slowing down their collective success.

Take a few minutes to think about the mental silos that are getting in your way. What one thing could you do today to start breaking down those silos? If we don't regularly ask ourselves this question, we make the hard work of leadership even harder.

Support the Success of Your Peers and Colleagues

At a recent conference, I was part of a lineup of speakers that included Sir Ken Robinson, one of the world's greatest minds on the topics of creativity, innovation, and education. I have followed his work through his books and TED talks, so I was thrilled to get a chance to hear him speak. Robinson said that in today's world, we need to think about organizations as organisms instead of as machines. He said an organization is not the buildings, offices, or factories; it's the people inside, and that culture is the relationships, patterns of behavior, and common beliefs held among those people.

When you see an organization in this way, it becomes apparent to me that we will need leaders who excel at supporting the success of others and accomplish this by investing in building relationships with peers and knowing how to be a good follower, as well as knowing when to lead.

Invest in Relationships

Has this ever happened to you? You are out running errands and bump into a friend you haven't seen for some time. You are both excited to see one another. You spend a few minutes catching up. You bring the conversation to an end and one of you says, "We should make a point of getting together for a coffee." You both agree wholeheartedly. It's a great idea. You leave and go on with the rest of your day. What happens next? In most cases, nothing. You both have the best intentions to reach out, but life gets in the way and you don't.

The same kind of thing happens in organizations. Every single time I talk with senior leaders about building a strong leadership culture, one revelation emerges—they admit to doing a poor job of building relationships with one another. In some cases, they say they are downright awful. At least they don't deny it. Now they have good intentions. They want to do it, but as I said many times in *The Leadership Contract*, "Good intentions are not good enough when it comes to leadership."

We need to start investing in building relationships with our peers and colleagues. We need to go beyond good intentions. The reasons are many. So much of the way we work today is collaborative and team-based. We are more interdependent than ever before. You can only succeed if I help you succeed. I can only succeed if you help me succeed. We need each other to deliver results. What I've also learned in my client work is that many problems leaders face in executing strategy come down to poor relationships with their colleagues. You can't build a sense of community among a group of strangers. It's not how we are wired as human beings. When we encounter strangers, we tend to be apprehensive and fearful. It's a good survival mechanism that has served humanity well for thousands of years. But in organizations, it's a killer.

In *The Leadership Contract*, I shared the five most frequently cited tactics for building relationships with internal colleagues. In *The Leadership Contract Field Guide,* I also provided a template that you can use to assess the strengths of your current relationships. I'd encourage you to review those activities as a way of helping you invest in relationship-building with your colleagues. We use these templates in our Leadership Contract seminars, and leaders always walk away with surprising insights.

But for now, think about the priorities you and your team must deliver on for your organization. Ask yourself which relationships are critical to your success? Is it an individual leader? Another group or department? Now think about the status of the relationship: Is it strong, weak, strained, or even nonexistent? What are you doing to make the relationship as strong as it can be?

Be a Good Follower

One of the things you realize as you work to build community in your organization is that you need to be good at leading, but you also need to know how to follow. This may sound counterintuitive. After all, this is a leadership book, you might be saying to yourself. But a lot of recent research has examined the concept of *followership*. My personal take on this work is that it perpetuates the idea that organizations are made up of two kinds of people—those who lead and those who follow. These researchers tend to define *followership* as those who are in subordinate roles, directed by someone who is the leader. This leads to a limited view of how leadership unfolds in organizations today.

A few years back, I jumped on a conference call with a colleague who was new to our company. He was in Europe, and we were having our first discussion about a significant proposal for a leadership development opportunity. My colleague was spearheading the process, and our team had other colleagues on the line who represented different internal functions and geographies. Many of these colleagues had never worked with each other before.

It was fascinating to see my new colleague in action. He was quite adept at moving the agenda forward and pushing people when required. I also found there were times when I had to jump in and take the lead, and other times when I had to step back and follow the lead of my colleagues. I needed to take direction from a colleague who wasn't my direct manager. I needed to align and support the course of the entire team. I also needed to deliver on my commitments. Finally, I needed to support the success of my colleagues in their efforts to help us win. I found myself moving back and forth from leading to following and saw my colleagues doing the same. It was like a dance. I discovered that I needed to pay attention and be very deliberate in how I showed up to add value to the team.

The next time you find yourself in a meeting with peers from across your organization, observe yourself in action. Do you find yourself always leading and taking charge? Are you doing all the talking or are you allowing others time to speak? Do you see opportunities where you need to shift to be more of a follower?

In today's complex organizations, a leader who is a lousy follower can be just as much of a liability as a leader who is not stepping up. I would argue that good followership is part of being an accountable leader today. Ultimately, being part of a *community of leaders* is all about knowing when to lead and when to follow, when to push forward, and when to pull back and let someone else lead the way.

Final Thoughts

"It takes a village" is a common proverb founded on the belief that it takes a community to raise a healthy child. It is not uncommon for an entire village to be concerned about the welfare of every child.[1] This same fundamental idea applies to organizations as well. Gone are the days when one leader can make every decision or drive every change. Leading companies today and in the future will realize that it will take a village of accountable leaders who will step up to be community builders. Will you be one of them?

Gut Check for Leaders: Be a Community Builder

As you think about the ideas in this chapter, reflect on your answers to the following Gut Check for Leaders questions:

1. To what extent are you committed to the concept of being a community builder?
2. Are you wired to be a community builder?
3. Do you bring a one-company mindset and work in the best interest of your organization?
4. To what extent have you built strong credibility with your peers and colleagues?
5. Are you a leader known to invest in building relationships with others?

Note

1. Joel Goldberg, "It Takes A Village To Determine The Origins Of An African Proverb," *National Public Radio*. July 30, 2016, https://www.npr.org/sections/goatsandsoda/2016/07/30/487925796/it-takes-a-village-to-determine-the-origins-of-an-african-proverb.

PART 4
The Organizational Response for Senior Executives and Directors

Section four includes four chapters that explore how the board of directors, the chief executive officer (CEO), other senior executives, and the chief human resources officer (CHRO) must step up to implement several foundational strategies to build strong leadership accountability.

Chapter 10: Make Leadership Accountability a Priority in Your Company

This chapter discusses the role that boards, the CEO, senior executives, and the CHRO must play in making leadership accountability a priority in their organizations. It also discusses the need to conduct a leadership accountability audit.

Chapter 11: Define and Embed Clear Leadership Expectations

This chapter discusses the five steps that organizations can implement to define and then embed clear leadership expectations for all leaders.

Chapter 12: Do the Hard Work to Sustain Momentum

This chapter presents strategies that organizations must implement to sustain momentum to drive strong leadership accountability. It presents four strategies, including how to demonstrate zero tolerance for bad and abusive leadership behavior, not ignoring unaccountable and mediocre leaders, being mindful of who is put into leadership roles, and supporting leaders during critical leadership turning points.

Chapter 13: Foster a Community of Leaders Across Your Organization

This chapter presents strategies to help create a community of leaders across the entire organization. First it shows how your organization needs to assess the leadership culture, then how to look for leaks in the culture, followed by encouraging relationship building among the leaders through leader forums, and finally knowing how to evolve the leadership culture as the company experiences change and transformation.

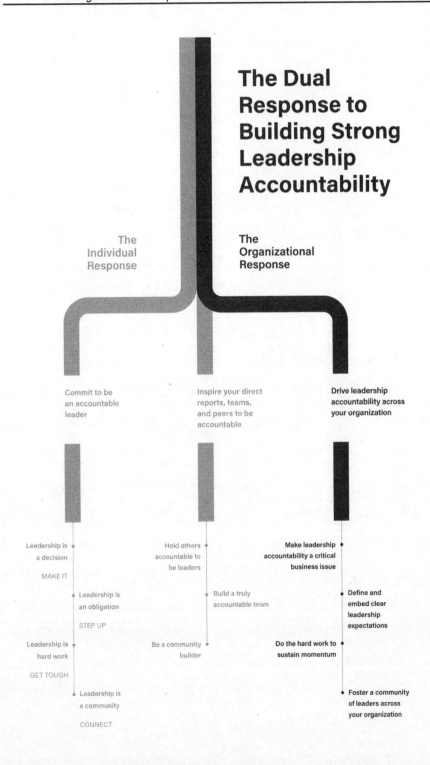

The Dual Response to Building Strong Leadership Accountability

The
Individual
Response

**The
Organizational
Response**

Commit to be
an accountable
leader

Inspire your direct
reports, teams,
and peers to be
accountable

**Drive leadership
accountability across
your organization**

Leadership is
a decision

MAKE IT

Hold others
accountable to
be leaders

**Make leadership
accountability a critical
business issue**

Leadership is
an obligation

STEP UP

Build a truly
accountable team

**Define and
embed clear
leadership
expectations**

Leadership is
hard work

GET TOUGH

Be a community
builder

**Do the hard work to
sustain momentum**

Leadership is
a community

CONNECT

**Foster a community
of leaders across
your organization**

CHAPTER 10

Make Leadership Accountability a Priority in Your Company

M ost CEOs I work with express frustration over the lack of accountability they see in their organizations. I find this is especially true of CEOs new to their companies. They usually arrive with a mandate to drive significant change. They know they will need leaders to step up in new ways to drive success. However, after they spend time getting to know the state of their organization, they realize there are many leadership accountability gaps. The gaps may exist with the executive team or leaders at other levels of the organization. At other times, they recognize that the human resources function isn't doing its job. Unless they address these gaps, progress will be difficult. However, to address leadership accountability gaps effectively requires commitment on the part of the board, the CEO, the CHRO, and other senior executives. This chapter explores how these leaders must work together to drive success.

Leadership Accountability—the Critical Business Issue

In my experience, leadership accountability is a new business issue that many companies are beginning to understand. As a result, there is high variability in whether companies are thinking about it, discussing it, and ultimately doing something about it. I've learned that many stakeholders must step up. If they don't, it will be hard to achieve success. For example, in one company, the CEO made leadership accountability a priority. He single-handedly tried to push this into his organization; however, progress was slow because other leaders in the company were not on board. One person can create a spark, but you need a whole community of leaders to drive sustained impact, even if that one person is the CEO. I've also seen cases where the head of human resources is the champion for leadership accountability, but the senior executive team is neither interested nor engaged. In these cases, very little progress happens.

The first step, then, is to help key stakeholders understand their accountability. We will start by examining what this looks like from the perspective of the board, the CEO, the senior executives, and the HR function (see Figure 10.1).

Figure 10.1 The Critical Roles Needed to Build Strong Leadership Accountability

The Role of the Board

I was chatting recently with the director of a board of a global engineering company. She had served on the board when the company had experienced a significant financial scandal. It was a "nightmare" and "disaster" for the company—her words. It consumed the directors as they were overseeing the aftermath and engaging in damage control. She described it as a trying and stressful period, something she would never want to experience again in her life.

Boards that have had to deal with scandal, misconduct, or corruption on the part of senior executives know the costs and reputational damage that can occur. These issues fall squarely on the board to address and resolve.[1] Increasingly, boards are therefore assuming greater oversight of leadership accountability and culture.

A recent report produced by the National Association of Corporate Directors (NACD) states that culture is a unifying force and, when it is healthy and robust, it will positively reinforce the strategy and business model of an organization.[2] In contrast, a dysfunctional or weak leadership culture can undermine strategy execution, and thereby create significant risk for a company. Boards need to think about leadership accountability in the same way—as a risk issue requiring their oversight. If leadership accountability in an organization is weak, this creates risk for the execution of the business strategy, the ability to attract and retain the best talent in the industry, and the reputation of the company.

Drawing on my conversations and work with boards, I believe they need to pay attention to the following areas:

- **Hire a CEO who is an accountable leader.** One of the primary responsibilities of a board is succession and ensuring the selection of the right CEO for the company. They typically look for a proven track record, industry experience, key relationships with external stakeholders, and several other essential capabilities and traits. Boards also need to assess whether the individual is an accountable leader at a personal level.
- **Encourage the CEO to be accountable for leadership accountability.** The board then needs to ensure that the CEO pays attention to leadership accountability and makes it an organizational priority. The board and CEO need to engage in conversations about

the leadership accountability of the organization. The CEO must share relevant information and metrics on the state of leadership accountability for the organization. They need to also engage the board in helping to shape the thinking around the leadership expectations for the organization.

- **Recruit new directors to the board who are committed to being accountable leaders.** Boards will increasingly be looking to recruit new directors through the lens of leadership accountability. They will need to ensure that directors are personally committed to being accountable and setting the tone for the board and the rest of the organization.

- **Ensure the board has a director with solid human resources experience.** Many boards struggle to fully appreciate talent, leadership, and human resources issues, as they typically do not have a director with depth and expertise in these areas. Having a director they can rely on to bring knowledgeable perspectives on how to think about these crucial issues is invaluable.

- **Ensure the board sets the tone for the rest of the organization.** I recently interviewed the chair of the board for a large higher education institution. I was working with them to create a company-specific leadership contract. In my interview with the chair, I asked whether the board saw itself as being part of the organization's leadership. He paused and said it was a great question, and he didn't know the answer. He speculated that some directors did, in fact, see themselves as leaders and part of the organization's leadership. He also knew that others did not. The question and our discussion prompted him to have this conversation with the other directors. Directors are increasingly being expected to step up and set the tone of leadership accountability for the rest of the organization.

The Role of the Chief Executive Officer (CEO)

CEOs must make leadership accountability a priority and see it as part of their efforts to leave the organization in a stronger and better place than they found it. Here are some strategies to consider:

- **Demonstrate strong leadership accountability at a personal level.** The CEO must be an example to all the leaders and employees of the organization they lead. I have found that when the CEO isn't accountable personally, it creates havoc at other levels in the organization. At the same time, when the CEO is accountable and holds others accountable, a positive ripple effect takes hold across the organization.

- **Hire a strong head of human resources.** I believe hiring the right person to lead human resources may be the most crucial decision a CEO ever makes. Unfortunately, this isn't always a strength for some CEOs. Of course, it's essential to look for candidates with a depth of human resources expertise—that's a given. However, it is also vital that they demonstrate strong leadership accountability at a personal level, and that they can partner with the CEO, the board, and the executive team to put practices in place that help build strong leadership accountability. I've seen too many companies limited or even crippled by weak and mediocre human resources leaders and teams.

- **Build a truly accountable executive team.** I've talked to many CEOs who admit that building a truly accountable executive team is one of the toughest challenges they face. When a CEO can build an accountable executive team, amazing things happen across the organization. The clarity, the commitment, and the alignment they demonstrate set a powerful tone that inspires employees and creates confidence in everyone's ability to drive success. When the team is mediocre, terrible, or even toxic, then a CEO doesn't have a chance.

- **Set clear leadership expectations and pay attention to your leadership culture.** We have already explored the importance of having a strong leadership culture, and the CEO must be vigilant in ensuring it is robust and healthy. It's about creating clear leadership expectations for all leaders. You can do this by creating a company-specific leadership contract. It's also about building a community of leaders across the organization. Finally, it is about having the courage to have zero tolerance for bad behavior and misconduct.

The Role of the Senior Executives

As we just discussed, the CEO plays a critical role in making leadership accountability a priority in the organization. These efforts get amplified when senior executives and the extended leadership team (usually the direct reports of the executive team) also rally around to support the CEO. Let's look at the strategies to consider:

- **Demonstrate strong leadership accountability at a personal level.** Just like the CEO, all senior executives and leaders must step up as accountable leaders. I find that many senior executives do not fully appreciate how much they set the tone for the behavior of other leaders and employees.
- **Build truly accountable teams.** The senior leaders need to be seen to work well with each other. They must also build accountable teams within their divisions, functions, or departments. As we discussed earlier, when employees observe the top leaders setting the right tone and working effectively together, this significantly increases their level of engagement.
- **Address leadership accountability gaps.** Senior leaders must be vigilant in addressing leadership accountability gaps within their departments, functions, or divisions. They need to ensure their leaders do their job in stepping up and holding others accountable for being leaders.
- **Ensure the extended leadership team sets the right tone for others.** As we learned earlier in this book, when employees see their senior leaders working well together, it has an immediate impact on their engagement. The extended leadership team has a critical role to play to set a positive tone for the rest of the organization. Everyone looks at them to see the extent to which they are accountable, and that they are leading effectively and working together to deliver results. When this isn't happening, it undermines everyone's sense of engagement and commitment, as well as their willingness to step up and be accountable.

The Role of the Chief Human Resources Officer (CHRO)

The head of human resources has a pivotal role in helping an organization build strong leadership accountability. As I described above, when a company has a strong HR leader in place, amazing things happen for the organization. When the HR leaders are weak or mediocre, little progress is made. Here are some suggestions to pay attention to:

- **Set the tone at a personal level.** Much like the CEO, the CHRO must demonstrate accountability. I find that the expectations for HR leaders are often even higher than for the CEO in many respects. As the leader of the people function of an organization, employees expect the top HR leader to be above reproach, to be the guiding light, and even be the conscience for everyone else. It's a significant obligation, but this is what it means to be an HR leader in today's world.

- **Build a truly accountable HR team.** Too many times, I find that some CHROs are not viewed as effective leaders by others in the organization. It is unfortunate, and it serves to undermine any attempt to do good work. Just as the CEO must build a truly accountable executive team, so too must the head of HR. The expectations are high for all HR leaders.

- **Encourage senior executives to address weak and unaccountable leadership on their teams.** Heads of HR can play a crucial role in helping senior executives address weak leadership in their teams, functions, or divisions. Many executives may shy away from this work. Some expect they can delegate it to the HR function. HR leaders need to resist this and support senior leaders in doing their jobs. When the CHRO sets the right tone and is a trusted adviser, executives do a better job of coming to terms with the accountability gaps that exist on their teams.

- **Ensure the organization commits to creating clear leadership expectations.** If the CEO isn't addressing this at a personal level, then HR must take the lead. The next chapter will explain how to do this, but HR leaders can create tremendous value for their organizations when they support a process to set clear leadership expectations. The next chapter will explain how to do this by creating a company-specific leadership contract.

- **Establish a balanced compensation strategy.** The CHRO must work with the CEO and the board's compensation committee to ensure that the strategy is balanced. By balanced, I mean that leaders are compensated both on the "what" and the "how" of leadership. The what is about measuring and compensating leaders for their ability to deliver desired business results. The how is about measuring and compensating leaders on how they step up as leaders, building strong leadership accountability and a strong culture across their teams and organization.

- **Provide metrics to the board.** The CHRO needs to regularly provide metrics to the board on the state of leadership accountability and culture within the organization. Also, HR needs to provide metrics on the state of the organization's leadership culture. These are vital to help the board and CEO not only understand these critical business issues but also be ready to discuss the risk implications should there be weakness evident in the data.
- **Make sure your team does not enable mediocre leadership.** I've seen too many examples where well-meaning and well-intended HR practitioners enable leaders to be mediocre. How? They jump in and do the hard work of leadership on their behalf. These mediocre leaders get used to it and in turn wimp out and avoid doing the hard work themselves. They rely on their HR business partners to have the tough conversations with poor performers, to give candid feedback, or to intervene to manage conflicts between colleagues. If your HR team is doing this, have them stop. Even though they think they are adding value and serving their internal customers, the reality is that they are not. HR needs to be a sounding board for leaders to help them do their jobs and tackle their own hard work.
- **Implement practices to help drive strong leadership accountability.** The HR team must work to create and implement several practices that help ensure the organization has strong leadership accountability. Throughout the remaining chapters in this section, we will explore the practices that the HR team can implement.

It is vitally important to be explicit in how the board, the CEO, senior executives, and the CHRO need to think about their roles in building strong leadership accountability. Figure 10.2 presents a set of Gut Check questions that can be used to help bring this level of clarity within your organization.

Once the decision is made to see leadership accountability as a critical business priority, then it's essential to understand where you stand as an organization. That's what we will explore next.

Conduct a Leadership Accountability Audit

Once an organization is committed and has made leadership accountability a priority, it is crucial to understand the current state

THE GUT CHECK QUESTIONS

The Role of the Board

01   Is the board confident that it is getting good information about the organization's current state of leadership accountability?

02   Can directors describe the organization's leadership culture?

03   To what extent would directors say that the culture of the board aligns with the leadership culture of the organization?

04   Is the board engaged to help shape the leadership expectations of the organization?

05   To what extent does the board's leadership culture enable robust discussion and debate on important organizational issues?

The Role of the CEO

01   Do you make leadership accountability a critical business issue within your organization?

02   To what extent do you have a clear sense of the leadership culture needed to achieve your strategic objectives?

03   Do you and your senior executive team set the tone as accountable leaders?

04   Are you confident that you have a human resources leader in place capable of helping you build strong leadership accountability across your organization?

05   Do you share information with the board about the state of leadership accountability?

06   Have you set the expectation of addressing performance issues and those leaders who are unaccountable and mediocre?

The Role of Senior Executives

01   Are you confident you are setting the tone as a truly accountable leader?

02   Do you see the opportunity to make your executive team stronger and more accountable? What are you doing about it?

03   Have you built truly accountable teams within your division, function, or lines of business?

04   Are you moving fast enough to address weak leadership within your team?

05   Do your teams model the leadership expectations of your organization?

The Role of the CHRO

01   Do you personally set the tone as a truly accountable leader? Can directors describe the organization's leadership culture?

02   To what extent have you built an effective and accountable HR team?

03   Have you, the CEO, and the executive team worked together to create a set of clear leadership expectations for all leaders?

04   Do you support leaders at all levels to effectively address leadership accountability gaps on their teams?

05   Does your team create effective processes and programs that help build and sustain strong leadership accountability across your organization?

Figure 10.2   Gut Check Questions to Help Make Leadership Accountability a Priority

of leadership. An ideal way to do this is by conducting a Leadership Accountability Audit.[3] Figure 10.3 presents the questions for the audit. As you review them, reflect on the current state of your organization. If you prefer, you can visit www.drvincemolinaro.com to download this Leadership Accountability Audit and other resources.

What insights did you gain based on your responses to the Leadership Accountability Audit questions? Where is your organization demonstrating strength? Where are the weaknesses and gaps that need attention and action? How can you go about engaging others in conducting this audit? Below are some suggestions for you to consider:

- **Engage the executive team.** Involving the senior executive team in conducting the Leadership Accountability Audit is an excellent first step. Their results will give you a good sense of how they are thinking about this issue and areas you may need to address.
- **Engage the extended leadership team.** Some organizations engage a broader group of leaders in completing the audit. Your organization's extended leadership team is an ideal group. Typically, they represent the direct reports of the executive team and should have a good read on the functions they lead. This will give you a complete picture of where your organization stands.
- **Tap into middle and front-line leaders.** I have also had clients engage with a smaller group of middle and front-line leaders to get their perspectives. The Leadership Accountability Audit can be sent out as a survey or conducted through a set of focus groups. Engaging leaders at this level usually provides excellent insights and a more granular perspective on the issues and opportunities to address.
- **Aggregate the data.** Summarize the results of your audit. Identify the areas of strength that can be better leveraged to build strong leadership accountability. Then identify the gap areas that need immediate attention. Now you are ready for the next critical step—to share the findings with key stakeholders.

Lead a Strategic Leadership Conversation

I'm often asked to come in and speak with boards or senior executive teams on the topic of leadership accountability. It's a great way to

The Leadership Accountability Audit

Rate each question (1 = not at all, 5 = to a very great extent)

01	Is leadership accountability a critical business priority in our organization?	01	02	03	04	05
02	Are you satisfied with the degree of leadership accountability displayed by our leaders?	01	02	03	04	05
03	Have we set clear leadership expectations for our leaders?	01	02	03	04	05
04	Does our organization tolerate leaders who behave badly?	01	02	03	04	05
05	Does our organization have the courage to identify and address unaccountable and mediocre leaders?	01	02	03	04	05
06	Do we allow terrible teams to exist across our organization?	01	02	03	04	05
07	Does our organization have a strong leadership culture in place?	01	02	03	04	05
08	To what extent are you satisfied with the leadership accountability demonstrated by:	01	02	03	04	05
	A Board directors	01	02	03	04	05
	B Executive-level leaders	01	02	03	04	05
	C Mid-level leaders	01	02	03	04	05
	D Front-line leaders	01	02	03	04	05

Open-ended questions

09	In what specific ways are leaders currently stepping up and demonstrating strong leadership accountability?	
10	In what specific ways are leaders struggling to step up and demonstrate strong leadership accountability? What risks is this creating for the organization?	
11	What are the barriers to leadership accountability in our organization?	
12	What are the most significant opportunities to drive stronger leadership accountability?	

Figure 10.3   The Leadership Accountability Audit

start what I would call a strategic leadership conversation. Having a meaningful dialogue with a board or senior executive team (or both) is critical.

For example, my team and I recently met with a longstanding client. The meeting included the head of HR and the leader of enterprise learning. They told us about a big meeting they had coming up with the senior management team. The CEO had asked them to spend 90 minutes providing an update on how the company was tracking on their learning and leadership development strategy. The CEO also wanted to learn what was new and hear about some hot topics in the field. We worked with them to design an agenda for their meeting.

Since they were looking to foster meaningful dialogue, they conducted the Leadership Accountability Audit with the senior management team and aggregated the results. Before the meeting, they sent a one-page briefing document to provide a common foundation for the discussion. It included ideas from *The Leadership Contract* and presented some of the high-level findings from their Leadership Accountability Audit. The agenda for the 90-minute discussion was as follows:

- **Introductions and Setting Context (5 minutes).** They began by reinforcing the context for a discussion about leadership and explaining how it connects to the existing set of strategic priorities. In the case of this client, the company had just made a significant acquisition, and cultural alignment was top of mind for the executives. As a result, the CHRO and head of enterprise learning anchored the discussion of leadership accountability to drive cultural alignment.
- **Review the Data from the Leadership Accountability Audit (20 minutes).** They provided an update on their priorities and began to position the leadership accountability gaps they saw in their organization.
- **Facilitated Discussion (50 minutes).** They began to ask a series of questions designed to engage senior management with the topic. Here are the questions they used:
  - Based on the data, are we confident that we have the leadership culture in place that will ensure our future success?
  - To what extent do we believe our leaders are fully committed to their roles as leaders?

- Where is leadership accountability strong in the organization (explore strengths by level: front-line, mid-level, executive ranks)?
- Where is leadership accountability weak in the organization (explore strengths by level: front-line, mid-level, executive ranks)? How might this create risk in delivering our strategic objectives?
- Are we addressing mediocre and unaccountable leaders quickly enough? Do we tolerate (and therefore condone) leaders who misbehave and are misaligned?
- What recommendations do you have to strengthen leadership accountability across the organization?
- How can we strengthen the cultural alignment among the new leaders who have joined our company after the acquisition?
- What will be our outcome measures of success? In other words, how will we know when we have strong leadership accountability in place across the organization?
- **Discuss Implications and Next Steps (15 minutes).** They spent the remaining time considering any next steps stemming from the dialogue.

This session was a huge success. The senior management team confronted some of the gaps they found by completing the audit. They also realized they needed to do a better job at setting clear leadership expectations, especially to help drive cultural alignment. The outcomes of this discussion were positive, and it opened an opportunity for a similar dialogue with the board.

Based on the example above, think about whether you could use the same approach within your organization. You will most likely find it will spark a robust and meaningful dialogue, possibly even a much-needed healthy debate. In my experience, most senior management teams and boards rarely get the opportunity to engage in strategic leadership conversations. When they do, you will find they have plenty of valuable insights and perspectives to share. You may also find it worthwhile to repeat the leadership accountability audit every 12 to 18 months to gauge your progress in improving leadership accountability.

When you are ready to address the issues and act, review the ideas in the next three chapters of this book. They will provide a valuable road map for strengthening leadership accountability across your entire organization.

Final Thoughts

Working through the ideas and exercises in this chapter will give you much food for thought. You may feel daunted—you have a lot of tough conversations ahead of you. The questions may have opened up important conversations that you have never had or have been avoiding. Some of you may also feel daunted as you realize you may have a lot of hard work ahead to build stronger leadership accountability in your organization. In many ways, that is good news! You can't improve your organization until you understand where it currently stands and where you may be falling short. The more you can get into a practice of engaging in these important and strategic conversations, the easier it will get. Remember it's your obligation to your organization, leaders, and employees to tackle these issues head-on.

Gut Check for Leaders: Make Leadership Accountability a Priority in Your Company

As you think about the ideas in this chapter, reflect on your answers to the following Gut Check for Leaders questions:

1. To what extent has your company made leadership accountability a priority?
2. Is there clarity among the board, CEO, extended leadership team, and the CHRO on the role each plays to drive strong leadership accountability in your organization?
3. Does your organization conduct a Leadership Accountability Audit and generate metrics to gauge the strength of leadership accountability?
4. Do the board and the senior executive team have strategic conversations about leadership accountability?

Notes

1. Laurie Hays Edelman, "The Board, CEO Misconduct, and Corporate Culture," *Harvard Law School Forum on Corporate Governance and Financial Regulation*, January 12, 2019, https://corpgov.law.harvard.edu/2019/01/12/the-board-ceo-misconduct-and-corporate-culture/.
2. "NACD Blue Ribbon Report on Culture as a Corporate Asset," National Association of Corporate Directors (2017).
3. Visit www.drvincemolinaro.com to learn more about an online version of the Leadership Accountability Audit.

CHAPTER 11

Define and Embed Clear Leadership Expectations

When an organization defines a clear set of leadership expectations, it makes explicit the behaviors that leaders need to demonstrate. These desired behaviors, consistently evident, will create the desired leadership culture. I believe defining and reinforcing clear leadership expectations to be a primary obligation of the senior leaders of any organization. However, here's the challenge. As we have already seen, my research reveals only about half of organizations do this consistently. Imagine for a moment what happens in a company when leadership expectations are not clear. There is a high degree of confusion, on the part of both leaders and employees. The leadership experience for employees is inconsistent. There is no mechanism to hold leaders accountable for their behavior.

Depending on how you look at this, it could be either a missed opportunity or an excellent chance to set your company apart from others. This chapter will help you understand your obligation to create, communicate, and embed a clear set of leadership expectations for your leaders.

Leadership Expectations in Action—the Amazon Story

Before we explore how to define and embed a clear set of leadership expectations in your organization, let's look at a company that has done this with success—Amazon. Now, it's important to state that their story is controversial. Not everyone supports Amazon's unique culture. I share their story because they provide an example of a company that has been unrelenting in using clear leadership expectations to sustain its desired culture.

Let's start back in August of 2015 when the company made headlines in the *New York Times.* An article ran that described the punishing pace at which the company operated, burning out many of its employees.[1] Stories of employees crying at their desks, getting text messages from their bosses after midnight, or being criticized by co-workers for leaving to pick up their kids were featured. However, other employees celebrated the company's intense, hard-core work ethic, for teaching them to excel and find success in their careers.

When the story broke, many people vehemently condemned the company's culture, arguing that no company should completely ignore the work-life balance needs of employees. However, others defended the company, saying this is what it takes to run a successful company in today's hyper-competitive world. These voices argued that Amazon is an ambitious organization that sets the bar high for its employees. Not every employee can thrive in that climate, but the company succeeds because of its high standards. The debate over Amazon's culture got so heated that Jeff Bezos, founder and CEO, weighed in to defend his company.[2]

As I reflected on the story at the time, I felt that something was missing in the entire debate. This demanding, even harsh environment did not emerge by accident. The company was always clear and transparent on its leadership expectations and the kind of culture they wanted to create. You can go to their corporate website to see their 14 leadership principles.[3] When you do, you will learn of the company's desire for their leaders to:

- Be obsessed with the customer
- Demonstrate ownership
- Learn and be curious
- Hire the best talent
- Set high standards
- Think big
- Have a bias for action
- Be frugal and accomplish more with less

- Speak candidly
- Be "vocally self-critical" even when doing so is embarrassing
- Have the backbone to challenge one another
- Have conviction
- Be tenacious and not compromise "for the sake of social cohesion"
- Deliver results

When I reviewed these leadership principles, I immediately saw how they could lead to the hard-driving leadership culture described in the *New York Times* article. However, this is precisely the leadership culture Amazon wanted to create. Some will find this type of culture exciting and will relish the chance to push themselves to achieve more and more. Others will find it a harsh and even punishing environment. Regardless, Amazon provides us with an example of the importance of setting clear leadership expectations and the role they play in establishing a strong culture. By making their desired leadership principles clear, Amazon has set its standard for how leaders are expected to behave. In many ways, Amazon's leadership principles represent their leadership contract for the organization—this is what leaders must live up to every single day. When you get this right, there are many benefits. Now this type of leadership culture isn't for everyone. However, it's important to state that Amazon has been clear and transparent about what it expects from leaders and employees. In many ways, that's the whole point of setting clear leadership expectations.

The Benefits of Having a Simple, Clear, and Inspiring Leadership Contract

When an organization creates a compelling set of leadership expectations that is framed as a leadership contract, many terrific benefits emerge:

- **Increases clarity and commitment.** There is an immediate sense of increased clarity and commitment among your leaders, which in turn enables them to demonstrate considerable excitement and passion for your company on the part of leaders. It also strengthens their commitment to executing your strategic priorities.
- **Creates a more consistent leadership experience.** A compelling set of leadership expectations creates a common language and way of thinking about leadership. Everyone knows what it means to be a leader in your company. As a result, you improve the leadership experience in your company, as you will see greater consistency in how leaders lead their employees and teams.
- **Establishes a unified culture.** A leadership contract creates a more unified leadership culture and helps drive the engagement of your leaders. This is especially valuable if your organization is attempting to transform itself and needs to evolve toward a new culture. This benefit is also essential if your organization has completed a merger or acquisition, and now needs to establish a more harmonized leadership culture.
- **Puts a spotlight on unaccountable leaders.** The leadership contract provides you with a mechanism to identify unaccountable leaders. It's important to recognize that having a clear leadership contract will move some people in leadership roles to opt out. Once they see the heightened expectations, they will make a personal decision to step down from their leadership roles. Some will ask to go back to a technical position. Others may decide to leave your organization. In the end, this is a positive outcome because few organizations today can carry people in leadership roles who are not fully committed to being truly accountable.
- **Inspires aspiring leaders.** Those employees aspiring to move into leadership roles in the future now have personal clarity as to what your organization expects. Many people struggle to understand what it really means to be a leader. Your leadership contract facilitates better career discussions and helps mentors and managers determine ways to support the growth and development of aspiring leaders.

Who wouldn't want these benefits in an organization? Next, we will explore how to go about creating a leadership contract with a clear set of leadership expectations. However, before we do that, it's essential to consider a potential failure path in doing this critical work.

The Failure Path to Avoid

Historically, many organizations have gone about setting clear leadership expectations by creating leadership competency models. However, clients I've worked with have not found this approach as valuable in today's environment. The chief complaint is that traditional competency models are just too complicated. I've seen leadership competency models with up to 15 competencies, each defined and then further delineated into four different managerial levels. Another complaint is that the language used is often academic, sterile, and filled with jargon, which makes the model inaccessible and uninspiring to the intended audience—your leaders. As a result, many competency models end up sitting on a company server, never seeing the light of day. They are not living documents that leaders embrace or that the organization uses to set clear expectations and drive strong accountability.

Keep this in mind as you begin to create your set of leadership expectations; you must do it in a way that is simple, clear, and inspirational.

Create a Clear Set of Leadership Expectations

In this section, we will explore how to go about creating a clear set of leadership expectations for your organization. Essentially, you are creating a company-specific leadership contract. The steps outlined below are the same ones that my teams and I have used with countless organizations around the world. In this work, we generally partner with the CEO and CHRO. We also engage with the senior executive team and other senior leaders of the organization. Some clients also engage with their boards to gain their perspective. There are five steps to the overall process shown in Figure 11.1.

Step 1: Use Your Business Context and Strategy to Identify Leadership Expectations

As we discussed earlier in the book, leadership is rooted in context. The specific business environment and strategic imperatives define what it means to be a leader in an organization. In *The Leadership*

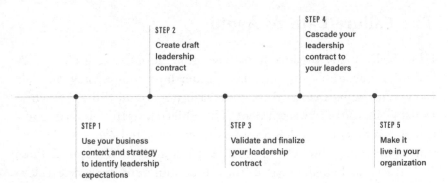

Figure 11.1   The Five Steps to Create a Company-Specific Leadership Contract

Contract Field Guide, I introduced an exercise that helps leaders gain clarity about their business context and define leadership expectations. The process to create a company-specific leadership contract follows the same approach:

- **Your business context.** Begin with a good understanding of your emerging business environment—the emerging trends and drivers that are expected to impact your organization over the next three to five years.
- **Your business strategy.** Review your business strategy and the strategic imperatives of your organization.
- **Your desired leadership expectations.** Articulate what you expect from your leaders and how they will need to step up individually and collectively to successfully lead your organization.

Think about your emerging context and business environment over the next three to five years. Consider several macro trends such as economic, political, technology, industry, regulator, or social issues and specific industry-related trends. Next, determine any organizational challenges and opportunities you anticipate emerging. Thinking about these broad issues will give you a clear sense of your context. Shift your focus to identifying and confirming the strategic priorities and imperatives for your company. Based on these insights, you will begin to identify the specific ways that leaders will need to step up, individually and collectively, to help your organization be successful.

In our client work, we typically use a guided-interview approach, which gives us a robust understanding of how senior leaders are thinking about the business, the strategy, and leadership expectations. Here are the questions you can use within your organization. As you can see, the questions connect to the business context, the strategy, and then to defining the leadership expectations:

1. What do you believe are the primary external opportunities and threats impacting the organization currently and over the next three to five years?
2. What strategic priorities are critical to the organization's success over the next three to five years?
3. Describe the elements of the leadership culture you need in your company to effectively execute your business strategy and create enduring value.
4. What aspects of this leadership culture currently exist in your organization? What aspects need to be made stronger?
5. In what specific ways do your leaders need to step up now in their leadership roles and demonstrate real accountability?
6. What specific behaviors will leaders need to demonstrate consistently across the organization?
7. In what ways do your core values need to be reflected in our leadership expectations?
8. What is the tone that this leadership contract needs to strike to gain the most traction with your leaders?
9. In what ways must you roll out the leadership contract so that it is fully embraced by your leaders?
10. What specific outcomes and measures (tangible and intangible) will demonstrate to you that leadership accountability within your organization has become stronger?

Once you have collected all your data, you will aggregate the themes you see across all the interviews. You'll immediately be able to determine the degree of alignment that exists among your senior management. You will also start to see a story emerge regarding the leadership expectations for your leaders.

At this point, it will be helpful to integrate any data that you may have also gathered through the Leadership Accountability Audit (discussed in Chapter 10). Connecting the dots between the two sets of data will make your work more concrete and substantial.

Step 2: Create a Draft Leadership Contract

You now have what you need to start creating a draft leadership contract. In many ways, this second step is a blend of art and science. Here are some factors to consider as you start to create your company-specific leadership contract:

- **Identify a meaningful set of leadership expectations.** In practice, I find that it's best to identify the top five to seven leadership expectations. However, you should not be limited by this. Some companies have more. We have already seen that Amazon has 14. While my preference is to keep the number smaller, you will need to define what best works for your organization.
- **Leverage the four terms of the leadership contract.** Many organizations use the four terms of the leadership contract as inspiration when they create their expectations for leaders. Some make the four terms explicitly prominent in their company's leadership contract. Others use it merely to test out their leadership expectations to ensure that nothing substantial is left out.
- **Use direct and straightforward language.** If the language used is complex, filled with jargon, or uninspiring, then leaders will not embrace your leadership contract. The key is to make the language of your leadership contract as accessible and user-friendly as possible, and not laden with jargon.
- **Articulate why the expectations matter.** Define each leadership expectation and make it clear why it is essential to the organization. Tie everything back to your business context and strategy. You can cite why each expectation matters for the successful execution of the business strategy. You may also want to stress how the leadership expectations reinforce your company's vision, mission, and core values. The more leaders see the leadership expectations tied to several existing priorities, the better it will be.
- **Decide on the tone and language of the leadership contract.** Some companies want their leadership contract to be direct, to the point, and even a little hard-hitting. Some prefer a more

inspirational tone. Others want it to be very informal. In the end, I have learned there is no one best approach—you must decide what will work for you, your leaders, and your culture. An organization can genuinely make the leadership contract its own. That's what is great about the process. I've seen clients have success calling this their Leadership Contract. Others have used words like leadership expectations, leadership charter, leadership pledge, leadership principles, or leadership commitments. Again, decide what will work best for your organization. Regardless of the language and tone used, you are still creating clear expectations that act as a contract for your leaders.

Step 3: Validate and Finalize Your Leadership Contract

It's essential to gain buy-in from the senior management team. You want the senior executive team feeling good about the leadership contract and understanding how it will be a primary driver of strong accountability among leaders. With support from your senior executive team in place, you may then want to engage other leaders in the organization. Consider conducting focus groups with a cross-section of other leaders from different levels and functions. This will help you drive broader buy-in, and ensure the tone and language of your leadership contract will resonate with other leaders.

Incorporate feedback from your focus groups and then finalize your leadership contract. Based on my experience, you will know that you got your leadership contract right when two emotions emerge at the same time when you read it. First, it immediately generates *excitement*. The statements are aspirational and inspirational. You instinctively want to strive to be a better leader. Second, it *scares* you a little because you now know you are being held accountable to a higher standard of leadership behavior.

Step 4: Cascade Your Leadership Contract to All Your Leaders

With your leadership contract complete, now the significant work begins: You need to cascade it across your organization. Here are some of the many strategies that I've seen implemented with a high degree of success:

- **Ensure the CEO and senior executives genuinely embrace it.** The CEO and senior executive team must play a key role in rolling out the leadership contract. They must own it. If HR solely owns it, there is a risk your leaders won't embrace it. It's best if the CEO and the senior executive team are front and center in cascading the leadership contract. The head of human resources must also be visible. You want your leaders to know that the company's most senior leaders are invested and are leading the way for everyone else. While they are doing this, it's also important to reinforce that the leadership contract also applies to them. I've seen senior executives cascade a leadership contract in a way that communicates it's for everyone else but them. They project an attitude that they have already arrived as leaders. I can tell you with all certainty that this is a failure path and will impede your efforts.
- **Focus on the extended leadership team.** Many companies bring their top two to three levels of leaders together for a leadership forum, summit, or conference (the language differs from company to company). Typically, these meetings are intended to help educate leaders on the emerging business context and the strategic priorities of the organization. They are great venues to explain, discuss, and help leaders begin to internalize the new leadership expectations. You may, as many clients have done, ask your leaders to show their commitment by signing it.
- **Cascade to all other leaders.** It's crucial to then communicate the leadership contract more broadly to all leaders. Depending on the size of the organization, this can be done through a series of town hall sessions, video broadcasts, or by asking senior leaders to speak with their teams. For example, one client placed the expectation on all the senior leaders to communicate the leadership expectations to their teams. HR created a toolkit that allowed leaders to have a series of discussions over three months in regular standing team meetings. I like this strategy a lot, as it reinforces leadership accountability at a team level.

How Cisco Cascaded Their Leadership Expectations at Scale

One company that did an amazing job of cascading their new leadership expectations was Cisco. The worldwide leader in IT and networking created "Cisco Leaders Day," and it represented the first time in the company's history that they took all 8,000 leaders offline for a day. The purpose of the live event was to align everyone on what it means to be a leader at the company. The day included 38 hours of discussions, six broadcasts in as many time zones, and 18 in-person locations. In a recent LinkedIn post, Fran Katsoudas, Cisco's EVP and "Chief People Officer," explained that in this new era of work, where everything is changing at an exponential pace, how we communicate, engage, and show up to our teams has never been more important.[4] She wrote: "At Cisco, we know our leaders play a crucial role and are accountable to both the business and their people… we know that making the investment in our leaders and enabling them to better lead their teams has a huge impact on how we drive our strategy and deliver amazing results for our partners, customers, and shareholders." Using their own technology, the company engaged thousands of leaders around the world, in multiple time zones and at various levels. Katsoudas also said that their Leader Day was not an isolated event, but rather part of a journey. "Leading is about constant learning," she said, "and this is our next step in that journey—resetting expectations and engaging with all leaders… When you're a leader, you cannot opt out of leading."

Step 5: Make It Live in Your Organization

Once you have created and cascaded your leadership contract, then you need to ensure you embed it and make it live within your organization. Here are some strategies to consider:

• **Recruitment and selection.** Your leadership contract can be a valuable guide in recruiting external candidates coming into leadership positions. One client of mine told me that once they created their leadership contract, they included it with the offer letters to external candidates. They also included a copy of my book *The Leadership*

Contract. The new leaders were instructed to read the book and carefully consider the company's leadership contract. Then they were asked to sign it. They wanted these individuals to submit it along with their signed employment contracts. My client learned the value of helping new leaders joining their organization to be absolutely clear on what it meant to be a leader in their company and the leadership expectations they would be held accountable for demonstrating day-to-day.

- **Compensation of leaders.** I have many clients engage in discussions about how their leadership contract can be embedded in their compensation strategy for leaders. Increasingly, I see organizations balance their compensation formula between what leaders deliver (business outcomes, strategic priorities) and how they deliver (degree to which leaders are stepping up to the organization's leadership contract). This is a worthwhile conversation to have in your own organization.

- **Performance and development conversations.** Your leadership contract needs to be visible in performance discussions held with leaders. This provides an ideal way to give and solicit feedback, coach leaders, and reinforce their accountability.

- **Career development.** Your leadership contract can be a meaningful way to help leaders understand what it really means to be a leader. Use this information to guide career discussions. As we've already explored in this book, focusing these conversations at critical leadership turning points is valuable for individuals. The clearer they become about what it means to be a leader, the more they will be able to make better leadership decisions about their careers.

- **Anchor in leadership development programs.** Your leadership contract needs to be part of any development program that your leaders experience. If you partner with external vendors to design and deliver some of these programs, it's vital they understand your leadership contract. Discuss the implications for program development, as they need to make specific links to your leadership contract in their program delivery.

- **Anchor your leadership contract in teams.** Encourage all leaders of teams to leverage the leadership contract to help build truly accountable teams. We explored how to do this in Chapter 8. If teams can embrace the leadership contract to create clear expectations for the team, this will increase their commitment and clarity, while helping them deliver results.

- **Recognize and celebrate accountable leadership.** Some organizations have used their leadership contract to create recognition and award programs. Many are peer-nominated. Leaders and teams who are seen to be living the leadership expectations and demonstrating real accountability receive recognition for their efforts and the example they set.
- **Evolve your contract as your company evolves.** Many companies change their leadership contracts as their organizations grow and change. For example, one client refreshed their leadership contract when they introduced a new strategy, which changed the company's direction. In turn, this required leaders to step up in new ways. Given the amount of change that companies face today, it's prudent to review your leadership contract every three years. Make sure it is still relevant and that it is articulating the leadership expectations you need your leaders to live up to at an individual and collective level.

A Company-Specific Leadership Contract in Action

Over the years, I've seen many companies be deliberate in creating clear leadership expectations for their leaders. In this section, we will briefly explore an example of a company that created a clear set of expectations for their leaders by establishing a leadership contract.

The Adecco Group is one of the world's largest human resources firms and a Fortune Global 500 company. It offers end-to-end career and HR advisory services that include staffing and recruitment, career transition, reskilling, and talent development, as well as HR outsourcing and consulting.

They began a strategic journey a few years back to reshape how the world works. The company has been reinventing how it delivers its core services to customers, while at the same time establishing new businesses in emerging growth areas like digital reskilling, the gig economy, and workforce transformation. All these crucial efforts focused on helping the company to enable and empower their clients and candidates to embrace and succeed in the future of work, under the vision of Making the Future Work for Everyone.

This transformation required a strong focus on fostering the right culture. It all started with company CEO Alain Dehaze. In a personal interview,[5] he shared with me his belief that "Everyone is a leader and has a responsibility to do the right thing and set an example for others." He also stressed that culture starts at the top and, therefore, he and his leadership team must model the behaviors they expect from their colleagues around the world. With this perspective in place, Dehaze and the company's executive committee created a company-specific leadership contract for their organization that makes explicit what the company expects of leaders. It also represents a commitment by each leader to personally be accountable for their performance and for driving the desired culture.

The process was inclusive and collaborative. Dehaze wanted to ensure that each senior executive felt a deep sense of ownership and that they were also personally invested in and connected to their leadership contract. In the case of The Adecco Group, their executive committee came together as one team to co-create their leadership contract. They spent an intensive day-long session that featured healthy debate and deep engagement. They defined and aligned around 10 leadership expectations that were rooted in the company's core values of Passion, Entrepreneurship, Responsibility, Team Spirit, and Customer Centricity. The Adecco Group Leadership Contract is shown in Figure 11.2.

Once they created their company-specific leadership contract, they started to cascade it to their leaders. They wanted to make sure they were fully embedding the leadership contract as the bedrock of the culture they aspired to create at the company, today and in the future.

The rollout strategy was a collaborative process that began by working with the extended leadership team or the top 300 leaders of the organization. During a three-day Global Leadership Conference in 2018, they engaged these leaders in a half-day workshop led by executive committee members. They created interactive workshops to bring The Adecco Group Leadership Contract to life. These sessions focused on three pillars of the leadership contract—*what we value, how we act,* and *how we lead.* After the workshops, all 300 leaders voluntarily signed The Adecco Group Leadership Contract. It was a powerful way to show their commitment to embrace the 10 leadership expectations and drive them forward into the rest of the company.

At the Adecco Group:

Our strategy sets our direction for shaping the future of work, while our values provide the foundation for our culture.

Our leaders are key to the execution of our strategy and in creating our culture. As a company, we are committed to recruiting and growing leaders - the best in our industry - who are genuinely passionate about our mission of "Making the future work for everyone". The actions and decisions of our leaders are guided by our core values of Passion, Entrepreneurship, Responsibility, Team Spirit and Customer Centricity.

We expect our leaders at every level to take personal accountability to fulfil our vision to be the "Most admired workforce solutions partner thanks to talent and technology".

As a Group, we have embarked on a journey to Perform, Transform and Innovate. To ensure this is a success, we have set out the following ten leadership expectations that we all must live up to and which should also inspire our teams across the Adecco Group.

As leaders of the Adecco Group, we will:

1. Develop our organisational capabilities and drive commitment and passion to deliver our strategy aligned to OGSM* - while fostering solidarity and a 'One Company' mindset.
2. Bring our values to life with Customer Centricity at the heart. We must listen to and understand our clients, candidates and associates to generate profitable and sustainable growth while applying the frugality principle in how we operate.
3. Build an undisputed leadership position by attracting, developing and growing high-performing and responsible leaders and teams at all levels of our organization, thereby ensuring that strong successors are in place.
4. Be accessible and hands-on, fostering an open culture of dialogue, inclusion, diversity and respect that fuels our passion and our winning company culture.
5. Provide clarity to colleagues on roles and responsibilities, helping them understand our strategy, setting clear targets and expectations that allow us to drive results.
6. Be personally accountable and hold others to best-in-class standards of financial, commercial, and talent targets as well as performance.
7. Recognise high performers while also addressing ineffective leadership in a direct, swift, courageous and respectful manner.
8. Clearly communicate and engage all our stakeholders around a shared sense of purpose, focusing on what truly matters and is relevant to our customers, colleagues and shareholders.
9. Ensure that integrity and ethics are a cornerstone of how we lead. We will not tolerate any infringements of any legal requirements or company standards.
10. Embrace sustainability as being at the heart of our work and a competitive asset for our company evolving from a culture of compliance to one of integrated sustainability.

*OGSM- Objective,Goals,Strategies,Measures

These are the ten leadership expectations for all leaders at the Adecco Group. We commit to these principles at a personal and collective level to help us drive the Group's future success and to continue to be the world leader in HR solutions.

I thank you all for making the future work for everyone.

Alain Dehaze
CEO of the Adecco Group

Figure 11.2   The Adecco Group Leadership Contract

A toolkit was created to support the rollout deeper into the organization. Country managers were accountable for leading workshops within their regional leadership meetings. The workshops modeled the approach used at their 2018 Global Leadership Conference to ensure consistency and alignment.

Overall, the leaders at The Adecco Group have embraced the contract as a robust framework for positive culture creation. Across the company, leaders are personally bringing this to life in their work. Just six months after the launch of the leadership contract, close to one-third of their global workforce of 34,000 is already familiar with it. In 2018, the company was once again ranked in the top five global companies to work for by *Fortune*'s Great Places to Work® Survey. For Dehaze, these outcomes demonstrate the power of the cohesive leadership community that is required to drive a real cultural transformation.

Many leaders began to see an immediate impact. Many saw the leadership contract as an essential reminder of the shared commitment leaders have to the business and to one another. Other leaders find it helpful to guide their efforts to be mindful in daily interactions with employees. Other Adecco Group leaders are discovering that the leadership contract provides a valuable way to have conversations with future leaders about what it means to be a leader at the company. Others are excited to see the messages reflected in the company's global vision, which communicates that they have one team working, growing, and succeeding together.

Through the entire process, the human resources team was a crucial partner in helping make the leadership contract part of the company's DNA. The leadership expectations are part of the company's performance management process and integrated into leadership development programs. In turn, this helps to inspire the right behaviors and show leaders how to embrace the expectations every day with their teams. All new leaders joining the company receive The Adecco Group Leadership Contract as part of their on-boarding, training, and development (such as mandatory ethics training and e-learning programs). New hires are expected to read, internalize, and sign the leadership contract.

The Adecco Group is undergoing an exciting transformation, and strong leadership has never been more critical. Their leadership contract defines the qualities that each leader needs to embody to ensure their current and future success.

Final Thoughts

Creating a company-specific leadership contract is a crucial strategy that companies must implement. As I shared, my global research reveals only about half of companies do this, which means there is a tremendous opportunity for companies that commit to this strategy. It helps bring clarity, inspires leaders to step up, and creates a more consistent leadership experience across an organization.

Gut Check for Leaders: Define Clear Leadership Expectations

As you think about the ideas in this chapter, reflect on your answers to the following Gut Check for Leaders questions:

1. To what extent have you and your organization created a clear set of leadership expectations for your leaders?
2. How might your organization benefit from having a company-specific leadership contract?
3. Does your organization do an excellent job of embedding leadership expectations in the way it operates through several key human resources practices?
4. Does your organization regularly review your leadership expectations to evolve them as your business context and strategy change?

Notes

1. Jodi Kantor and David Streitfeld, "Inside Amazon: Wrestling Big Ideas in a Bruising Workplace," *New York Times*, August 15, 2015, https://www.nytimes.com/2015/08/16/technology/inside-amazon-wrestling-big-ideas-in-a-bruising-workplace.html?module=inline.
2. David Streitfeld and Jodi Kantor, "Jeff Bezos and Amazon Employees Join Debate Over Its Culture," *New York Times*, August, 17, 2015, https://www.nytimes.com/2015/08/18/technology/amazon-bezos-workplace-management-practices.html?module=inline.

3. Amazon, "Leadership Principles," https://www.amazon.jobs/en /principles.

4. Francine Katsoudas, "The Future of Leadership," September 26, 2017, https://www.linkedin.com/pulse/future-leadership-francine -katsoudas/.

5. Personal interview with Alain Dehaze, June 2019.

CHAPTER 12

Do the Hard Work to Sustain Momentum

The third term of the leadership contract states that leadership is hard work and leaders need to be tough and have the resilience and resolve to tackle it. If they don't, it will undermine their efforts to be accountable leaders. The same idea applies to organizations. Many organizations make leadership accountability a business priority. They may also invest time to define and embed a clear set of leadership expectations for leaders. Sustaining all this effort takes dedicated focus. Much of it involves hard work. Unfortunately, just like individual leaders, many organizations avoid this hard work. As we already explored earlier in this book, my global research found that only 20 percent of organizations deal with the leaders seen to be unaccountable and mediocre. This is not acceptable in my opinion. Avoiding this hard work undermines all efforts to build strong leadership accountability and establish a robust leadership culture.

This chapter will focus on the four strategies that must be tackled to sustain strong leadership accountability (see Figure 12.1).

Demonstrate Zero Tolerance for Bad and Abusive Leadership Behavior

The global consulting firm PwC has done quite a bit of research over the years on the reasons why companies fire their CEOs. In 2019, they reported that, for the first time, misconduct was the number one

The Hard Work Needed to Sustain Strong Leadership Accountability

01 Demonstrate zero tolerance for bad and abusive leadership behavior

02 Don't ignore unaccountable and mediocre leaders

03 Address your unaccountable and mediocre leaders head-on

04 Support leaders during critical leadership turning points

Figure 12.1 The Hard Work Needed to Sustain Strong Leadership Accountability

reason, over poor company performance.[1] The *bad behaviors* demonstrated by these leaders and cited in their report include:

- Having a sexual affair or relations with subordinates
- Using corporate funds in a questionable manner
- Engaging in objectionable personal behavior
- Using abusive language or making public statements that are offensive to customers or social groups

These are all solid reasons to fire a CEO from a company. However, plenty of leaders engage in other behaviors that are not as dramatic as the ones just listed, but still create serious problems for companies. Consider some of the following:

- Leaders abusing their power for personal benefit or gain
- Leaders routinely mistreating, demeaning, or bullying others
- Leaders who are simply not team players
- Leaders who do not consistently model the organization's values or leadership expectations
- Leaders who use company assets for personal purposes

The critical question is: Why does an organization tolerate these kinds of behaviors from their leaders? By doing so, they severely undermine their efforts to build strong leadership accountability. These behaviors can also contribute to creating toxic work environments.

The good news is that demonstrating zero tolerance for bad behavior can be enormously powerful. Let's take a look at a story from the U.S. Navy Seals. In September of 2019, the Admiral of this elite special operations force fired three senior leaders after members of their teams were accused of severe discipline breaches.[2] The alleged misconduct included sexual assault and drinking while deployed in Iraq. Some Navy officials commented that they could not recall an instance when the leadership of a SEAL team was fired for misconduct committed by their team members. However, the Admiral had lost confidence in these senior leaders because of their failure to control their teams. He was also no longer confident in the ability of these teams to accomplish their missions. The Admiral also commented that these incidents made it clear that the special force had drifted from the Navy's core values of Honor, Courage, and Commitment. The Admiral knew that it was crucial to send a message that this kind of behavior would not be tolerated—and that leaders are ultimately accountable for their teams.

We have seen many examples of bad leadership in recent years, and some organizations have dragged their heels in responding to toxic behavior. Companies pay the price when they don't react quickly, perhaps because the individual is still seen as adding value or may be a "brilliant jerk." Or they may be hard-driving managers who obtain business results but do so at a cost seen in terms of abused employees, burnout, or loss of great talent. None of these reasons should be enough to not respond to these circumstances.

When you demonstrate zero tolerance for lousy leadership behavior, something remarkable happens. You find other leaders step up even more. They recognize that the organization is serious about leadership accountability. They see that the organization will not tolerate bad behavior, and they work to be more accountable. You may also find that leaders who are not motivated to step up will leave, which in the end is also a good outcome.

Take a few minutes to think about the leaders in your organization who are not living up to your leadership expectations or are leading in a way that is misaligned to your core values. What has your organization done about this behavior? What are you going to do now?

Address Your Unaccountable and Mediocre Leaders Head-On

As I shared earlier in this chapter, only 20 percent of organizations surveyed in our global research said they do a good job of addressing their unaccountable and mediocre leaders. This is something that organizations must improve upon. I have had many clients ask for my ideas on how to help them get better. The first step is that you have to commit to address the unaccountable leaders head-on. A good starting point is by having a framework to help you better diagnose those leaders you sense may be struggling in their roles.

To help our clients, we developed a leadership accountability nine-box. This borrows from the traditional nine-box frameworks that many companies use during talent planning, which assess leaders based on their performance and potential.

I created this model on the fly after reflecting as the team was struggling with having robust and honest talent discussions about their leaders. Everyone seemed to be able to identify and agree on who their high-potential leaders were. These individuals were hard to dispute. However, they struggled when they began to talk about other leaders who were not stepping up. I discovered a lot of nuance and subtlety surrounding a leader who may be seen as being unaccountable and mediocre in his role. The nine-box addresses this by providing more granularity to assess leaders and then guide a discussion.

The nine-box uses two dimensions: *leadership accountability* and *creating enduring value*. The *leadership accountability* dimension describes the extent to which leaders are committed to being truly accountable in their roles. The *creating enduring value* dimension describes the extent to which leaders drive strong results, both in *what* they're accomplishing and in *how* they deliver those results.

As we played with the nine boxes and the labels, the team was able to have a fruitful conversation. I found that it forced senior teams to address the leaders who are struggling in their roles. Once this was done, most teams acknowledged that they had been avoiding doing anything about this because they really didn't know how to assess their leaders and what to do next.

Figure 12.2 shows the nine-box model I created, with each box described in detail. Take some time to read through it now.

Let's briefly review each box, starting at the lower-left quadrant:

- **Incompetent.** This individual is a weak leader, both in terms of the ability to create enduring value and in the ability to demonstrate

Figure 12.2   The Leadership Accountability Nine-Box

leadership accountability. If you have leaders who show up in this box, the question is: Why are they still in your organization?

- **Ineffective.** This individual is weak in creating enduring value and moderate in leadership accountability. The person will most likely struggle to be effective in their role and so you will need to address it head-on.

- **Inconsistent.** This individual is weak in creating enduring value but strong in leadership accountability. This leader most likely is largely well-intentioned, but that alone isn't enough. This person cannot consistently generate value, and this undermines their overall effectiveness. Many people will misinterpret an inconsistent leader's good intentions as effectiveness. However, they would be wrong. In most organizations, these leaders are ignored. Nothing is done to address the situation. As I've always said, when it comes to leadership, good intentions are not enough.

- **Acceptable.** This individual is moderate at creating enduring value and weak at demonstrating leadership accountability. Again, another mediocre leader. One needs to assess whether this individual is in the right role and whether they can improve. If the answer is no, then the next step should be clear.

- **Adequate.** This individual is moderate in creating enduring value and moderate in demonstrating leadership accountability. I have found that many competent managers get slotted in this box. They add the right level of value to the organization but may not have the desire or capability to move into a more senior leadership role. You'll need to figure out whether they do have the potential to move up to determine whether investing in them will help elevate them.

- **Average.** This individual creates moderate enduring value and demonstrates strong leadership accountability. This individual performs at a relatively high level. The opportunity here is to strengthen their ability to create value for the organization.

- **Adept.** This individual creates substantial enduring value but demonstrates weak leadership accountability. Typically, strong technical experts fit in this box. They bring exceptional value to the organization through their expertise, but they do not have the interest or desire to be in a formal leadership role. The critical approach here is to have a candid conversation with the individual and reinforce the value they bring to the organization. You can reassess whether their career aspirations change over time and if they can make the leadership decision to step up.

- **Able.** This individual is reliable at creating enduring value and moderate in demonstrating leadership accountability. The key here is to understand what is getting in their way, as there may be barriers impeding their ability to step up.

- **Accountable.** This individual is strong at creating enduring value and is demonstrating strong leadership accountability. The key is to ensure they remain in this box. These leaders should be considered role models for others in the organization. They might also be good mentors for the Solid Leader and the Above Average leader.

How to Take Action and Support Your Leaders

If you are considering using this model within your organization, here are some ideas to consider. Begin by reviewing the results from your Leadership Accountability Audit, as it will give you a big-picture look at the broader leadership accountability issues in your organization. Next, review your company-specific leadership contract and use it as the anchor to think about leadership accountability. Then begin to examine the leadership population that needs focus and attention. I suspect you'll start some fascinating discussions. Here are some additional ideas on next steps that you may want to consider.

First, those leaders identified as Inept, Inconsistent, Ineffective, and Acceptable should get immediate action. The organization needs to determine whether there is any chance of helping these individuals get stronger. If not, then you need to act because keeping them in their roles undermines your ability to create a strong leadership culture.

The individuals who fall into the Adequate box need a closer look as well. You want to determine whether they can move to other quadrants in the top-right direction of the nine-box. If you learn that they're trending to the lower-left quadrants, that will give you a good sense of what you may need to do next.

After discussing the individuals who fall into these five boxes, the risk that an organization faces in having future leaders reporting to and working with these individuals should be clear. Remember, mediocrity breeds mediocrity. You want, whenever possible, your future leaders to never be working with leaders deemed to be Inept, Inconsistent, or Ineffective. Never, ever put a strong or high-potential leader under a mediocre one!

Individuals that fall into the Adept, Able, and Accountable boxes warrant further investment and development. These will be the leaders you can lean on to help you set the right tone and create a strong leadership culture.

Take some time to review the grid in the figure and reflect on some of the leaders in your organization. What does this exercise tell you about your leaders and your leadership culture? Once you are clear on where you stand, then you need to act. The leaders you see as mediocre need your support. You may find they shouldn't be in a leadership role. You may find they don't want to be in their leadership roles and are looking for a way out. Some may find they are better suited for individual contributor roles or roles that enable them to be technical experts. Then again, they may need to leave your organization entirely to pursue a different career path. Whatever the outcome, nothing will happen if your organization doesn't act. Too often, attempts to sustain strong leadership accountability are undermined because we fail to act on leaders who are not willing or are unable to be accountable. Keeping these leaders in their roles has consequences. It sends the message to other leaders and employees that you are prepared to tolerate mediocrity in your organization. It also disengages your high performers who are truly accountable, as their contributions are minimized. It is also difficult for those leaders, as they don't feel like they are at their best. Remember, as I've stated many times already in this book, mediocrity breeds mediocrity.

How Not to Address the Mediocre and Unaccountable Leaders

When you see a leader engaged in bad behavior, you typically know it and can immediately sense the negative impact on your culture and people. You may also be driven to act to avoid losing great talent and eroding your culture, as well as the risk to your company's reputation. However, mediocre leaders can be just as problematic. They are managers and executives in leadership roles who don't have what it takes to lead. In comparison to lousy leaders, the mediocre ones tend to fly under the radar in most organizations. I've come to learn through my leadership role and through my work with clients that organizations pay the price for mediocrity, and it's significant. I've also seen organizations take actions that create the appearance that they are doing something, but in reality, they are not. Here are some examples.

I've seen many companies identify mediocre leaders but keep them in their roles. Usually, this happens because of personal loyalty to the individual. I'm all for loyalty, but when a leader is inept and cannot perform in a leadership role, then you need to take real action.

Sometimes the company delays taking action because they are unwilling to pay severance if a decision is to exit a leader. Yes, severance costs can be a material issue; however, what are the other costs to your culture, to employee engagement, for having people in roles they simply are not cut out for? You need to weigh all costs in these situations.

Another popular non-action is to move the leader in question to another role in another function or department within the organization. It's typically an area of the company where the person is going to be less of a liability. That's just really passing the problem to another colleague or function. No one wins.

Another startling practice I've heard countless times is moving mediocre leaders out of "the business" and into the human resources function. The thinking is simply to mitigate the negative impact on the business and customers by moving the person to a less valued part of the organization. I don't think I have to tell you that this approach creates a huge problem. Maybe this was a suitable strategy a decade ago. But in today's world, the HR function is critical to a company's success. You need your strongest leaders there, not the mediocre ones. Just imagine if your HR department were filled with a bunch of mediocre leaders. What impact would this have on your company?

I have also found that in large organizations, there are lots of places for mediocre and unaccountable leaders to hide. Their ineffectiveness can be overshadowed by the strength of other leaders. But don't fool yourself: They are still there lurking and hiding in the tall grass. I heard an interesting story from a client of mine a while back. She worked with the illustrious Sergio Marchionne, former CEO of Fiat Chrysler. He was known to have an eccentric, unorthodox style and was a leader who had a passion for tackling complex problems.[3] He also had a reputation as being a tough leader, with little patience for mediocrity. My client shared that one of Marchionne's regular lines to his leaders was: "I will find you in the tall grass!" This meant that if a leader were trying to hide under the radar or get by with minimal effort, Marchionne would find that individual and deal with them.

Who is hiding in the tall grass of your organization? Who are the mediocre leaders in your company whom you are ignoring or failing to address?

The Power of Taking the Right Approach

Let's consider a different and much better approach. A senior leader, John, worked in a manufacturing company outside Chicago. I met him a while back after I delivered a keynote on *The Leadership Contract* at a conference. We talked after that event about a senior finance leader, Marcelo, in his organization who was mediocre.

As a person, Marcelo was well-liked but not really competent in the leadership part of his role. To complicate things, he had a personal relationship with the founder and CEO of the company. John kept pressing his CEO to do something about this mediocre leader, but to no avail. So John gave up. After John and I spoke, he realized he needed to keep pressing. He finally convinced his CEO to at least have a conversation with Marcelo, which he did. He found that Marcelo never wanted or liked having a leadership role. He did it because his CEO (and friend) asked him to do the job. John was able to uncover that Marcelo had a real passion—data analytics. Marcelo was a technical superstar who had in-depth subject matter and industry knowledge the company really required. However, all of this was being diminished because of the leadership role that Marcelo didn't even want to do.

No one was winning. Not Marcelo. Not the team he led, and certainly not the company. John and Marcelo discussed a new way forward, which he presented to the CEO. They collectively decided that they would create a new role for him as a subject matter expert in finance and data analytics. Marcelo would be able to concentrate on what he loved and did best. He would also act as a subject matter expert and mentor to younger employees in the finance department, which he enjoyed. However, he wasn't going to manage a team. This move allowed the company to keep an employee who did not have passion for being an accountable leader while allowing John the opportunity to bring in the leadership talent his company desperately needed.

This story had a happy ending. However, sometimes, mediocre leaders need to leave your organization entirely because they are inept. In these cases, you need courage and resolve to make this happen. I've learned that most of these individuals aren't happy in their roles anyway, but they keep hanging on. Organizations keep hoping they will step up one day, but that approach is futile at best. It all started because John had the resolve and courage to keep pressing his CEO. He was holding his CEO accountable for addressing a mediocre leader. Once he was able to have an honest conversation with Marcelo, the truth came out that he wasn't happy in his role, but he kept hanging on. This is a great example of how an organization can address a tough situation head on and do it to drive a positive outcome for everyone.

Be Mindful of Whom You Put into Leadership Roles

A few years ago, I worked with a startup technology company. The company had developed a core set of values that were compelling and differentiated from competitors. In the early days, the company was extremely mindful of every new leader they hired into the organizations. The search firm they worked with would do in-depth assessments. Candidates would have many interviews with potential co-workers. It wasn't uncommon for a candidate to have 10 to 15 interviews. I thought that seemed excessive when I first heard about the practice. However, the new leaders I worked with all spoke about how valuable the process was because, when they joined, they felt like they had been with the company forever. They said it helped them hit the ground running in their new roles.

That company realized that every new hire, especially those being hired into leadership roles, really mattered in the early days. They were getting ready to drive accelerated growth, and they couldn't afford to have any missteps along the way. Their values were fundamental to them, so they had put candidates through multiple interviews to gauge for culture fit. To me, that is an excellent example of getting it right and being mindful of whom you put into a leadership role.

However, after a few years, the company wasn't as mindful as they had been in their early days. Growth continued to accelerate. Managers were under pressure to fill the many vacant roles; they started to take shortcuts. Speed was the priority now. Hiring for culture fit took a back seat. Over time, lousy behavior emerged. Things began to happen that the company never experienced before: leaders who bullied and demeaned others or who demonstrated a lack of collegiality. This problem kept coming up again and again. At the core, it was about leaders and their misaligned leadership behavior. Morale and employee engagement, which were always strong, began to decline. This story has an important lesson for us as leaders: to be mindful of whom we place into leadership roles. If we don't get it right, the costs can be significant.

A recent survey of over 2,000 chief financial officers found that all the costs of a bad hire may not be financial.[4] Most CFOs were concerned about the degradation of staff morale and a decrease in productivity. A poor hiring decision has costs for any role, but when it's a leadership role, the costs are exponentially higher. Also, those costs are not just financial, but also cultural in nature.

Sometimes an organization is experiencing hyper-growth, like the organization described above. As a result, it must hire a lot of new talent to keep up. The pace is so frantic that the checks and balances typically put in place when hiring new leaders go by the wayside. Alternatively, maybe you have weak leaders who aren't committed to leadership accountability hiring brilliant jerks, without paying attention to culture fit or leadership expectations.

Regardless of the reason, it's critical to be mindful when putting people into leadership roles. Sure, it may be easier to be expedient and to take shortcuts. It's easier not to take the time to assess for culture fit. It's

easier to hire a brilliant jerk who may be a disaster with the team. It's easier to promote someone when he or she may not be willing or ready to
take on the role. These are all easy choices, but in the end, there is a good
chance you, your employees, and your organization will pay the price.

You must be tough with yourself and resist the temptation to take
the easy way out. Here are some ideas to consider:

- **Use your company's leadership contract as a guide.** Your
  organization's leadership contract spells out the expectations for all
  leaders. Use this to determine fit and whether you are looking to
  bring a leader on board who is prepared to be an accountable leader.
- **Stay away from brilliant jerks.** As we explored earlier in the
  book, many organizations have had a longstanding practice of promoting strong technical performers into leadership roles. An implicit
  assumption is made that exceptional individual and technical performance will translate to strong leadership performance. Indeed, this
  happens sometimes; but many times, it does not. Plus, when you have
  many brilliant jerks around, they can leave a trail of destruction to
  your culture and erode the engagement of your employees.
- **Make it acceptable for someone to say no to a leadership
  role.** At times a candidate, especially an internal one, may feel tremendous pressure to say yes to a leadership role. In many organizations, people feel, when the opportunity emerges, the only acceptable
  answer is yes. We need to make it okay for people to say "No!" or
  "I'm not ready." Employees must be able to say no without fear that
  they will be written off or taken off a high-potential list, or never
  asked to take on a leadership role in the future. You may be keen to
  put someone in the role, but if the person's not ready, you need to
  respect that. Remember that saying no to a leadership role that one
  isn't ready for is, in fact, a mature leadership decision.

Support Leaders at Critical Turning Points

As we discussed earlier in the book, many leaders get into leadership
roles by accident. Not only have organizations thrust individuals into
these roles, but many have also done so without providing any support or development. I can't tell you how many times I've heard leaders
lament the first time they went into leadership roles. For many, it felt

like being thrown into the deep end of a pool when you don't know how to swim. Most new leaders are ignored and left on their own with little to no training, coaching, or support. There's lots of thrashing about and frantic attempts to stay afloat. Some eventually catch on and learn to tread water. Some start to sink. All of this is much more painful than it needs to be. In the end, it's a colossal waste of time, talent, and energy.

As we explored earlier in the book, my team and I have identified four critical turning points that require special attention:

- The first time one is identified as having leadership potential
- The first time one assumes a front-line leadership role
- The first time one becomes a mid-level manager
- The first time one assumes an executive-level leadership role

At these turning points, what it means to be a leader changes dramatically. The expectations increase significantly. I was working recently with a group of senior leaders at on off-site. They admitted they did a terrible job of supporting their people in new leadership roles. As a result, they saw much churn: leaders failing, others leaving, and numerous examples of eroded engagement and culture. As one leader said, "We need to wrap our arms around these leaders to ensure they will be successful." That's exactly right.

You need to embrace your leaders as they assume new leadership roles, especially those at critical turning points. Provide them with the support, coaching, and mentoring they will need to thrive and be successful. Sit down with them to discuss how the leadership expectations will evolve for their new roles. One client of mine also had their leaders re-sign the company-specific leadership contract. This was a great way to force a leader to recommit to being a truly accountable leader in the new role.

Final Thoughts

Sustaining strong leadership accountability in an organization takes hard work. Most companies I work with struggle with this. Typically, they invest most of their energy up-front in defining clear leadership expectations. However, many fail to spend the time necessary to ensure things sustain over the long term. The strategies in this chapter will help you avoid this common pitfall.

Gut Check for Leaders: Do the Hard Work to Sustain Momentum

As you think about the ideas in this chapter, reflect on your answers to the following Gut Check for Leaders questions:

1. To what extent do you and your organization demonstrate zero tolerance for bad and abusive leadership behavior?
2. Do you and your organization address unaccountable and mediocre leaders effectively?
3. To what extent are you and your organization mindful and careful of who you put into a leadership role?
4. Do you and your organization effectively support leaders during critical leadership turning points?

Notes

1. Per-Ola Karlsson, Martha Turner, and Peter Gassmann, "Succeeding the Long-Serving Legend in the Corner Office," *Strategy & Business*, May 15, 2019, https://www.strategy-business.com/article /Succeeding-the-long-serving-legend-in-the-corner-office.

2. Ryan Browne and Barbara Starr, "First on CNN: Navy SEAL Leaders Fired after Allegations of Sexual Assault and Drinking Among Team," *CNN*, September 6, 2019, https://www.cnn .com/2019/09/06/politics/us-navy-seal-leaders-fired/index.html.

3. Sam Walker, "The Leader of the Future: Why Sergio Marchionne Fit the Profile," *Wall Street Journal*, August 11, 2018, https://www.wsj.com/articles/why-the-future-belongs-to-challenge -driven-leaders-1533960001.

4. Roy Maurer, "Morale, Productivity Suffer from Bad Hires," *SHRM*, February 2, 2015, https://www.shrm.org/resourcesandtools/hr-topics /talent-acquisition/pages/morale-productivity-bad-hires.aspx.

CHAPTER 13

Foster a Community of Leaders Across Your Organization

My team and I have had the privilege to work with many kinds of organizations with very different leadership cultures. I've seen cultures where leaders were accountable, shared an aspiration to be great leaders, and supported one another to execute the company's strategy. Unfortunately, in my experience, these leadership cultures are the minority.

I've also worked with many organizations where leaders were at war with one another or caught up in petty politics, power struggles, working at cross-purposes, or protecting turf. These kinds of leadership cultures distract leaders and employees, erode engagement, and create a significant barrier to strategy execution and achieving extraordinary results.

Through all these experiences, I have learned that you don't have to settle for an ineffective leadership culture. Change is possible. It's not an easy journey, but an organization can transform its leadership culture. It starts by making leadership accountability a priority, defining clear leadership expectations, and doing the hard work to sustain momentum.

The last area of focus is to foster a community of leaders across your organization. Four strategies that we will explore are in Figure 13.1.

Foster a Community of Leaders Across Your Organization

01 Assess your leadership culture

02 Be on the lookout for leaks in your leadership culture

03 Enable relationship-building among your leaders

04 Evolve your leadership culture as your company changes

Figure 13.1 The Four Strategies to Build a Strong Community of Accountable Leaders

Assess Your Leadership Culture

The first step is to know what the current state of your organization's leadership culture is. You can use the Community of Leaders Survey to help you with this.

Set up some time to have your executive team or extended leadership team complete the survey (see Figure 13.2).

The results from this survey will generate an important discussion that will help align the senior executives on how they see the leadership culture of the organization. As you review the responses from the completed survey with your executive team, reflect on the following questions:

- What overall patterns do you observe?
- Do any findings surprise you?
- What areas of strength exist? What are some of the weak areas?
- Do the results worry you, or are you encouraged by them?

The 10 Characteristics of a Strong Community of Leaders

Let's now spend some time discussing each of the 10 items. I will share some of the patterns I have seen in other organizations. You may find this context valuable for understanding your own organization's results.

1. **Leaders are clear on the strategic direction of the organization.** Without strategic clarity, it is hard to align leaders and

Assess Your Leadership Culture

Rate your organization's leadership culture on each of the statements below

		NOT AT ALL TRUE	SOMEWHAT TRUE			COMPLETELY TRUE
01	Our leaders are clear on the strategic direction of our organization.	01	02	03	04	05
02	Our leaders create excitement about the future of our company.	01	02	03	04	05
03	Our leaders share a common aspiration to be great leaders.	01	02	03	04	05
04	Our leaders lead as a united front with a one-company mindset.	01	02	03	04	05
05	Our leaders hold one another accountable and call out unproductive leadership behavior.	01	02	03	04	05
06	Our leaders celebrate success and key milestones.	01	02	03	04	05
07	Our leaders break down silos and collaborate effectively.	01	02	03	04	05
08	Our leaders make sure that internal politics and personal agendas take a backseat.	01	02	03	04	05
09	Our leaders demonstrate resilience and resolve in the face of adversity.	01	02	03	04	05
10	Our leaders support one another; they have each other's backs.	01	02	03	04	05

Figure 13.2   The Community of Leaders Survey

drive their commitment. If your survey revealed a very high score, congratulations; now focus on keeping it at a high level. However, if this was rated low for your organization, you'll need to understand what might be happening. First, you may find that the leaders are unclear whether it has a strategy in place. This may sound strange, but I can't tell you how often leaders are unaware that a strategy even exists. Second, you need to understand whether the communication of the strategy is clear and done effectively. At times, senior executives "communicate" the strategy without actually ensuring that anyone understands it. They may use a lot of financial terms, talking about operating margin, earnings per share, and so on. Many other leaders struggle to appreciate what this language means, and more importantly, what they specifically must do to drive the strategy. Ultimately, clarity is not a communication challenge; it's a translation challenge. Senior executives must *translate* the strategy so that leaders can understand it and in turn explain it to the people they lead.

2. **Leaders create excitement about the future.** If this rating is low, then there may be engagement issues taking place with your leaders. Connect this finding with results from your employee engagement survey to see whether there are parallels between the two sets of data. The real risk here is that if your leaders are not excited about the future, every employee will know it. That will impact their engagement and excitement about the company and its future. If you are fortunate to have high scores on this item, make sure you leverage the excitement of your leaders to engage your employees and accelerate efforts to deliver results.

3. **Leaders share a common aspiration to be great leaders.** When this item is rated low, I generally find it's because the organization has not communicated a clear set of leadership expectations. Once you do, you will see this item get stronger. It's critical to not just communicate your company-specific leadership contract but to also provide a road map for how the organization intends to support the development of leaders. If they do not see a plan and do not feel the company is investing in them, this will impact their aspirations and willingness to step up.

4. **Leaders lead with a united front and a one-company mindset.** When this item is low, you may find you have a "stable of thoroughbreds" type of culture (as we discussed earlier in the book), where leaders are focused on their own business, department, or function. You must help your leaders understand how the business operates as a whole, how departments come together, and how they must act as ambassadors of the entire organization, not just their functional units.

5. **Leaders hold each other accountable by calling out unproductive leadership behavior.** As we've already seen, this was the lowest-rated item in my global research. In fact, it's the lowest-rated item at an individual, team, and culture level. It is always the lowest-rated item in every organization where we have conducted this survey. I believe this happens because we haven't made this an expectation of leaders. Many have been trained to stay focused on

their work, team, or function. They also may believe that calling out unproductive leadership behavior is the responsibility of senior executives or the HR department. You may find it valuable to equip leaders with the skills to be able to have tough conversations with one another. You may also need to address those leaders (bullies, brilliant jerks) who don't play well with others and are not stepping up in their roles.

6. **Leaders celebrate success and key milestones.** When this item gets a low rating, there is a risk that leaders do not know whether they are winning or losing. This item is, in many ways, the easiest to implement, and yet it's the one most neglected. Leaders get busy focusing on delivering results, and they do not take time to pause and celebrate their successes. This undermines efforts to drive the engagement of employees. If they don't see their leaders acknowledging key milestones, they begin to disengage.

7. **Leaders break down silos and collaborate effectively.** When this item is low, leaders are stuck in their functional areas. Many may not feel empowered or feel they need permission to break down silos. If this is critical to your success, then you need to set this as an expectation. You also need to highlight examples of leaders who have busted silos and driven stronger business outcomes as a result.

8. **Leaders keep internal politics and personal agendas to a minimum.** If this item is low, then you may have a highly political culture on your hands. There are always politics in companies, but if it becomes the primary focus of leaders, then you have problems. The work here is to ensure you make your expectations clear—particularly the expectation to have a one-company mindset. You may also need to keep your eye on individuals who may be highly political. When you address this behavior head-on, you will find that drama and distraction decrease and productivity rises.

9. **Leaders demonstrate resilience and resolve in the face of adversity.** Whenever we conduct the Community of Leaders Survey, this item gets the highest rating. In most organizations, leaders find a way to come together in the face of a crisis. All the issues, frustrations, politics, and drama that occupy them during regular periods tend to disappear in a crisis. Unfortunately, once the crisis is averted or resolved, they go back to internal bickering, infighting, and politicking. A crisis can create a false sense of community. Leaders

need to come together in good times and in bad. Otherwise, you create an organization of "crisis junkies," where leaders believe the only time they need to lead is in the face of trouble.

10. **Leaders support each other—they have each other's backs.** If this item is rated low, then you have some serious work on your hands. Without a sense of deep trust, it will be hard to create community. There may be a few things going on. First, the expectation has never been set for leaders to support one another. The second is that leaders may not know each other well. It's hard to build a sense of trust and community with strangers. The focus here is to foster relationship-building among your leader population.

Use the Community of Leaders Survey as a 360 Assessment of Your Leadership Culture

Consider using the Community of Leaders Survey as a 360 assessment of the leadership culture among the senior leaders in your organization. I have had clients do this, and it is a valuable exercise. They have their senior executives complete the survey based on their perceptions of how they demonstrate the 10 characteristics. Then the next level of leaders (usually VP or director level) complete the survey based on how they see the senior leaders stepping up as a community of leaders. This makes for a robust discussion and clearly will show you whether the senior team is setting the right tone for the rest of the organization.

Look for Leaks in Your Leadership Culture

The Community of Leaders Survey gives you a baseline of where your organization stands. Once you have that level of insight, then you must be hyper-vigilant and even unrelenting in looking for what I call *leaks* in your leadership culture. Think of a stainless-steel drum filled with precious oil. If the drum is in good condition, it will retain the precious oil and preserve its value. On the other hand, imagine if the drum is neglected and over time begins to decay and even develop holes. What will happen? The precious oil will start to drip out. If the holes increase in number and size, then the oil will begin to gush out and spill all over the place.

It's helpful to think of your leadership culture like this oil drum. If you neglect it, leaks can happen and weaken your leadership culture. Misaligned behaviors demonstrated by your leaders are the leaks that erode your leadership culture. The good news is that you can leverage the 10 characteristics of a community of leaders to help you be vigilant and spot the leaks. Let's start by having a look at Figure 13.3. You will see the 10 characteristics of a community of leaders. I have also identified some key behaviors that are both aligned and misaligned behaviors for each of the 10 characteristics. Think about your organization as you review the table. You may identify other behaviors that you have seen as you read through the list.

Ideally, you want your leaders to be demonstrating the aligned behaviors consistently. But if you identified many misaligned behaviors, then you have "leaks." These leaks are weakening your ability to build community. One of the ways to spot leaks is by seeing leaders in action. The other is by looking at employee engagement data or themes emerging from exit interviews with employees leaving your company. When an issue starts surfacing with regularity, then you need to nip it in the bud before it becomes entrenched in your culture.

Enable Relationship-Building Among Your Leaders

As I've said many times to leaders I work with, "You can't build a sense of community and a strong leadership culture among a group of strangers." That's why some of the most important strategies for sustaining your efforts are ones that connect leaders. Mike Fucci, chairman of the board for Deloitte, stressed this in a recent article. He said companies today need leaders who can create leadership ecosystems that help move strategic priorities forward. He continued: "This means building diverse leadership alliances through inclusive relationship management. Leaders who are effective in developing the organization's ecosystem often spend a great deal of time and attention reaching up, down, and sideways internally and externally. Leaders who are able to build relationships on this scale are able to act more decisively and efficiently."[1]

THE 10 CHARACTERISTICS OF A STRONG COMMUNITY OF LEADERS	ALIGNED BEHAVIORS	MISALIGNED BEHAVIORS
01 Leaders are clear on the strategic direction of the organization	• Leaders are clear on how their priorities align with overall company strategy • Everyone is laser-focused on delivering on the most important strategic outcomes for the company	• Confusion or lack of clarity on the desired outcomes • Leaders are working at cross-purposes to one another
02 Leaders create excitement about the future	• Leaders are optimistic about the company and spread optimism to those they lead • Leaders are upbeat in the face of challenges and obstacles	• Leaders are apathetic and going through the motions • Leaders disengage those they lead by lack of inspiration
03 Leaders share a common aspiration to be great as leaders	• Leaders are fully committed to their roles as leaders • Leaders act as role models for other leaders in the organization	• Leaders not stepping up as leaders • Tolerating bad bosses and mediocre managers
04 Leaders lead with a united front and a one-company mindset	• Leaders lead in the best interest of the whole organization • Leaders reinforce messages in an aligned manner	• Animosity is high between leaders, departments, and functions, creating barriers to execution • Leaders act as bystanders, not owning company-wide challenges and problems
05 Leaders hold each other accountable by calling out unproductive leadership behavior	• Leaders have the tough conversations with one another • Leaders recognize when aligned leadership behaviors exist, and challenge others when they don't	• Passive-aggressive behavior is rampant among leaders • Leaders are not open to feedback and get defensive when challenged
06 Leaders celebrate success and key milestones	• Leaders leverage recognition to help others see progress toward goals and ignite passion • Leaders are happy for the success of other departments and functions in the organization	• Little time is made to acknowledge progress toward milestones • Leaders are envious of colleagues' success
07 Leaders break down silos and collaborate effectively	• Leaders look for leadership accountability leaks across the organization • Leaders work to build connections between teams and departments	• Departmental infighting and turf wars • Teams going ahead without engaging stakeholders
08 Leaders keep internal politics and personal agendas to a minimum	• Leaders have little time for grandstanding and political games • Leaders are transparent and direct in how they relate with one another	• Leaders focus all their energy on jockeying for recognition, prestige, and power • Gossiping, posturing, and bad-mouthing one another
09 Leaders demonstrate resilience and resolve in the face of adversity	• Leaders turn to each other in the face of adversity • Leaders support one another during trying times	• Leaders turn on each other in the face of adversity • Throwing colleagues and other teams under the bus
10 Leaders support one another; they have each other's backs	• Leaders build high-trust relationships with one another • Leaders look out for one another	• Leaders don't care when colleagues are struggling or need help • Backstabbing is rampant

Figure 13.3   The Aligned and Misaligned Leadership Behaviors

Some of your leaders may already be doing this on their own, especially if they put into practice the strategies I presented in Chapter 9. Other leaders will need to be nudged along and supported. While you need to make your expectations about relationship-building clear, it's also important that you support relationship-building at an organizational level. Let's explore some strategies.

Hold Regular Leadership Forums

All my research and client experiences have taught me that regularly bringing leaders together in forums is a powerful strategy for relationship-building as well as establishing and reinforcing a strong leadership culture. These forums or leadership conferences provide leaders with the opportunity to come together to network and build relationships. These forums help counter the isolation that many leaders experience day-to-day.

When done right, leader forums can help clarify your business strategy and reinforce your leadership expectations. Over time, you will find your leaders are better able to collaborate, innovate, and hold themselves and one another accountable for their performance.

So what makes for a great leader forum? Here are some lessons gathered from working with many clients around the world:

1. **Decide who needs to attend.** First, it's essential to be clear on who should be in the room. My clients usually convene the top two or three layers of leaders and selected high potentials. These people should be in leadership roles and have a key mandate for advancing the strategy of the organization. This doesn't always mean that a leader must have direct reports. At times, leaders play critical integrator roles or possess deep subject matter expertise vital to the company. These leaders are not often invited to these events, which is a missed opportunity.
2. **Determine the best frequency for your leader forums.** The frequency is an important decision you need to make. I've seen some organizations hold leader forums annually, biannually, or even quarterly. Gathering your senior leaders is costly and requires a commitment. I find it's important to determine the frequency that works for your organization and be consistent.

3. **The senior executives must set the context and be engaged.**
The event should begin with opening remarks, usually from the
CEO to provide an update on the state of the business, a review of
the corporate strategy, and a reinforcement of the leadership expectations. It's helpful for all the senior executives to have some exposure when it makes sense. It is also critical for them to demonstrate
passion and excitement for the company. It's also essential for them
to remain actively engaged throughout the event.

4. **Bring the voice of the customer.** Some of the most compelling sessions happen when customers are invited to talk about their
experiences in working with an organization. Don't just invite customers who like you and who have worked with you for years.
Bring in customers who will challenge you and your leaders to step
up in new and different ways to create enduring value for them.

5. **Tackle tough business issues.** Don't fly leaders from around the
world or the country just to put them in a dark meeting room and
subject them to talking heads and PowerPoint slides for three days.
This is a surefire way to suck any energy, passion, or commitment
out of every single leader in attendance. Instead, the agenda should
include a balance of brief presentations with lots of opportunities
for leaders to discuss and debate critical business issues. Usually
these are not divisional or operational priorities, but challenges
facing leaders across the enterprise. These discussions can't just be
about empty talk. Ensure that leaders can drive to actions that will
form the basis for personal commitments.

6. **Build in some fun.** The best leader forums find a way to build
fun into the agenda. Every organization needs to define for themselves what this means. For some it's talent shows, golfing, tours of
the local city, or activities to support charitable organizations. The
key is to ensure the event fosters relationship-building and networking among your leaders.

7. **Wrap up with a call to action.** Finally, I find the best leader
forums close out with a compelling *call to action* by the CEO. Set
the bar high for your leaders. Reinforce the importance of individual and collective leadership accountability. The call to action should
include the responsibility of leaders to cascade key messages back to

their teams. Too often, these events happen and little information gets back to employees, which is a missed opportunity.

Ultimately, great leader forums achieve two critical outcomes: clarity and commitment. First, they should drive increased clarity about the company's strategy and leadership expectations. Second, they should deepen the commitment of leaders to execute the strategy and work together to build a strong community of leaders, which in turn will help you build a strong leadership culture.

Build Community During Leadership Development Programs and Other Events

Leadership development programs offer another powerful opportunity that helps leaders to connect and build relationships. This can be accomplished several ways. First, you can use a cohort approach to leadership development whereby your leaders experience your programs as an intact group. Over the duration of the program, they get to build relationships with one another. You will find these relationships can become quite strong. The positive effects can carry over into the workplace, as leaders start working more collaboratively with one another. We had one client who also reported that the relationships carried over to their leaders' personal lives, many of whom became friends.

Another strategy is to embed social tools in your leadership programs that are delivered virtually. While the physical face-to-face element may not be present, a social platform can still yield positive outcomes with respect to relationship-building, learning, and mutual support.

Hold periodic events for leaders to come together to discuss the organization's strategy and leadership expectations. These events are shorter in duration than leadership forums, but also serve as a way for leaders to connect and get to know one another. These events can also be held for targeted groups of leaders such as front-line and middle managers. Many clients I have worked with hold regular events for women leaders to give them their own space to connect, build relationships, and learn from one another.

Evolve Your Leadership Expectations as Your Company Changes

In August 2018, I was in South America to promote the launch of the Spanish translation of my book *The Leadership Contract*. During my time there, I was in Peru, Chile, and Panama. I spent about two to three days in each country. I did 20 presentations and meetings with senior leaders. In one of those meetings, I spent time with the Latin American team of a global company in the agricultural products industry. As we arrived at the head office, we saw banners throughout the headquarters emblazoned with the words "One Company." They were hard to miss.

As we started our meeting with the executive team, we quickly learned that the day before was their "Day One." You see, their company was acquired 18 months earlier by another company. It took all that time for the acquisition to gain approval by regulators and various governments. By chance, we happened to visit the team on day two. How lucky was I?

We learned during our conversation that each of the executives was deeply involved in crafting the new strategy of the combined companies. It also became evident that all of that work hadn't prepared them for how they should lead. They had questions for me about how they should show up as leaders. They also wanted answers because their teams were asking them the same questions. Could they drive ahead on priorities as they always had? Did they need to seek permission for specific actions? Should they be proactive in reaching out to colleagues from the acquiring company? Some openly acknowledged that they were not fully embracing their new organization. The culture of their old organization, which some had spent 10 to 15 years with, still coursed through their blood. Despite all the banners and posters, their loyalty was still to the old company and its brand. Now what I didn't tell you is that these two companies were fierce competitors before the acquisition. You can imagine how much work they had ahead of them to integrate the two cultures and create a new unified leadership culture.

Despite all the integration work they were doing, they hadn't spent much time discussing the desired leadership expectations and culture for the leaders and the new combined company. They asked me to explain how they might do this, and I told them a lot about what you have read in the previous four chapters of this book. They got excited about this work. They then discussed how they were going to reach out to their colleagues to start having meaningful discussions. They were aligned around a goal to bring clarity to their leaders and drive their commitment when it mattered most.

In my experience, there are several triggers that will push you to reexamine the expectations of leaders in your organization. Like the example above, a merger and acquisition should initiate a company to review leadership expectations, determine how to build community, and create a strong leadership culture. Bringing two companies together after a merger or acquisition isn't easy. I know this through my client work. I also know this through my own leadership experience with 13 acquisitions (both in acquiring other companies and in being acquired). The key lesson is that the sooner your company can create a new set of expectations for leaders, the better and even easier things will be post-merger. Failure to move on this quickly leads to internal confusion, conflict, and an "us versus them" mentality among leaders. This, in turn, will erode progress and undermine success.

Here are some other triggers that a company can face:

- **A new CEO joins the organization.** Typically, when a new CEO joins a company, the person comes in with an agenda to drive change. I've never worked with a CEO who was appointed to maintain the status quo. Driving change will mean a shift in strategy, and that will likely translate into a change of leadership expectations.
- **Poor company performance.** If a company is experiencing poor performance lasting several quarters, then change is required. As you know, doing what you've always done won't get you to a different place. This will result in a shift in strategy, which creates the need for leaders to step up in new and different ways.
- **Drive accelerated growth.** Sometimes companies experience an opportunity to drive accelerated growth due to market demand or the chance to expand globally or into new markets. This, too, increases the expectations of leaders and requires you to evolve your leadership culture.
- **Transforming business models.** Many companies find they have to change their business model in response to external changes,

whether those changes come from regulators, technology, competitor threats, or evolving industry dynamics. These days, many companies are transforming their business models due to digital technologies, AI, and machine learning. Again, new business models will also create new expectations for leaders.

Final Thoughts

As you might appreciate by now, this work of making leadership accountability a priority, defining clear leadership expectations, tackling the hard work to sustain momentum, and building community among your leaders is an ongoing effort. As we discussed in Chapter 1, the future for leaders will continue to be a challenge for them. They will need to continually be thinking about how to drive strong leadership accountability to help everyone to step up, take ownership, and deliver results.

Gut Check for Leaders: Foster a Community of Leaders Across Your Organization

As you think about the ideas in this chapter, reflect on your answers to the following Gut Check for Leaders questions:

1. To what extent do you and your organization regularly assess your leadership culture?
2. Do you regularly look for leaks in your leadership culture?
3. Do you implement practices that foster relationship-building among your leaders?
4. To what extent does your organization evolve its leadership expectations and culture in the face of key changes?

Note

1. Mike Fucci, "Addressing the Leadership Gap: Diversity Is an Essential Ingredient to Development, Succession," *Huffpost*, December 2017, https://www.huffpost.com/entry/addressing-the-leadership-gap -diversity-is-an-essential_b_5a2fe4bbe4b0bad787127018.

CONCLUSION

A while back, I saw a commercial for the Chartered Professional Accountants of Canada (CPA).[1] Entitled *Record Label*, the ad re-creates a fictional meeting in the office of the president of a record label back in the early 1990s. He is lamenting the fact that his company is being "killed by this Internet fad." The CEO asks his executive team to give him ideas on how to revive their flagging business.

One suggests a mail-order CD club where members get 10 CDs for $1. Another suggests they invest heavily in laserdisc technology, as he holds up this massive-looking CD. Finally, a seemingly sensible woman pipes up with a radical idea: abandon CD sales and instead create an online platform to stream music to customers for a monthly subscription fee.

There is a pause as everyone looks at her with a sense of confusion and contempt. Then the annoyed CEO asks, "How is that going to help us sell CDs?" The ad finishes with a devastating tag line read by a narrator: "Are you on the right side of change?"

This commercial showed a company confronting a fundamental shift in its business environment. Their old business model was becoming less and less successful. CD sales were down. Something new was emerging, but they couldn't see it. One person in the room had the way forward, but the rest of the leaders couldn't think of or see their business differently.

To me, this commercial sums up the leadership challenge of our time. We are living through a period of significant change in our organizations, our economies, and our world. Companies everywhere are experiencing a higher degree of disruptive change. These include the onset of new technologies, intensifying global competition, sweeping demographic changes, increased regulatory pressures, climate, social and environmental challenges, and geopolitical and economic uncertainty. Add to all this the emerging influence of AI, big data, and robotization. Many of my clients describe it as a VUCA world where things are more volatile, uncertain, complex, and ambiguous than ever before.[2]

In a period of radical change and disruption, we desperately need our leaders, at all levels, to be better than ever before. Leadership has always been critical to the success of any enterprise. However, as we have explored earlier in this book, at the very time we need all leaders to be stronger, the reality is that they are not.

Publilius Syrus was a Latin writer who lived from 85 to 43 B.C. He wrote, "Anyone can hold the helm when the sea is calm." He got it right way back then. Anyone can lead when times are good, when the world is stable, and the sea is calm. It takes real and accountable leaders to lead in today's and tomorrow's world. All leaders will need to be stronger than they have ever been to deal with this world of change. Also, at a time when we need leaders to be stronger, they are not. Many leaders today are overwhelmed, disengaged, and underprepared.

I believe that the way forward is to focus on leadership accountability. It is and will always be what sets the truly great leaders apart from the rest. There is a dual response that will be required: individual and organizational.

At a personal level, you will need to embrace the four terms of the leadership contract. You will need to decide to be an accountable leader. You will need to step up to your obligations as a leader. You will need to develop the resolve and resilience to tackle the hard work of leadership. You will need to connect with your colleagues to build a sense of community because this is the model of leadership for the future.

You will need to go beyond yourself to hold others accountable for being leaders. You will need to build truly accountable teams. You will also need to play a role within and across your organization to build a strong leadership culture and community of leaders.

At an organizational level, the dual response demands that you make leadership accountability a priority within a company. Senior leaders need to define clear leadership expectations for all their leaders. They must also do the hard work to sustain their momentum in building a strong leadership culture. Finally, they must invest the time to help leaders create a sense of community across the entire organization.

I have learned that no matter how bad a situation may be, there's always hope. An ineffective leader can improve, a terrible team can become a great one, and an uninspiring culture can become amazing. It's all possible, but it isn't easy. Change never happens by accident or merely hoping for it to happen. It takes a deep desire and real determination —and one other important element—leadership accountability. How you respond to the challenges of the next decade will be critical not only to the success of your organization but also to the success of our society as a whole. Are you ready to commit to and be an accountable leader? If you answer yes, then congratulations. I invite you to join me and other accountable leaders as we lead the way for our companies and our world!

Notes

1. Justin Dallaire, "Check It Out: Chartered Accountants Tackle the 'Internet Fad,'" October 13, 2017, http://strategyonline .ca/2017/10/13/check-it-out-chartered-accountants-tackle-the -internet-fad/.

2. Brigadier General George Forsythe, Karen Kuhla, and Daniel Rice, "Understanding the Challenges of a VUCA Environment," May 15, 2018, https://chiefexecutive.net/understanding-vuca -environment/.

ACKNOWLEDGMENTS

I have had the good fortune throughout my career to work with some of the brightest minds and outstanding business professionals in the world. Every day I am inspired and challenged by you.

To my many clients. Thank you for your support and your longstanding relationships. I am indebted to you for bringing the ideas of *The Leadership Contract* to your leaders.

Thank you to the many readers of my books and blogs. I sincerely appreciate your encouragement. Nothing excites me more than when readers reach out to share how the ideas in my books, presentations, blogs, and seminars have helped them become better leaders and people.

Thanks so much to Gina Bianchini, Giulia Cirillo, Kurt Ekert, Brad Furtney, Olga Giovanniello, Matthias Goebel, Josh Linkner, Laura A. Liswood, Tricia Naddaff, Andrew Pateman, Dan Schawbel, and Ricardo Viana Vargas for your generosity in providing endorsements for my book. I admire and deeply respect each of you for the impact you are having in your organizations and the world.

A big thank you goes to the team at John Wiley & Sons, who contributed significantly to this project. A special thank you to Shannon Vargo, my editor for the past seven years. Thanks also to Sally Baker, Peter Knox, Vicki Adang, Dawn Kilgore, Tim Gallan, Paul Reese, and the rest of the team. Thanks also to Olivier Terree from Cross Knowledge for his support in creating the Fulfilling the Leadership Contract program.

Thank you to Dr. Nick Morgan, Sarah Morgan, Nicola Lindsay, Emma Wyatt, and Jennifer Montfort. Your full commitment and support are always valued and appreciated. To Kevin Youngsaye for bringing your design gifts to this project.

I wish to express my sincere appreciation and gratitude to my colleagues and friends who supported this work: Dr. Alex Vincent, Tess Reimann, Tammy Heermann, Razia Garda, Alicia Lambier, and Dan Lett. First, to Tess Reimann and Carole Clarke for your dedication and amazing work. To Dr. Alex Vincent and Dan Lett for their contribution to our work and research on accountable teams.

Thank you to Alain Dehaze, Stephan Howeg, and Libby Archell from The Adecco Group. I have always appreciated your support of my work and for bringing *The Leadership Contract* into your great company.

I would also like to acknowledge the many professionals at LHH around the world. I wish to thank Ranjit de Sousa, John Morgan, Razia Garda, Alicia Lambier, Claudio Garcia, Chris Rice, Michelle Moore, Philippe Michecoppin, Carole Blades, Michelle Anthony, Helene Cavalli, and José Augusto Figueiredo.

Finally, I wish to acknowledge my family. To my parents for being examples of accountability and supporting me to do my life's work. To my children, Mateo, Tomas, and Alessia—you continue to amaze me, and I wish you continued success in your future.

Finally, to Elizabeth, my wife, partner, and friend. I am fortunate and grateful to have you in my life. Everything I do is only possible because of you.

INDEX

Note: Page references in *italics* refer to figures.

ABOUT THE AUTHOR

Vince Molinaro, PhD, is the founder and CEO of Leadership Contract Inc. As a global leadership adviser, speaker, and researcher on leadership accountability, Vince travels the world helping organizations build vibrant leadership cultures with truly accountable leaders.

Vince experienced a defining moment early in his career when he saw a respected colleague and mentor succumb to cancer that she believed was the byproduct of a stressful, toxic work environment. As a result, he has made it his life's work to boldly confront mediocre and unaccountable leadership.

Vince calls out the global leadership crisis today and thoughtfully lays out the strategy to address it head-on. His unique combination of provocative storytelling, evidence-based principles and grounded practicality has leaders at all levels stepping up to fulfill their obligations to drive the success of their organizations.

He is a *New York Times* best-selling author and has published several books including *Accountable Leaders* (Wiley, 2020), *The Leadership Contract* (3rd ed., Wiley, 2018) and *The Leadership Contract Field Guide* (Wiley, 2018). He has also co-authored two other books: *Leadership Solutions* (Jossey-Bass, 2007) and *The Leadership Gap* (Wiley, 2005).

Vince lives leadership accountability every day as an entrepreneur and global executive. His research and writing on leadership accountability are featured in some of the world's leading business publications. He also shares his insights in his Gut Check for Leaders blog and through the Accountable Leaders App available from the Apple and Google App Stores.

Vince and his family live near Toronto, Canada.

SOLUTIONS TO

BUILD STRONG
LEADERSHIP
ACCOUNTABILITY

IN YOUR ORGANIZATION

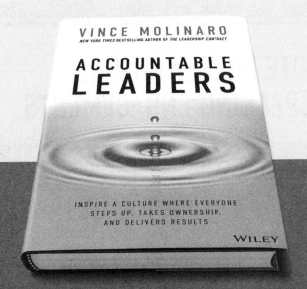

We offer leadership accountability solutions to help your organization build and develop accountable leaders and teams at every level.

KEYNOTE PRESENTATIONS AND SPEAKING ENGAGEMENTS

Dr. Vince Molinaro and his team deliver compelling keynotes and interactive sessions for your leaders, executives and board directors. Each session leverages the ideas in the books: *Accountable Leaders*, *The Leadership Contract* and *The Leadership Contract Field Guide*. Topics include:

THE LEADERSHIP CONTRACT™

The Four Steps to Becoming a More Accountable Leader

A COMMUNITY OF LEADERS™

How To Make Leadership Culture Your Ultimate Differentiator

ACCOUNTABLE LEADERS™

How to Create a Culture Where Leaders and Teams Step Up, Own and Deliver Results

ACCOUNTABLE LEADERS™ DEVELOPMENT PROGRAMS

Organizations need leaders to raise their game and have more impact at a personal, team and organizational level. Our series of award winning learning programs are designed to help leaders at all levels step up and become truly accountable in their roles:

The Leadership Contract™: Our hands-on Leadership Contract seminars and workshops (instructor-led, virtual instructor-led, and blended) transform how leaders think about their roles and shift their mindset of what it means to be a truly accountable leader.

Build a Truly Accountable Team: This learning program helps leaders develop the skills to build and sustain an accountable team. Leaders will explore how to drive greater team clarity and team commitment.

Be a Community Builder: This learning program helps leaders develop the skills to work across an organization and embrace their role in building a strong leadership culture.

ADVISORY SOLUTIONS

We offer a series of consulting solutions to help organizations build strong leadership accountability.

Strategic Leadership Conversations™. This solution is designed to help boards and senior management teams understand why leadership accountability is a critical business priority. We can also conduct a Leadership Accountability Audit to identify current strengths and gaps within organizations.

Accountable Teams™. A process to increase the clarity and commitment of a team through increased personal and collective accountability.

Create a Custom Leadership Contract. We can work with you to design and roll out a clear set of expectations for your leaders.

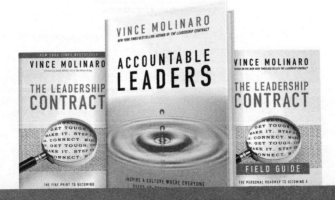

BRING OUR DEVELOPMENT AND ADVISORY SOLUTIONS INTO YOUR ORGANIZATION
For more information: info@drvincemolinaro.com

THE EFFECTIVE WAY TO
BECOME A
BETTER LEADER

The Accountable Leaders App will help you develop and sustain the mindset of a truly accountable leader.

Access exclusive content like blogs, courses, discussion groups, all designed specifically for members of our community.

Meet like-minded leaders who are committed to support one another to the be best accountable leaders they can be.

Be the leader others want to emulate by putting new insights into practice within your own leadership role.